Praise for Deena Kastor and Michelle Hamilton's
LET YOUR MIND RUN

"A candid account about the self-doubt that enters the mind of an elite athlete and how positive thinking made [Kastor] a champion both on and off the course."

—*Athletes Quarterly*

"Long-distance runner Deena Kastor shows the secret to her success—and as an Olympic medalist and the American female record holder in the marathon, she's had more than a few—relies less on any inborn talents [and more] on 'the power of thought, attitude and perspective.' Through race day and training anecdotes, she reveals the mental habits anyone can use to unleash their physical and mental potential."

—*Furthermore from Equinox* ("5 Books High Performers Should Read This Month")

"Deena Kastor is one of the greatest bodies in distance running, but this book captures what is so groundbreaking about her mind. *Let Your Mind Run* gives us the privilege of watching Deena's mind become her greatest asset as an athlete and as a positive, thriving, well-balanced person—from her earliest races to her Olympic career and beyond. Living and training with Deena in Mammoth Lakes has been a great joy of my career and has certainly shaped me into the athlete I am today. I invite you to explore *Let Your Mind Run* and peer into the life of my greatest mentor."

—*Alexi Pappas, Olympian, writer, and filmmaker*

"I have been savoring every story, every morsel of motivation and empowerment; [Kastor] is one of my longtime running heroes, and I never want this one to end!"

—*Running 'N' Reading*

"Inspiring . . . [*Let Your Mind Run*] details the mental techniques [Kastor] used to improve not just as an athlete but as a person."

—*Connecticut Magazine*

"In *Let Your Mind Run*, Deena Kastor captures the essence of the relationship between life and running, bringing her mental strategies and joie de vivre within stride for all of us. This is more than a memoir—it's a gift to everyone who looks to find balance and a healthy pace in life and sport."

—Joan Benoit Samuelson, gold-medal Olympic marathoner and
author of *Running Tide*

"*Let Your Mind Run* is a fascinating read that has applications for all athletes in all sports. . . . It's about cultivating positivity as the launching pad for achieving great performances."

—*Sporting Kid Live*, National Alliance for Youth Sports

"Engaging . . . [*Let Your Mind Run*] is a gift to all who are passionate about running and who seek to find balance with mental conditioning . . . A heartfelt and impressive memoir from one of America's treasured runners."

—*Booklist*

"*Let Your Mind Run* shares the mentality of a champion without the clichés and platitudes we've come to expect from books on sports. This is something entirely different, a fascinating collection of specific moments of discovery and the ways they come to life on the run. Whether you're a runner or not, this book will change you. Required reading for anyone in pursuit of excellence."

—Lauren Fleshman, coauthor of the *Believe Training Journal*

"Deena Kastor showed great promise as a high school runner but lost her confidence. In *Let Your Mind Run*, she explains how she changed her thinking, got back on track, and became America's greatest-ever woman distance runner. It's not about doing harder workouts; it's about taking charge of your mind. Through her journey, we learn how to use her techniques to reach new heights in our own pursuits."

—Amby Burfoot, winner of the 1968 Boston marathon and author of *Run Forever*

LET YOUR
MIND RUN

A MEMOIR *of*
THINKING MY WAY
to VICTORY

DEENA KASTOR
and MICHELLE HAMILTON

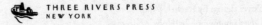 THREE RIVERS PRESS
NEW YORK

Published in the United States by Three Rivers Press, an imprint of the
Crown Publishing Group, a division of Penguin Random House LLC,
New York.
crownpublishing.com

Three Rivers Press and the Tugboat design are registered trademarks of
Penguin Random House LLC.

Originally published in hardcover and in slightly different form in
the United States by Crown Archetype, an imprint of the Crown
Publishing Group, a division of Penguin Random House LLC,
New York, in 2018.

Photographs by Heleana Drossin (page 5), Andrew Kastor (page 55),
PhotoRun.net/Victor Sailer (page 147), and John Barnhart Stylecraft
(page 257).

Library of Congress Cataloging-in-Publication Data
Names: Kastor, Deena, author.
Title: Let your mind run : a memoir of thinking my way to victory /
    Deena Kastor with Michelle Hamilton.
Description: First edition. | New York : Crown Archetype, 2018.
Identifiers: LCCN 2017037828 (print) | LCCN 2018005712 (ebook) |
    ISBN 9781524760779 (ebook) | ISBN 9781524760755 (hardback) |
    ISBN 9781524760762 (trade paperback)
Subjects: LCSH: Kastor, Deena. | Running—Psychological aspects. |
    Runners (Sports) —Psychology. | Women runners—United States—
    Biography. | BISAC: SPORTS & RECREATION / Running &
    Jogging. | BIOGRAPHY & AUTOBIOGRAPHY / Sports. |
    PSYCHOLOGY / Emotions.
Classification: LCC GV1061.15.K394 (ebook) | LCC GV1061.15.K394 A3
    2018 (print) | DDC 796.42092 [B]—dc23
LC record available at https://lccn.loc.gov/2017037828

ISBN 978-1-5247-6076-2
Ebook ISBN 978-1-5247-6077-9

Printed in the United States of America

Illustration (page 293) by iStock/sportpoint
Cover design by Rachel Willey
Cover photograph by Holly Andres

10 9 8 7 6 5

First Paperback Edition

To Coach,

for teaching me that the value of all we know

increases the moment it is shared

Our life is what our thoughts make it.

—MARCUS AURELIUS

CONTENTS

■■■■■■■■

PROLOGUE

Olympic Marathon, Athens, Greece, 2004

Wow, that's a big lead pack.

All the players are there. Paula. Catherine. Her arm carriage is so tight, distinct.

The Japanese look strong. Rumor is they're well prepared.

I don't belong back here. I belong up there.

Pick up the pace then.

But heat is rising off the pavement.

Oh, Miss Morocco is throwing up and it's only 10K.

I don't want to end up like that.

Okay, hold back.

Wow, she's really staggering—where's she from?—I hope a medic is nearby.

The leaders are getting farther away. You need to pick it up.

But if I pick it up, I could end up like these other girls dropping off like flies.

You're thinking too much about the heat.

You know, I actually don't feel that hot.

Forget the heat, then. Focus on staying cool instead.

Just fluids and sponges.

Oh, this Cytomax is hot. Couldn't the IOC afford refrigeration?

Chug it anyway.

Shit, it's the half and the leaders are gone.

You can't medal from back here. You need to get moving.

Reel in the girl ahead.

Strong and steady.

Gotcha, good, now go after the next girl.

Bingo.

One at a time.

Her back's a target. Fast as you can.

I hope this strategy works.

Believe it will.

Now, go.

GO!

When I first became a professional runner, I thought the hardest part would be the physical training. After all, what could be tougher than running to the top of an 11,000-foot peak while trying to fend off a pack of highly trained male distance runners? What could be more taxing than interval workouts so intense you taste blood in the back of your throat?

The answer quickly became clear: wrestling with my mind. Starting out, I had no idea running would be so mental, no idea that the most important aspect of my success would come down to how I thought.

My early successes as a runner came as a child and filled me with great joy, but they were driven by talent and the fun of winning. At the college level, I doubted my ability and was ready to move on from running simply because I didn't understand that my own thinking was blocking my potential.

An unexpected turn of events sparked my curiosity and had me driving to Alamosa, Colorado, to pursue professional running. Shortly after arriving, I noticed that my coach kept emphasizing a good attitude. At first, I thought this meant being upbeat. Eventually, though, I realized a good attitude went far beyond the general idea of staying positive. It was part of a discipline, a long-cultivated habit of building and sustaining a positive mind capable of turning every experience into fuel.

I'd always considered myself a happy, mostly cheerful person, but when I started paying attention to my thoughts, I was surprised to find there was a lot of negativity in my head. In a workout, I focused on the struggle or was judgmental. Discovering this thrilled me because I realized that I could change my thinking. Every aspect of a run, from the pain it produced to the weather conditions, offered me a choice: Is this a thought that will slow me down? Or can I find a perspective that will speed me up?

Replacing negative reactions with positive ones infused me with energy and offered a boost in motivation. With a single thought, I realized, I could change the outcome of a workout, drawing out more strength and speed from my body. So whenever I caught myself thinking negatively, I found a positive alternative. Each day, thought after thought and action after action showed me I could get to the top of that hill, I could finish a workout faster, and I could barrel past the competition.

The physical and mental effects were so powerful that alongside managing negativity, I began to create positive moments by bringing gratitude and enjoyment to the day. Focusing on positive emotions further increased my drive and self-belief, powering my training. I became fitter and faster and began reaching goals I'd originally believed were improbable. So I set new ones.

I thought I had discovered the secret to success—because I had. By identifying a thought that was holding me back and replacing it with a new one to help me move forward, I undid years of self-destructive thinking patterns that had left me unhappy and injury prone. And I built better mental habits that not only propelled my success but also prepared me to handle setbacks and challenges.

Positive thinking has long been considered a powerful life tool, to the point that it has almost become a cliché. Yet its great power emerges when applied as a lifelong process. Changing a single thought improved the moment I was in, but years of dedicated practice changed my career, my life, and ultimately me.

All of this left me in awe at the power of choosing perspective, the way it can crack open physical and mental potential. During my career, no one could see the turns of thought, the diligent choosing of words, the monotonous shifting of perspective, yet it was apparent in my performance, and the joy I felt for life. Over the years, I realized we have it within us, no matter our passion or career, to build a better stage for success. Building a positive mind gives any pursuit surprising ease, lifting one to unimaginable heights. Here's how it lifted me.

PART I

Open

I.

WINNING

There is no instinct like the heart.

—LORD BYRON

When I was a kid, running was play. I accelerated on the trails, making a game of keeping pace over rocks and roots. I took blind turns with my arms raised high to avoid the encroaching chaparral, and craned my neck trying to find the hawk whose cry echoed in the canyon. Cresting a hill, I imagined I had similar views as that hawk. Running down the backside, I was a coyote chasing its prey. In the field, I was a deer prancing over tall grasses. These moments thrilled me, but I loved even more the buzz of racing. It seemed wild, even reckless to run to the point of straining, to be chased and to fend off competitors in a primitive game of speed. Each race I charged off the line eager to see if I could extend the gap between me and my challengers. The rush of adrenaline and urgency, of fear and delight, of pride and satisfaction, was the most emotion I had ever felt as a child.

I was eleven and a new member of the youth track program in Agoura Hills, a Southern California town bordered by the Santa Monica Mountains. My parents had enrolled me. Sports were, in their minds, the antidote to my quiet, solitary ways. I liked sitting alone on the hillside pulling weeds between the flower beds, pretending I was a gardener while the neighborhood kids played in the cul-de-sac. I spent hours in our playroom having Barbie redecorate her dream house or staging plays with my stuffed animals. Once, I sucked the colored candy coating off a pair of M&Ms and held them in the palm of my hand, pretending they were bird eggs. I told my sister Lesley, who was seven, four years younger than me, and gullible, that I'd found them in a nest outside my bedroom window. A few days later, after I'd secretly bitten into them, we were excited to find a crack in the shell. I pulled on the opening and pried off a chunk of chocolate to reveal the peanut inside, which I told Lesley was a tiny bird. For shock value, I ate it.

My parents were worried I spent too much time in my head, and sports were a logical solution. They didn't start with track, but with softball when I was eight. My dad got into it and signed on to coach. He was a quiet man, with a stout belly and skinny legs, and an obsessively trimmed beard and mustache. At practice he wore a polo shirt and shorts, with white socks pulled high to cover his thin ankles. He jokingly referred to himself as an olive on a toothpick. Among my teammates, he was known for his bear hugs. My mom brought the snacks. A lively Jewish woman with a thick Boston accent and a freckled face from being raised at the beach, she appeared at each game with an ice chest filled with orange slices, Capri Sun drinks, and enough Big League Chew for the entire team.

Softball was boring to me, so I passed the time in the outfield making dandelion necklaces for my teammates. Once, parents and coaches started shouting my name. The ball had whizzed by and I ran to pick it up. Then, unsure of what to do, I held it. My dad frantically pointed to first base, but by the time I threw the ball, the runner was already approaching second base. My dad and the other coach just shook their heads.

Ice-skating was more promising at first. I could go backward, spin without traveling, and abruptly stop by catching the thin edge of my skate's blade on the ice. I loved skating so much, my mom hired someone to make the frilly, sequined outfits I wore for competitions, complete with matching boot covers. But one morning, when it became clear I was never going to execute an axel, my instructor quit, walking off the ice in the middle of practice. She told my mom it didn't really matter, I was too skinny to be graceful anyway.

My mom was convinced these experiences were ruining my self-esteem, and in a bid to right this, she and my dad enrolled me in youth track. Running seemed fail-proof. There were no tryouts, no one was cut, everyone participated and got a ribbon. Most kids started with the sprints, but my mom ruled them out because a few girls in the valley were already racing at a national level, including future Olympian Marion Jones. Ever protective, my mom thought if I got clobbered in the sprints, my self-esteem would plummet, so she had me join the distance-running group.

My dad drove us all to the track on the first day. I was braiding Lesley's hair when we pulled in to the school and the chaotic scene caught our attention. Kids were jumping into sandboxes, arching over bars, falling into big blue mattresses. Coaches were shouting and pointing and clapping. My mom, with a plush stadium cushion in one hand and my sister's hand in the other, made a beeline toward the bleachers. I followed my dad, who had offered again to be a volunteer coach. We scanned the field to find the distance team and were eventually directed to a group of about eight boys and girls huddled around head coach Sal Pratts.

Coach Pratts was a big personality stuffed into a short, strong frame. "Today's warm-up is a half mile on the track, then five minutes on the trail," he said.

Wary of doing something wrong, I asked, "How many laps is a half mile?"

"Two," he said.

My dad held up two fingers.

"Where's the trail?"

Coach Pratts started to give me directions, but then said, "Just follow Noelle, if you can keep her in your sights."

Noelle was tall and leggy, with short, curly brown hair and big white teeth highlighting a friendly smile. We hit the track. Noelle had been running for a few years and her experience showed, but I found I could keep up with her. This was a relief; I just had to watch her to know what to do.

Our half mile complete, I followed Noelle out the gate. The school abutted the foothills of the Santa Monica Mountains, and we followed a dusty trail a short way into the hills. I looked up and was taken aback. The land was open and wild. There were fields of dry grasses and chaparral broken only by large arching oak trees. Rattlesnakes hidden in yellow flowering brush shook their tails, and horses grazed in the fenced-off meadows. I'd seen the mountains on the drive to the mall and thought they were pretty, but never knew you could go into them. When it was time to turn around, I didn't want to.

I loved running right from the start. It was simple and fun. It lacked rules and structure. There was no equipment to fuss with, no technique to learn. While the kids on the infield waited for their turn to jump or throw, Noelle and I and the other kids ran single file on the dusty cinder track. I remember thinking how lucky we runners were to be in constant motion. We were part of the action all the time. Running was also, to my surprise and delight, both solitary and social. One minute I was dashing down the track as if by myself on the side of the hill. The next, I was whipping around and making funny faces, trying to make my teammates laugh.

Best of all, running didn't make me feel foolish or ridiculous, like I'd done something wrong. The ease of it made me feel competent and free. Everything we were asked to do, I could do. I ran and counted my laps. I warmed up on the trails, happily shooting out the gate with my teammates to the wild open space, and ran among the rabbits and deer. Sometimes, Coach Pratts let us run through the neighborhood. We stretched across the whole street, a pack of scrawny kids exploring manicured suburbia, unfettered, adventurous, going where none of the other kids got to go.

―――――――

Our team, the Las Virgenes Comets, competed against other valley track clubs. Meets lasted a full day, 10:00 a.m. to 4:00 or 5:00 p.m. on Saturdays, with the distance events sprinkled throughout the day.

A couple of days before my first race, I overheard my parents talking in the kitchen. "The coaches want Deena to run the fast heat in the 880," my dad told my mom.

"No, no," my mom insisted. "It could destroy her self-esteem."

"Deena seemed fine when the coaches suggested it at practice. They think she has promise. Let's let her do it."

I had promise? The idea was shocking. I didn't know what they saw in me, but since I had been following Noelle, I decided I'd keep doing that. At the meet, my mom, dad, Lesley, and I found spots in the bleachers and watched the field competitions and the races until Noelle came up and said it was time to warm up with the team. As we ran on the grassy infield, I wondered why Noelle was wearing sweats when it was hot out. I was already dressed in our new red, white, and blue uniform. Back at the bleachers for a sip of water, I heard the first call. "Ten minutes until the Midget Girls' 880."

I followed Noelle as she made her way to the staging area on the side of the track, and watched as she took off her running shoes and slid into the sleeker look of spikes, all while engrossed in the music playing on her Walkman. She seemed like a real pro, operating with the ease of knowledge.

"Second and final call for Midget Girls in the 880."

Noelle stripped off her sweats to reveal her uniform. *Ah, okay*, I thought, *that's what you do.* She bent down to double-knot her shoes, so I bent down and double-knotted my own shoes. Racing seemed pretty simple so far. The officials handed out numbers to each of us and I watched Noelle peel off the back and stick the number onto her shorts' left side. My dad came over wearing his new Comets trucker cap. "Okay, honey, let me rub your legs for good luck." He knelt, gave each leg a quick shake. "Go get 'em, kiddo," he said with a wink.

We filed out of the holding area and lined up on the track in numerical order. Noelle wore bib number 1 and was first on the inside rail. I was five or six girls away. The starting official stepped onto a metal podium and blew his whistle, quieting the parents and coaches in the bleachers.

"Runners set."

Noelle put her toe on the line, bent her knees a little, and leaned forward. I did the same.

"GO!"

Noelle shot forward. I leapt, making a frantic bid to pass everyone and get on her shoulder. The two of us ran one-two around the first and second turns and headed down the backstretch. I looked around, wondering if there was more I should be doing, and noticed Noelle was breathing hard. I wasn't breathing hard and this surprised me. She was the fastest girl on the team, the one everyone said was going to win. *Oh, maybe this is the promise the coaches were talking about.*

Noelle and I shot down the straightaway as an official rang a large metal bell, indicating we were heading into the final lap. The smell of hot dogs drifted onto the track as we blew past the concession stand. Nauseated, I gulped air. Dust from Noelle's back-kick settled on my teeth, so I stepped into the second lane, and pulled up beside her. The parents went silent. Noelle surged, so I surged. She picked up the pace again. I matched her stride. This back-and-forth, this taunting of each other, was fun. But then I looked over and saw that Noelle was straining and I knew I'd gone too far, like when you're teasing your little sister and you know you've crossed a line, so I didn't pass her. Besides, I had no clue how to lead a race or win one. Was the leader supposed to do something other than run? Was there a protocol at the finish line? Following was safer.

We ran side by side down the homestretch and I trailed Noelle to the tape. My dad was right there at the finish to give me a high five.

"Wow," he said. "You don't even look tired."

"I'm not that tired," I said.

He handed me a Snickers bar. "Do you think you could've won today?"

I shrugged, mumbling, *Yes, I don't know, maybe.*

As we watched the rest of the meet, I thought about what my dad had asked. He didn't say he thought I could win, but his tone implied it. I didn't know if I could've won, but I knew I could've run faster. *Okay,* I thought, *next time I'll try.*

The following weekend when kids from the West Valley Track Club poured into the stadium, the race already had a different feel. Not only was I sporting a new bright-yellow Walkman and racing shoes, but going in with the intent to win gave racing an electric, exciting feel.

This race was a mile long, double the distance of the previous week. I was a little uncertain about whether I could run that far. We were also facing a different team, and while I knew Noelle was good, I was unsure about the other girls. Parents in the stands around me were making predictions about who would win, so as we waited for my race to start, I eavesdropped:

Did you see she almost beat Noelle last week?

In her first race? Wow, she's very talented.

Yes, she's going to be good.

Wow, I thought, *they're talking about me. Maybe I can do this, maybe winning is possible.*

When the starter shouted "GO!" I came alive, hitching myself onto Noelle's shoulder with an authority that took me by surprise.

During the first lap I realized I hadn't thought the race through. I had no tactic, no clear idea on how I planned to win. So I stayed on Noelle's shoulder again, waiting for some indication that it was okay to run faster. At the half, my breathing was fine and steady. This seemed reason enough to pick up the pace, but I hesitated, wondering if it was the proper time to pass. I spent much of the third lap in a mental debate on the matter, eventually settling on surging in the final straightaway. When Noelle and I rounded the last turn, I bolted and won.

Winning must have been rewarding, because it was what I set out to do. But I don't remember crossing the finish line. I remember the reaction in the stands. Climbing up the bleachers toward my family, I saw the other dads slapping my dad on the back. The other moms were congratulating my mom. My parents were smiling so wide it was like I was seeing their full sets of teeth for the first time.

"I can't believe you just started running," the adults said to me.

"You're clearly very talented."

"Keep it up!"

There was Cheryl Goldstine, the mom of Lauren, our team's prized sprinter. And Jackie Flashberg, the mom of a teammate who'd encouraged my mom to sign me up for track. "Look at that," she said, proud of herself. My dad nudged my mom in the side with his eyebrows raised as if to say, *I told you so.*

It was an uncomfortable amount of attention. It was also extraordinary. The approval told me that winning was exactly what I was supposed to do. It was the point of racing. So the following weekend, I set out to win again. Noelle and the other girls now knew I would push in the final stretch, so I surged with a half lap to go and won. The next race, I pushed the whole final lap. Before I knew it, I was running hard right from the gun, pressing so much that my chin thrust forward, my fists flew in front of my face, and my breathing was labored. I kept pushing until the fiery effort in my body was all I felt. My mind, though, didn't register the discomfort. It was simply the feeling of winning. Along the backstretch, the farthest away from the stands, where it was quiet, I'd gaze across the infield and see the second-place competitor half a lap behind me and push harder, thinking how embarrassing it would be to lose when I already had such a large lead.

Soon running started coming up in conversation all the time, even when I wasn't on the track. The families in our cul-de-sac asked me what kind of shoes I wore. People in my dad's office asked about my upcoming races. The kids at school said they couldn't believe I liked running; they thought it was hard. Teachers told the entire class I'd won and made word problems out of the miles I ran. At home, my dad wanted to know which workouts I liked best, and my mom asked if I'd met anyone new at practice. Even in line at the grocery store a friend's mom would notice the pasta in our cart and ask about carbo-loading. I normally compartmentalized things. When I was running, I was running. In math class, I thought about numbers. At the grocery store, my mind was on Cocoa Puffs. Winning, though, seemed to push running into every aspect of life. It heightened its importance, and by extension, made me feel important. So of course I wanted to keep winning.

One of my teammates, Hillary, got so nervous before races, she threw up in an unlucky trash can before each meet. I held her hair back a few times, but couldn't understand her fear. The pre-race adrenaline, the nerves, the effort had for me a delicious ring because what followed was the thrill of winning. I chased that nerves-effort-reward feeling and found it week after week my first year when I finished the season undefeated, save for that first race.

Winning took on even more urgency the second year. I was now experienced and at the top of my age group, the eleven-to-twelve-year-olds, so I was expected to win. Plus, my dad was really invested. He'd bought a stopwatch and stood on the track clocking every lap. The night before races, he didn't sleep well. He stared at the clock until it was time to wake me, and in the morning he gently ran his fingers through my hair, saying softly, "Deena, it's time." Then he headed to the kitchen to make me Eggo waffles. When I heard the toaster eject, I shuffled downstairs and ate at the table with heavy eyes and imperfect posture.

My parents had also purchased a camping van, the Merry Miler. We drove it all around Ventura County and up and down the state to my races. Lesley and I played Othello on the table in the back while my parents listened to Neil Diamond and Barbra Streisand singing "You Don't Bring Me Flowers" on repeat. When I got car sick, I crawled to the front and knelt between my parents in the captain's chairs. Other times, I'd fall asleep to the hum of the highway only to be ripped out of a dream by my sister's laughter at my drooling. We stopped at fun places like Big Sur, California's Great America, and Andersen's Pea Soup, which my dad loved. All of these adventures revolved around the fact that I was winning and I raced, wondering, *What if I got second, or tenth? Would my parents still want to come?* I didn't want to find out, so I drove harder, finishing the season un-defeated again.

In the fall, one of the track coaches, Bill Duley, started a cross-country team. Bill was a hippie in running shoes. Lean with a Lorax mustache, he sometimes got so excited watching races, his voice rose three octaves. He told my parents he believed I could be a national champion if I ran cross-country, a race contested on grass and trails. I didn't think anything could make running better, but cross-country turned out to be a lot more fun than track. Bill let us go farther down the trails and took us to other parks. We explored beyond the ranch houses into Cheseboro Canyon and ran through the staged western town of Paramount Ranch, where cameras had filmed movies starring Cary Grant, Bob Hope, and Mae West. We ran into the dry hills, discovering artifacts from the area's rich Chu-mash history—large domes made of willow branches, charcoal cave drawings, arrowheads, and cooking stones. The routes through Mal-ibu Creek State Park were flatter, but if you followed the creek long enough, you climbed a big hill and dropped into the canyon where the show *M*A*S*H* was shot. Rusted-out jeeps and disheveled picnic tables were scattered around the site. A vintage ambulance was taken over by brush and vines. Whenever I looked up to the familiar ridge-line from the show's opening scene, the theme song began playing in my head.

Bill emphasized the team aspect of cross-country. He explained that while we ran as individuals, each runner's place equaled the same number of points, which added up to a team score. One point for first place, two points for second, and so on. The team with the lowest score won. He told us horror stories about teams losing by one point. One point! "Remember," he said in the huddle before a race, "every runner counts, every place counts. So no matter how hard you think you're working, fight to catch the runner in front of you. Fight to the finish."

Running for a team gave winning greater purpose and I charged off the line with added fervor. I was often alone out front for the whole race, and the terrain became my main competitor. I wanted to conquer the hills and grass and mud as much as I wanted to beat the girl behind me. Being alone gave me the physical and mental space to push and explore my effort. Listening to my rapid breathing and the quick-footed touch of my shoes on the ground became the rhythm of each race. As my spikes chopped up the lumpy grass, and I cut tight turns around trees, I saw myself as powerful and strong, not the scrawny girl I actually was. I'd be immersed in the effort, then look up and see a teammate's mom cheering on a hilltop and wonder how on earth she'd gotten there. Then my eyes would drop back down and I'd be focused on pushing again. I let my legs run out of control on the downhill, and, ignoring the stepping-stones the organizers had laid for us, plowed through creeks, imagining myself a nimble puma crashing through the water.

I ran cross-country undefeated that year, which didn't go unnoticed: the local papers started doing stories about me. It was surreal to flip through articles on the American farm crisis, the AIDS epidemic, or the Colombian volcano eruption that killed 25,000 people, and then suddenly come to a full-length feature on me. What could be significant enough about a suburban kid to warrant being in the same paper as these important issues? Winning, it seemed.

Still, whether it belonged next to the news or not, seeing my name—Deena Drossin—always gave me a charge. I liked it when a story said my time would've beaten the boys that day. It was thrilling when reporters called me the "new distance star," a "girl with a bright future," and "a phenom." I loved that one, *phenom*. Once, a reporter wrote I had the sixth-best performance of the day. It was meant as a compliment because a couple hundred boys and girls, some older than me, had competed in multiple races throughout the day, but I didn't like it because it made it sound like I'd placed sixth when I'd actually won my race.

The cross-country national championships Bill had mentioned to my parents were held that year in Raleigh, North Carolina. The race was hosted by The Athletic Congress, the sport's national governing body, now called USA Track & Field, and included races at the professional, junior, and youth levels. In 1985, the elite fields included top runners like Olympians Pat Porter and Lynn Jennings, names I wouldn't know for another decade. I was twelve, and what was monumental to me was that we were in an airplane flying across the country so that I could run a race.

My mom and I were traveling with Bill and his stepson, Bryan, the fastest runner on the boys' team, who was also competing. On the flight, while Bryan shot spit wads at me, Bill told me my main competition would be a girl named Deresa Walters, the defending champion. He downplayed the championships, acting like the flight was just another thirty-minute drive across L.A. to another race on Saturday. "All you have to do," he said matter-of-factly, "is race like you always do."

I didn't know what Bill was worried about. I went up against unknown competitors on unfamiliar courses each weekend using a strategy that worked every time: run as hard as possible. This being the national championships, it seemed to me the only difference was that I was going to have to run even harder.

My mom and I woke in the hotel on race morning to the sound of rain pounding the window. Her first question to Bill when we met him and Bryan for breakfast was whether they'd cancel the race. "Is it safe?" she asked.

"It's ideal," Bill assured her. California's dry terrain was an exception, he explained. Everywhere else in the world, cross-country meant mud and obstacles, hay bales and gullies. Rain made it all the better. If the sky was clear, some organizers would hose down part of the course to create some interest.

The moment we arrived at Meredith College, we were drenched and cold. I tried squeezing the safety pins to put on my bib number, but my hands were too cold, so my mom did it while I held the useless umbrella above us.

A little more than a hundred of us stood on the starting line in the rain. I scanned the girls to my left and right trying to pick out Deresa. I imagined a national champion would look a certain, definable way. All of them, though, looked the same: small, wet, and a little miserable in the cold.

The gun cracked and a girl jumped to the lead. I had no idea if it was Deresa, but I got on her shoulder. We had one big 4K loop through the woodsy park, and the leader and I sprinted down the grass toward the wide lake. The girl's breathing quickly became heavy. By now I understood that this was a clue, a signal to press ahead, and I took off. There was tension and strain in the effort, but every feeling associated with racing was fun to me. The burning sensation in my chest, the flailing of my scrappy legs, my arms thrusting greatly, was me wildly at play. I whipped around turns, dug my spikes into the sodden grass, and held up my face to take the brunt of the rain. On the flat stretches, I lengthened my stride and ran hard. I shortened it through puddles, stomping to create big splashes. I ran on, feeling cold water squish between my toes.

At one point, I looked across the lake and saw a long line of girls moving through the trees. *Wow, I have a huge lead.*

Wait. Did I go the wrong way?

No, I couldn't have, because the course is roped off.

Satisfied I hadn't made a mistake, I kept running, my mind taking in the scene. I noticed the raindrops splashing on the lake were huge and that the water dripping down my face tasted like hairspray. The mud splattering up my calves was cold and gritty.

As I ran, I heard the muffled sound of spectators through the trees. The sound got louder, which meant the finish was drawing close. When my mom and Bill saw me approaching, they started screaming. I smiled so big it parted the wet hair plastered across my face. Parents and coaches created a funnel for the last 200 meters and I looked at the two officials holding the finish-line tape. *Wow, I'm going to break that.* I sprinted through the rain and crossed the finish with my hands over mouth, stunned by my own performance.

2.

LOSING

May your choices reflect your hopes, not your fears.
—ATTRIBUTED TO NELSON MANDELA

Winning on the national stage felt big. It was crazy. Up until that race, I had thought of my running ability as a cool thing. After nationals I understood it was something more. People wanted to know if I was going to run in high school. They asked if I wanted to be an Olympian. I had no idea. Some kids might know they have the capability of speed or endurance based on family history. But since I was adopted and had no knowledge of my genetic makeup, my talent had taken my parents and me by surprise. It seemed we'd uncovered a hidden treasure, a genetic secret. How much talent did I have? How big was it? How far would it take me?

The uncertainty of it, the question it posed, thrilled me. I pushed in each race, exploring the scope of my talent. Each time I won, I was elated, and a little surprised. *Wow, my talent was big enough to beat those girls.* That was how I thought of my ability, as a fixed trait, like having blond hair and freckles. In my mind, everyone had a set amount and whoever had the most would win.

I kept winning but never knew if my talent would hold up in the next race, against unknown competitors. So I toed the line of every competition with the anxious excitement of a kid unable to wait to open a present. The desire to see what I could do, to see if I could win, transformed me from a goofy girl tucking her shirt into cut-off sweats into a fierce competitor charging toward the finish. Bill once told a reporter I became a "monster" on the starting line. I probably would have gone with "lioness."

I ran undefeated again the next year and defended my national cross-country title. During track season, I set a national record in the 3,000 meters for girls aged thirteen to fourteen. *Oh my God*, I thought, a phrase I used a lot that year.

Heading into high school, running felt even more exciting. The team was bigger, about thirty boys and girls, and rather than practice two days a week, we ran five. I made the varsity team, along with two other freshmen, Tiffany and Stacy. The older girls fascinated me. They seemed like real runners. Their leg muscles were defined and they ran in actual running clothes, jog bras and split shorts. They also talked about their boyfriends and went to parties, which made them seem so mature. Bill, who'd started coaching high school the year before, thought that with the experience of the older girls and our freshmen talent, we had a chance at making it to the state cross-country championships that year. I wanted to contribute to that goal, to score for the team. But high school seemed like starting over as a competitor. Some of the girls were up to four years older than me and I had no idea how I'd stack up. So on the starting line of our first race, a dual meet against Buena Vista at a park in Ventura County, I was jittery and excited. Could I score? Could I win?

The sun was still hot, though low enough to relieve the oppression of the day. At the gun, I tore off the line and got to the front. I loved putting myself in this position. Being out front felt familiar and comfortable. I fought the urge to look back, assuming the field was hot on my heels, so I pushed and kept pushing. Halfway through, a parent on the sideline shouted that I had a huge lead. *Wow,* I thought, *I'm beating the older girls.* The effort began to feel hard and intuitively, I listened to my foot strikes, trying to keep the same fast cadence. It was both effortful and peaceful to tune in to the sound of racing. I pressed down the final stretch and broke the tape to cheers from my mom, dad, and Lesley.

Bill came over holding a clipboard. "Good job," he said, smiling. Tiffany crossed in second place, and Bill started shouting when he saw the rest of the team coming in, "Oh, Stacy and Cheyenne, and Tally! Wow, looks like we won this race."

After that, a strange thing happened. Just as I'd proven I could keep winning, everyone started speculating when I'd lose. Coaches and parents marveled at my winning streak, but wondered when it would end. A reporter wrote that I might have difficulty winning as the season grew in competitiveness. Bill, too, suddenly seemed concerned. He didn't say anything directly. He used a pep talk to address the matter a few days before the Kenny Staub Cross-Country Invitational, where we'd face the top schools in Southern California. "We're going to face big competition this weekend," he said to the team outside the locker rooms. "Don't expect to continue racing so dominantly as we have these previous races." He said those last lines while glancing at me and Bryan, who had also been winning his races.

At home, my parents started telling me they were proud of me no matter how I raced. "I know that," I said, cocking my head and thinking it peculiar that this new phrase—no matter how I raced—came on the heels of Bill's comment. They all seemed worried a loss would devastate me, but I'd heard Bill say "big" and "competition" and it made me want to go out and win, and win big.

Kenny Staub was held annually in Crescenta Valley, a small town north of L.A., where it was often unbearably hot. I wiggled myself into a front spot on the starting line so I could get off the line quickly. The gun fired and I shot ahead. The stampede behind me was loud and forceful, too close for comfort, so I worked to put some distance between me and the pack. The course was full of sharp turns and hills, like a roller coaster, and I pictured myself as a fast-flying car, zipping around turns, chugging up hills, and barreling down them. After a while, the dusty slap of the girls' footfalls behind me was gone, but my competitors' presence was a constant in my mind. I heard the stampede and tried to gain as much ground as possible. I flew around a grove of trees and down the final stretch, winning the race.

The next four races played out in similar fashion. Each race held the possibility that I would win and the chance that I would lose and the two played off each other, pushing me to run hard. I won the Fountain Valley Invitational and took the win at the Ventura County Cross-Country Championships. Everyone kept waiting for me to lose, but I kept winning.

Near the end of the season, we headed to San Antonio College in Walnut, California, for Mt. SAC, the West's largest cross-country invitational. Dozens of school buses lined the college's stadium when we pulled in, and you could see the big rolling hills we'd be running on. We followed Bill to the baseball field between the start and finish line and set up our blankets, coolers, and backpacks. The girls and I watched the boys start, then warmed up on the course's flat section so we could cheer them on. Back at the blankets, we pulled out my favorite part of our uniform, our blue-and-gold ribbons, and helped one another tie them to our ponytails, unifying us. We stacked our hands on top of each other, counted to three, shouted, "Go Chargers!" and took our place on the starting line.

The gun fired and I shot forward, but it was Kira Jorgensen who got out front. Kira was a junior at Rancho Buena Vista High in San Diego. She was tall and lanky, with dark-brown hair woven into two French braids that met in the back. Bill had told me about Kira. She was a strong runner who was on an impressive winning streak herself. He was, perhaps, preparing me to be chasing Kira. She was only a few strides ahead, though, within striking distance. *It's fine*, I told myself. *I'll catch her on the hills.*

Mt. SAC was notorious for its three climbs: the Switchbacks, which began just after the flat first mile; Poop-Out, which got its reputation from having a pitch so steep some runners used their hands to crawl up it; and Reservoir, a long, gradual climb on a dry, exposed slope. I pressed the pace, pumping my arms to keep the space between Kira and me from lengthening before the first hill. If I could stay in position, I'd set myself to catch her.

But Kira pulled away and expanded her lead on the Switchbacks just as I started climbing them. *She went out too fast. Stay on her, be ready to fly past when she tires.* Kira didn't tire. She kept inching ahead. I watched her, a tall figure in a maroon singlet, crest the hill and disappear. A half minute later, I hit the top and kept my eyes on her as momentum carried me down the hill.

My family, Bill, and the boys' team egged me on as I flew along the flat stretch toward Poop-Out Hill. Spectators huddled near the base of this next climb to catch the drama—who would use their hands? Who would have to stop and walk? Kira seemed to float up the hill. *Okay, there's time, she won't maintain that pace.* I ran in intense pursuit, imagining myself passing her on the quiet backstretch before Reservoir Hill. It'd be a dramatic show for the spectators, a runner who trailed the whole race emerging the leader in the final mile, a lone silhouette climbing the exposed slope of Reservoir.

The leading silhouette was Kira. I watched her press up the hill, and the fact of what was happening dawned as a simple thought: *Oh, here it is, the loss everyone has been talking about.* But even then losing didn't feel crushing. My winning streak had lasted longer than anyone had imagined. I'd already broken the usual hierarchy of high school running by beating the upperclassmen. Plus, once the older runners like Kira graduated, I'd be the one winning.

Kira made the sharp right onto the final stretch known as the gauntlet. I gained a few strides, but not enough to make up the entire distance, and she broke the tape. I followed 15 seconds later. Across the line, I put my hands on my knees, exhausted. Kira patted me on the back. "Good job today," she said. "You made me work for that."

"Thank you." I smiled, touched that she said something so nice to me. "Good job."

A booming voice came over the loudspeaker announcing that I'd broken the freshman course record. "We look forward to following her promising high school career. Congratulations, Deena," the voice said.

Bill rushed over. "A new freshman record!?"

My family was right behind him. "Great job, kiddo," my dad said. My mom was teary-eyed and handed me a bottle of water. Lesley said "good job" too, without looking up from the thumb war she was having with a friend. Tiffany finished fifth, helping secure Agoura the team win, and when she heard the news of my record, she said, "Oh my God, I can't believe it," squeezing my hands. Everyone was so impressed with the record, and made such a fuss about it that second place felt like a win.

The competitor in me didn't show up at practice. Practice to me was fun, and that was the whole point. We laughed our way through most runs and turned workouts into adventures. Sometimes at Paramount Ranch when Bill sent us off, we "borrowed" boats on Malibu Lake and tried tipping one another over, running back soaking wet. Other times, the boys' team jumped out from behind trees, trying to scare us as we ran by. The girls and I occasionally detoured mid-run to Bud's Ice Cream where my friend Annette, a shot-putter, slipped us a milkshake across the counter. We'd cram into a booth and eat the thick coffee-flavored shake with spoons. When the boys ran by, we ditched the cup and ran after them.

I loved goofing off, laughing with my teammates, and exploring the scenery. Racing, on the other hand, was competitive, highly charged, and intense. Practice and racing evoked such completely different emotions in me, they might as well have been separate sports, so my mind made no connection between them.

If my performance or the team's had suffered, and Bill had to work us harder to regain our places, the relationship between practice and racing might have clicked. But I ran well and the team ran well, which was perhaps another reason the true purpose of training stayed in my blind spot. I led the team to a Frontier League title, then we snagged the southern regional championship title. And just as Bill predicted, we made it to the state championships.

The team and I caravanned with our families north to Fresno the day after Thanksgiving for the state meet. By now our routine was familiar: set up blankets, warm up, fasten ribbons, run hard. I launched off the line at Woodward Park—a large, wooded stretch along the San Joaquin River—and into the lead with one other competitor. The two of us hit the mile in 5:18. I felt good, so I took off, blazing through the trees and into the sun-exposed section. I crested the course's only hill, ran back into the trees, and chased down the finish, winning the California State title as a freshman. The win reinforced what I was learning: if I ran hard, my talent would be big enough to beat the competition.

The team's season was over, but mine continued into the postseason. I took second at the West regional competition, which qualified me to compete at the Kinney National Cross-Country Championships, the pinnacle of high school running. Winning Kinney pegged you as the best in the nation. As a freshman, I now belonged to a small, exclusive group that made it to nationals their first year.

Kinney was in downtown San Diego at Morley Field, a collection of manicured fields flanked by eucalyptus groves in Balboa Park. All the runners stayed at the Hotel del Coronado, a fancy place with plush red carpets, crown-shaped chandeliers, and an ornately decorated Christmas tree that rose through the first three floors. The weekend was a highly orchestrated three-day event, with banquet dinners, panel discussions, and a trip to Sea World.

College recruiters moved about and media hovered around runners. The hype and grandeur built up the race's significance in my mind. It was big.

Kira was also competing; and off the line, I tried attaching myself to her, but she was already strides ahead, so I watched her run. She shot forward like a smooth and steady arrow. Her stride was tight and determined, so unlike her overexaggerated body language when she spoke. I tried to match her fluid style, tucking my elbows in and working to make my way through the runners between us. I couldn't catch her, though, and she disappeared out of sight. I ran the rest of the race with the chase pack and crossed the finish line in eleventh place.

Wow, that was hard, I thought as I walked through the finishing chute and into the media zone. Journalists and television crews were all huddled around a single runner, Kira. The fanfare could only mean one thing: she'd won. I squeezed my way through to reach her. "Congratulations!" I said, giving her a hug. Kira beamed, and I slipped out.

Standing next to my bag, I chugged a bottle of water and thought eleventh place wasn't all that impressive. But what excited me, what stayed with me, was that Kira had won. *I'm faster than she was as a freshman*, I thought, realizing then what I could do. *I can win this race someday.*

After Kinney, I didn't think my performance was something the papers would write about. But the *Ventura County Star* published a story saying my eleventh-place finish was a great cap to an incredible freshman year. Sophomore year, I missed the cross-country season opener due to injury and an article said our team would have to wait to be up to full speed until I returned. When I started competing again, the headlines read: *Healthy Drossin Leads Agoura Girls. Drossin Back in Top Form.*

Each story lifted me to a higher state of belief about my ability. The morning after each race, my mom would run out to the driveway to get the papers—we received three now—and we'd hover as a family in the kitchen reading the articles. Junior year, I had a few losses but I mostly won and the headline was: *Drossin's Future Bright Indeed*. I took second at the West regional championships that year, and the papers spun it as a success: *Drossin Qualifies 3 for 3. Drossin's Strategy Sets Her Up Well for Nationals*. I laughed at that one. The headline implied I'd held back in regionals to save myself for nationals. But I still had only one strategy: run hard.

Recruiters started calling. I visited the University of Arizona and the University of Oregon in Eugene, and had invitations from Arkansas, Wisconsin, and Villanova, too. Realizing that running was going to take me somewhere, I thought about it more. I started getting excited early in the week before a race, a contrast to my younger self, who only felt the charge to race when her toe hit the starting line. I practiced what it felt like to be strong and confident while walking across the quad between classes and I raced with more purpose and drive.

Heading into the Kinney championships junior year, I wanted to win. I already had local and state titles. What was missing was a national one. What better way to showcase my talent and prove my value to college recruiters than by being a national champion. At the race, I used my hard-from-the-gun tactic in the hope that Sarah Schwald, a junior from Spokane, Washington, who beat me at regionals, had a bad day. Sarah passed me, as did a number of others, and I placed thirteenth.

The papers didn't have much to say about that performance. That was okay. Shortly after finishing, I stood near the finish and watched my teammate Bryan, who was now a senior, win the boys' title. Bryan and I had shared headlines since middle school. I was following his winning path as much as Kira's. There was next year, my senior year, when I was sure the headline would read: *Drossin Crowned Queen of Kinney*.

I wanted to make that senior season flawless.

I signed with the University of Arkansas, largely because the women reminded me of my high school team. There was warmth and friendship among them. Lance Harter, the head coach, was working to build the Arkansas team into a national powerhouse, and he told me I'd be an important part of building that legacy. I could be valuable, a contributor, and lead the team to great heights. I liked that idea. All that was left was a winning senior year.

I pictured how it would unfold. It'd begin with a stamp of authority at the season opener. I'd charge out front and lead the team to its first victory of the year. An undefeated season would follow. I'd collect local, county, and state titles and stand with the team on the podium after delivering Agoura its first state title. The momentum would continue into the post-season. My victory at West regionals would be definitive, and breaking the tape at Kinney would be sensational. It was going to be perfect.

Tiffany, Kristie, Laura, Skye, and I—Agoura's top scorers that year—ripped off the line at the cross-country season opener. The girls followed close behind, securing the team win.

Off to a perfect start.

We collected another team win at the Woodbridge Rotary Invitational, where I set another course record. Our successes mounted. At the Marmonte League Championships, I broke the course record, and on the same course the following week, I bettered the record by winning the Ventura County title.

By the time I arrived at the state championships, a feeling of invincibility had settled inside me. Our routine—warming up, tying bows, walking together to the line—put me in an elevated state, my body hyperaware. I got off the line quickly, moving over the grass and into the shade. By now, the courses were familiar, and rather than focusing on the chalked arrows in the dirt, I used landmarks—a tree, a playground—to pull myself toward the finish line faster. *Get out of the trees as fast as you can,* I thought. Then: *Hurry, get to the hill, attack the hill.* My mind veered off the terrain at mile 2, where all the teams' families stood cheering: *Blaze past them!* I thought, and felt a swell of support as I went by. As I approached the final grassy stretch, I shouted inside, *Charge!*—pretending to be a storming frontline soldier in a historic war. Bill gave a fist pump as I broke the tape, winning again.

At West regionals, the race went off exactly how I imagined: I got in the lead, transitioned from grass to sidewalk to dirt smoothly, hearing only my footsteps, and won, advancing to Kinney.

The ballroom at the del Coronado was packed when my parents and I arrived. Within minutes, the media found me among the throng of runners and parents. "What's your goal this year, Deena?" a television reporter asked.

"I've had a great season so far, and want to cap it with a victory here at nationals," I said, thinking, *I want to crush it.*

"Do you feel running here the last three years gives you an advantage?" she asked.

"My only advantage is having lots of family and friends cheering for me on the course," I said. *I hope hearing so many* Go Deenas *will psyche me up and psyche out the competition.*

Bill and I headed to Balboa Park to walk the course. Kinney started with a slight ascent on grass, then descended into a eucalyptus grove. We stopped in the trees and Bill pointed out the tangents. As we made our way to the other side of the course to study the hill, Bill said, "These hills are nothing compared to what you've done at Paramount Ranch or Mt. SAC. Hills are your strength; you can use them to either take over the race or extend your lead."

My primary competitor was Melody Fairchild, a senior at Boulder High who'd won Kinney the previous year. Melody was a strong runner and I knew she'd be tough to beat. Bill knew it too, and before we reached the finish line, he stopped me in the grass.

"Nobody thinks they can beat Melody. Everyone is running for second place. Do you want to run for second, or do you want to run to win?"

"You know the answer to that," I said.

Bill nodded. "Okay, don't try to lead the race at the start. Hang on to her shoulder and let her do the work. When you take over, commit to the finish."

Race morning, the West team warmed up together, mostly in silence, so we could hear the announcer. He spoke of the uniqueness of the Kinney Championships, how it was the only national competition in high school athletics, how its champions went on to become NCAA champions, collegiate record holders, and Olympians.

We got in formation for the athlete parade. While the announcer rattled off the accolades of the other runners—state champion, regional champion, state record holder—all I could think was, *This is my last chance to win this race.*

"From Agoura Hills, California, Deena Drossin."

I waved to the crowd. As he read my accomplishments—Deena is a four-time state champion, the West regional champion, and making her fourth appearance at Kinney—I ran down the arced path, turning to smile at the camera, and took my place on the starting line. *I'm 3 miles away from a national championship.*

The final runner took her place.

"Runners set."

My toes hugged the white-painted line. *It's my time.*

POP!

I got out quickly and surged over the grass into the lead. A swarm of girls began to surround me. A second later, they swallowed me.

My God, what's happening? I shot into the trees toward the first turn—*Get there, take it hard*—and slipped on the woodchips.

Why are you so clumsy?

This isn't right, this isn't how I envisioned it.

Out of the trees, I charged toward the next turn. A couple of girls passed me.

Go with them. Get them.

I pushed, trying to turn my legs over faster, but the gap between us didn't close.

At mile 1, only about five girls were climbing the hill ahead of me, but I saw a hundred.

You're getting demolished.

I drove my arms to get my legs to move faster, but didn't gain any ground.

Is this really all you have?

I began to panic. I ran downhill, windmilling my arms, frantically trying to catch up. I did everything I knew to do. I chased and I charged. I practically lunged trying to catch the ponytail ahead of me. *I'm going to lose*, I thought, and this time my whole body went tense. My throat and stride tightened. I ran the last stretch pushing so hard to change the outcome my lips peeled back revealing the strain. I crossed the line in sixth place.

Get me out of here.

I ran through the finishing chute and media zone, stopping quickly to congratulate Melody on her win—I didn't want to be impolite—and disappeared into the trees before journalists, Bill, or my parents could find me.

Sixth place!

That's a far cry from national champion.

I kicked the woodchips at the base of the tree, keeping my head down. I don't know how long I stood there. Not too long because then my mom would've come looking for me. But long enough to try to find a reason for the loss. I'd won West regionals last weekend. I felt great on the starting line. I ran hard like I always did.

Your best isn't good enough.

You've been delusional.

Maybe you're just not that talented.

The next morning, my parents, Lesley, and I sat on the hotel's deck having breakfast. A story in one of the papers noted that a girl I'd beaten throughout high school had finally beaten me at Kinney.

"Wow," my mom beamed. "You may not have won, but you're still in the paper."

I was mortified.

Back at school, I walked the halls feeling like a fraud, like I had this secret. *I'm not the runner you think I am.* Coach Harter, I presumed, would no longer want me on his team and I came home after school braced for news that he'd called. I imagined he'd let me down easy, saying there had been budget cuts and that he was sorry, it was out of his hands.

News stories later in the week confirmed my fears. One reporter questioned whether I could handle the rigors of collegiate running. Another wondered if I was burned out. One got to the heart of it: High school, he wrote, could have been Drossin's best years.

I was confused. I didn't understand why I'd lost, and not understanding pained me. I replayed the race over in my mind, running through it from start to finish. I saw myself getting out hard, working to push with every step. To me, that was how talent was revealed, and mine had come up short.

Where were you? I whispered, suddenly feeling as if my ability had betrayed me, strung me along, only to stand me up when I needed it the most. *Can I trust you? Will you be there next time?*

I was worried. I had college races ahead, and a scholarship to maintain. I had a new coach who seemed sure I could lead his team. But how could I lead a collegiate team if I couldn't win a national high school championship?

Coach Harter did call. But only to wish me a happy birthday and tell me how excited he was for the fall. My parents bragged at every dinner party about my full scholarship. Bill said he looked forward to watching my progress in college. My senior class voted me "Most Likely to Succeed." Everyone seemed to think that Deena Drossin, star high school runner, was headed toward a promising college career. I wasn't so sure. For a long time after Kinney, I raced with excitement, but never without fear. And over time, it started to take its toll.

3

THE MAGICAL VISION OF THE MARLBORO MAN

To be what you must, you must give up what you are.

—YUSUF ISLAM (CAT STEVENS)

The sun was setting on the plains of Amarillo, Texas, when my mom and I pulled into the parking lot of the Best Western. She let out a sigh of relief at the silence, such a contrast to the rattle of my Jeep for the past eight hours. We were caravanning from California to the University of Arkansas with my new teammate, Jamie Parks, and her mom. Jamie was the reigning NCAA 10,000-meter champion, who had, the previous year, followed Coach Harter from Cal Poly San Luis Obispo to Arkansas. Everything about Jamie intimidated me. She was the team's distance star with a quintessential California look: blond, pretty, tan, and fit. Once we got to Arkansas, she would be moving into an off-campus apartment while I was moving into the dorms—clearly, I thought, a sign of my inferiority.

Jamie jumped out of her car and said to me, "We need to get out for a run before we lose the light." She grabbed her bag from the backseat.

"You can't run now," my mom said, alarmed. "It's getting dark."

"We'll run the main road, so headlights can light the way," Jamie said to my mom while looking at me.

According to Coach Harter's summer schedule, we needed to do a fartlek workout, a series of pickups within a run. It was the first real test of my talent since Kinney, and part of me was dreading it. Outwardly, I kept cool, but inside I was worried. *What if I can't keep up with her?* I imagined her telling Coach Harter afterward, *She's really not that talented.* But I wasn't going to not run. "Sure, sounds good," I said. "Meet you back here."

We disappeared into our respective motel rooms to change. My hands shook as I tied my shoes. *Is that you?* I whispered to my talent. *Please, please, be there for me.*

I found Jamie in the parking lot. "Ready?" she asked, hand poised over her watch. I nodded, and the two of us headed down a frontage road, making small talk during the warm-up. Jamie told me her mom was quiet and that they passed the time on the drive mostly listening to music. I told her my mom talked a lot and tried to rise above the Jeep's constant racket. She laughed. She warned me that Arkansas was a culture shock. There are churches everywhere, she said, and once you get a few miles out of Fayetteville, you'll see hog farmers in overalls with no shirt and missing teeth. I smiled, but didn't tell her I liked how different Fayetteville was from suburban L.A. I didn't want to be contradictory.

We began our pickups. She set the pace, and it was fast. I found myself having to press like I did in races to keep up. Jamie ran smoothly, steadily. I tried not to inhale too loudly. Her watch beeped and we backed off. *Made it through one.* I kept up with her during the second pickup, but during the third, I fell back. This was my test, and I needed to get through it, or at least think I had, so I got creative. I found that if I ran the recovery portion a little faster than I should have, I could narrow the gap between us. *A few steps behind an NCAA champion. Not bad.*

We finished the last repeat backlit by headlights and did a quick cool-down en route back to the hotel. I burst through the door and announced to my mom, who was sitting on the edge of the bed, "I just ran with Jamie!"

"Oh, thank God," she said, glad I'd made it back alive. I nodded, thinking, *Yeah, she didn't kill me.* Walking into the bathroom, I tapped my quads as if my talent lived there. *Thank you.*

Practice began a few days after Jamie and I arrived in Fayetteville with a trip to Holiday Island, a resort community on Table Rock Lake where the women's team, about a dozen of us, spent a week getting to know one another. Coach Harter set the tone on the first night. He stood in the living room of the condo resembling a fit version of the state's young governor, Bill Clinton, and had a similar upbeat voice. "This trip is going to be good for us," he said. "We're not trying to blow each other's doors off; we're going to run together and build camaraderie. We'll get the hard work in when we return to campus."

The town's roads were narrow and congested and the women and I ran mostly single file, doing goose runs—the runner in the back surges to the front, setting the pace and picking the direction until the lead is taken over by the next runner.

Evenings were spent cooking and talking. Margaret had a thick southern accent and said she was only in college to find a husband, preferably one who was educated. Claire was from Great Britain and revealed her first orgasm took place on a stationary bike in the weight room. Stephanie was a middle-distance runner from Vacaville, California, who had transferred from Cal Poly, like Jamie. She was a natural storyteller and used a lot of expletives ("hell yeah" and "screw that"), which I found funny. Pauline's short blond hair swung across her face when she got excited talking, but none of us could understand her thick Irish accent, so we all just laughed.

Conversations with the girls put me at ease. They were also often a primer on college athletics. To "walk on" meant showing up and proving you were good enough to be on the team. "Partials" and "fulls" referred to scholarship levels, but no matter your level, you were still obligated to run all three seasons: cross-country in the fall, indoor track in the winter, and outdoor track in the spring and summer. Someone mentioned a teammate was "redshirting" the cross-country season. "Which means what?" I asked. "Sitting out," the girls explained. We were all on the five-year plan, including me, and you could only compete in each season for four years, so by redshirting, you could run in your fifth year when you would be stronger and more mature.

Back in Fayetteville, running took on a serious tone. It no longer felt like the fun after-school activity it had been in high school; it felt like a profession. Lance told us to do 20-minute morning runs on our own before classes. He reminded us to build our class schedule around 3:00 p.m. practice time, and that we needed to come wearing our team warm-ups. After practice, we'd head to the arena to hydrate, lift weights, and ice any aches or pains.

On a tempo run on North Weddington Road, a flat stretch along farmland, Jamie ran ahead of the rest of us. Running with Jamie had assured me I could hold my own. But in my mind, my job was to lead the team as I had in high school and I felt the urge to catch her.

I held back, though, worried the other girls would think I was showing off, or if I couldn't keep up with Jamie, they'd think me a fool for trying. But mile by mile, the anxiousness to see if I could beat her built into a physical pressure, a hard pulsing through my body, so after the turnaround, I began gradually picking up speed, accelerating gently so as not to be obnoxious. Jamie was about a quarter mile ahead, and slowly her swinging ponytail came into view. I gave a little more and by the end closed the gap between us to a half dozen strides.

Stephanie came up to me afterward, slapping me on the back. "Wow, girl, where the hell did that come from?" I blushed.

A few days later, I ripped around Springdale Golf Course during a mile repeat workout without hesitation. Jamie and I worked together for the first few repetitions, pushing each other as our spikes ripped up the grass. On the next repeat, I felt so good I pushed past Jamie on the hill, finishing in the lead. Emboldened, I shot to the front in the next repeat, powered through the mile and crossed ahead of the team. When I turned, I saw them all coming at me. *Oh, God,* I thought, *why did I take the lead so soon? Now I have to keep it.*

Our cross-country season opener was an invitational on the University of Kansas's home course, Rim Rock Farm, known for the statues commemorating running legends like Billy Mills and Jim Ryun. About one hundred women were on the starting line. I stood with my team and shook out my legs, trying to let go of my nerves. *Just use this race to observe, see what happens,* I told myself. Just before the gun, Stephanie caught my eye. "Come on, Double D!" she said, smiling, the nickname a play off my initials, Deena Drossin, or ironic commentary on my small chest. Either way, her confidence channeled my nerves.

The gun fired, and I booked it off the line. *C'mon,* I thought, *be here, we have a job to do.* I launched an all-out assault on the grassy terrain, pulling ahead of the field. With each stride, I lengthened the gap, both surprised and relieved to be leading. I was out front, but anxious, no longer aiming to win, but trying not to lose. Wanting reassurance, I used a sharp turn to glance over my shoulder. I was far ahead but, afraid of getting caught, I continued pushing. I ran alone for the rest of the race, save for the grasshoppers jumping into my half-clenched hands. After breaking the tape, I caught my breath as the rest of the team followed. It was clear the Lady 'Backs won the team competition, and Lance was flushed with excitement. I celebrated with the team, but inside, I felt the pressure mounting. The season was going to get more competitive. *How are you going to keep winning?*

I pushed in workouts, trying to lead the team and bring out the best in my teammates. On easy days, we took to the trails above campus, loping through the lush woods and vines and into a wide horse pasture. Mid-run, Pauline said, "We can totally win an SEC title."

"My ring size is five and a half!" Margaret shouted, alluding to her conference ring.

"I was thinking more along the lines of an NCAA title," Stephanie chimed in.

Lance, who often joined us for these easy runs, smiled widely. "This is music to my ears."

I started having nightmares. Well, not exactly, more like frightening daydreams when my mind wandered during class or practice. I was in a high-stakes race, hammering as hard as I could, and runners flew past me at the end. Each race, I failed to win, disappointing my team and my coach.

We traveled to San Diego for the Aztec Invitational at Balboa Park, which was on the same course as Kinney. When I closed my eyes on the flight, I saw myself slip on the woodchips, unable to catch competitors on the hill. *The course doesn't have to be a demon*, I told myself as the plane touched down. *This is a different situation. You're in college now.*

When we arrived at the park on race morning, I looked around at the fields and down to the first grove of eucalyptus. It was beautiful. Families were strolling in the grass, dogs were playing around the trees, and fragrant wildflowers grew along the edges of the park. The course looked so benign. I rolled my eyes at the nerves I felt.

Still, the fear that I would fail hummed inside and I got off the line with urgency, taking the lead with no other goal than to redline the pace to keep the lead. The course was a flash of terrain, merely a checklist of start, trees, hill, repeat. Coming off the sharp turn at the base of the downhill, I checked over my shoulder. No one was chasing me. I was finally in front where I wanted to be every other time I'd run there, and peace flooded my body. The effort remained, but it was a fluid one, unlike the frantic push of high school. I made the final turn and allowed myself to enjoy what felt like a ceremonial passing between two towering palms. The long stretch to the finish came into view and with my mind calm, I heard the sound of my shoes pressing into the half-dry grass. My dad, in his cap and glasses, stood quietly on the sideline clapping. A "woo-hoo" came from my mom. "Go, Dee!" from Lesley. I raised my arms high and broke the tape with relief.

Afterward, I found Bill, who'd also come to watch.

"How much faster was my time?" I asked.

"You mean than senior year?" He paused. "Fifteen seconds I'd guess, maybe twenty."

"No, I mean exactly, do you know the exact number?"

Results were not yet online. Bill called the next day.

"Deena, it was thirty-six," he said. "You ran the course thirty-six seconds faster."

The win was as confusing as it was rewarding. I still didn't understand why I had lost Kinney in high school or why I was winning now. What made one runner better than another? How could I keep leading my team? I didn't know. But the men's team seemed to offer an answer. They would say, "The cream rises to the top," meaning the athletes who could sustain the hardest effort in practice emerged as the leaders and scorers. They were the winningest cross-country team in the nation. It seemed like a solid strategy.

And so I hammered every workout, even easy days. I'd rob myself of breath quickly, forcing my legs forward and my arms to pump so hard that my biceps and shoulders would go numb. The girls rallied behind me. "Keep it up, Deena!" "Go, Double D!" But on easy days, they tried enticing me to hold back. "I've got a good story to tell," Stephanie would promise.

But I couldn't hold back. By now, I'd led the team to an SEC title. I was winning, the team was winning, and I saw it was my job to keep us there.

I pushed my body to its limit. One morning when I woke, the

arch of my left foot was sore. It loosened up during the day, so I kept running on it. Eventually, though, it got my attention. Up on the trails with the team, the pain shot through my foot every time I pushed off the ground. I curled my toes to prevent the arch from stretching. But continuing to run only worsened the injury.

"Maybe you're running too hard," Lance said in the training room, where I stood with him and the athletic trainer, Kelli Sheffield, before practice. My mind dismissed the idea. Running hard was my job.

"Take the day off today," Kelli said. "Let's ice it and see how you feel tomorrow."

The pain was no better the next day or the one after that. "I think it's a classic case of plantar fasciitis," Kelli said, while I lay on a table in the training room. She added ultrasound and anti-inflammatories to my icing routine. I didn't worry. I figured "classic" meant "easily fixable." But by day five, I felt panicky.

Lance put me in the pool. At 6:00 a.m., with a floatation device around my waist, I ran back and forth along the edge of the diving pool, frustrated and feeling alone. The hour ticked by slowly. At practice later in the day, when the team started the workout, I returned to my table in the training room. Kelli or one of her staff rubbed the ultrasound wand along the bottom of my foot to increase blood flow, then I did towel curls and iced.

"You'll be better soon," the girls said when they stopped by after their workout.

"Yeah, it'll pass, thanks," I said.

But the injury held on, and the trainers were emphatic that if I competed in the upcoming NCAA districts, I'd risk being injured for the championships. Lance made the decision that I'd sit out the race.

The team was sweet. "We'll miss you!"

I smiled. "You can totally do this without me," I said, secretly worried it might be true.

"What can we bring you from Texas?"

"A big win," I said cheerfully.

The team crushed it. I wanted to be happy for them, but I worried that I was losing my place on the team. I jumped back into the full schedule even though my foot was still tight and tender, worsening the problem.

Before the championships, Lance asked the trainers, "Could racing with her foot like this be career-ending?"

No, was their consensus. "It could rip some fascia or scar tissue maybe, but she'll be fine," one of them said.

So I flew to Tucson with the team. At the starting line at El Conquistador Country Club, where runners from twenty-two universities had gathered for the NCAA Cross-Country Championships, I wished for more time to get ready. I ran near the middle of a crowded field. Every other stride, I pulled my foot off the ground as soon as it landed to avoid the pain. When my foot hit a rut and the arch stretched, the pain was crippling. Unable to find a rhythm, I finished forty-fourth.

I was humiliated. My place pulled the team's score down so much, we finished a distant second to Villanova. The loss felt like my fault. "Don't be so hard on yourself," Lance said, and he pointed out that even if I'd won, the team results would've been the same. "We're a young team and I'm proud of the entire season."

But I couldn't see it any other way: I'd let the team down, let Lance down, and had disappointed everyone.

Lance had me redshirt the indoor winter track season. The two months off only pulled me further away from the team. When I returned and ran in the outside lane while the women did workouts in lane one, I watched as an outsider looking in while the girls joked and laughed. To reinsert myself, I launched again into 60-mile weeks. Injury returned.

The cycle continued all through sophomore year and into junior year. During strong periods—winning another SEC title, leading the team to a second NCAA district title—I felt valued, like a contributor. Then another injury would hit and my judgment was quick and harsh: *You're fragile, totally worthless.* The headlines that went through my mind daily were something like, *Drossin Disappoints at Arkansas. Drossin Doesn't Live Up to Expectations. Drossin Can't Handle High-Level Training.*

Walking on campus or sitting in class, the negativity of such thoughts hummed at a low level, closing me off from other perspectives, like Lance's, who saw my stronger races as a boost to the team, and my injuries as the frustrating reality of collegiate athletics.

Berating myself was exhausting, and trying to keep up appearances was draining. If a teammate showed up wanting to do a different workout than planned, I was annoyed. If Lance pulled me out of the pool for 400s, I begrudged the workout. One afternoon, I walked onto the track and only a few of my teammates were there.

Where the hell is everyone?

Lance had given some of the girls permission to do their workouts on their own, so they could better balance running and schoolwork. Perfectly reasonable. But I snapped. *Screw it,* I thought. *Why am I working so hard to show up when no one else is?*

A protagonist on the big screen would have turned on her heels and walked out. I didn't leave; I just stopped caring. I redshirted again, taking my junior year off, ostensibly because my body and mind needed a break. In reality, I just wanted to get away from running.

So I focused on school.

I was a writing major and spent hours at a coffeehouse working on stories. I engrossed myself in the writings of Henry Miller, William Burroughs, and Flannery O'Connor. I found the troubled poetry of Edgar Allan Poe and Emily Dickinson somber and pleasing because it matched my mood. I researched for weeks the dark history of two great horror stories, learning how Lord Byron and his doctor, John Polidori, stayed on the shores of Lake Geneva in the Villa Diodati. Byron gathered his literary friends Percy Shelley, Mary Wollstonecraft Godwin, and Claire Clairmont and challenged them each to write a ghost story. Out of that stormy weekend of rancid meats and an abundance of wine came *Frankenstein* and *The Vampyre*. I tunneled into that darkness. *The Vampyre* was accidently attributed to Byron instead of Polidori and for my final assignment in creative writing I wrote *The Night the Lights Went Out in Old Main*, a fictional account of the murder of Byron by Polidori for taking credit for his work.

There was always a cappuccino and a pastry next to me while I wrote, and at one point I realized that the muffins were oily and the scones were dry and that I could do better. I'd always enjoyed baking and cooking. As a kid, I spent time in the kitchen with my dad, chopping garlic and creating a brown butter sauce for pre-race pasta. We often went shopping together and walked up and down the aisles looking for ingredients to try. Once I had moved into my own apartment my junior year in college, cooking became a hobby. I'd roast a whole chicken, plating myself a couple of pieces with garlic mashed potatoes, then I'd boil the carcass the next day to make soup, which my grandmother said could cure everything from the common cold to a broken heart. I started baking at home while I studied alone. I plucked recipes from *Gourmet*, *Cooking Light*, and *Vegetarian Times* and spun them into works of my own. Different flour or sugars changed the entire experience of a loaf of bread. Using coconut, oats, and dark chocolate could transform an everyday chocolate-chip cookie. Espresso grounds offered a fun alternative to a classic shortbread recipe.

So I went home and turned on the oven, thinking maybe I could sell my baked goods to the coffeehouses. I made a batch of blueberry muffins and whole-wheat bagels. In the morning, I went to class and hurried home to make raspberry–white-chocolate-chip scones and carrot cake. I placed one of each into several brown paper bags and stapled a business card to the top: SWEET EXPECTATIONS,

HOMEMADE GOODS DELIVERED DAILY. My logo was a muffin with a bite taken out of it. I dropped the bags off at seven coffeehouses and all of them called me back. The orders poured in. I was ecstatic.

A kind man who owned a local smokehouse let me use his commercial kitchen for free, so each morning at four, I drove through the empty streets of Fayetteville and lost myself in the rhythm of baking. Pouring flour into industrial-size mixers, fishing bagels out of big boiling pots of water, and gently smoothing cream cheese frosting on rich carrot cake had the same meditative flow as running—except when I burnt my finger or dropped a tray of cookies. I worked in silence, humming to the sound of the mixers churning, ovens clicking, and the shuffling of my feet.

I didn't run for almost a year and I didn't think about running. I didn't watch practice or attend team dinners. I didn't go to races to cheer on my teammates. As they ran the indoor season, the outdoor season, and started cross-country again, I baked, went to class, and wrote.

Customers at the coffeehouses said my flourless chocolate torte made them weak in the knees. Others claimed to have my bagels with the honey-whipped cream cheese every morning before work. Baking became my new effort, the compliments my new reward. Walking across the quad, I noticed my posture was taller and there was a little bounce in my step, such a contrast to the year before when I'd hugged my books to my chest, shoulders rounded, the perception of weakness causing me to carry myself in a weak way.

I might have just kept baking had my scholarship not obligated me to return for my final track season senior year. A month before I was due back at practice, I started heading out for twenty minutes or so in the afternoon. Running was hard and awkward. My breathing was labored even though the pace was slow. My muscles, particularly my quads and inner thighs, were tender and sore. I ran because I had to, but soon my muscles remembered the motion, though I think they were surprised at being weighed down by my softer baker's physique. I got up to forty-five minutes, then an hour, and my breathing evened out. At one point, my stride became smooth and fluid. It seemed like running was welcoming me back. I expected nothing from it, so I just ran, and it felt good enough that I smiled back.

Returning to the team was harder. I felt inadequate and fragile, fearful injury would return, and I didn't want to be there. I skipped the morning shakeout run so I could bake and then ran only in the afternoons with the team. Toward the end of the season, the conversation turned to what the seniors were doing after college. My teammates all had jobs or internships lined up. A few were pursuing professional running. "Deena, what are you going to do?" they inquired. The question made me sweat. I didn't know. I felt silly for having a college education and not knowing what to pursue. I liked creative writing, but it wasn't going to pay the rent. I'd actually run a few good races that spring, even won an SEC title. But I couldn't see those successes; all I saw was that I'd failed to bring Arkansas a national title. If I couldn't succeed in college, what chance did I have at turning pro? The only option presenting itself in my mind was to keep baking.

My parents came for graduation. They'd been good about not pressing too much about my plans. Now, the questions came over brunch. Mom: Are you going to get a job and stay in Fayetteville, or are you coming home? Dad: Have you thought about how you'll make a living? I told them I was thinking of staying in Arkansas and opening a little café.

"The restaurant business is the most difficult to be successful in," my dad said. "Most of them close within their first year. They're a money pit. You didn't study baking or business. Why don't you write for the athletic department?"

I spat back, "Baking is the only thing I'm good at."

Still, if I pushed aside the injuries and the black-and-white conclusion about my capability, I missed running. I missed the strong sense of purpose and pride of competing on a team. I missed the rush of racing, the push and the drive. Racing at times in college had still felt internal, instinctual, as if I were satisfying something essential.

There had been moments when I finished a race knowing I could have run better, sensing there was more in me that I didn't know how to access. None of that was conscious. But it was there.

Alone in my apartment one night after my parents left, I pulled out the *I Ching,* an ancient Chinese text full of wisdom and insight. I'd bought it one afternoon in the middle of college while browsing the self-help section of the student bookstore. I'd stood in the aisle that afternoon hoping a book would fly off the shelf and tell me how to handle stress, manage my time, succeed at something. Instead, I pulled out the *I Ching.* Flipping through it, I was drawn to its insights on constancy, self-mastery, and rhythm. To use this book, you ask a question, toss three coins six times, and connect the results with a corresponding message. I asked *Which will bring me more happiness and success—running or baking?* I tossed the coins. The oracle suggested *contemplating.*

I rolled my eyes and turned to my deck of tarot cards. Reflecting on my question, I placed one card on the table. The Two of Swords. It pictures a young woman seated on a cement bench holding two swords in her hands, which represent two sides of a situation. The blindfold around her eyes reveals that she cannot see the problem or the solution.

I sighed. I suppose I wanted a card that didn't exist: the Baker, featuring a fat, happy fool licking frosting off a spoon. Then I could open the café and tell my dad I had the backing of the cosmos.

In late May after graduation, Fayetteville emptied of students, save for those competing in the NCAA track championships in June. I was running the 10,000. After a hot and sticky workout on the track, the other girls walked to their cars. But with finals over, there was no need to rush, so I lingered on the grass, stretching.

Milan Donley, an assistant coach, was nearby watching his long jumpers practice. Milan was tall and lean, and when not in Razorback gear, he wore cowboy boots and a big belt buckle, looking like the Marlboro Man, if the Marlboro Man had been healthy and tended toward philosophical thinking.

Milan worked mostly with sprinters and field athletes, but as a former distance runner, he enjoyed watching our practices, and he and I had gotten to know each other. Whenever I asked his opinion about a workout or race, he would answer with "More important, what do you think?"

He walked over to where I was stretching. After a little small talk, Milan asked, "So what are your plans, Deena?" I was pretty sure he'd heard about the bakery, but I mentioned it anyway.

He nodded and asked, "Are you sure that's what you want? Are you sure you're done running?"

"I am," I said. "I've been running half my life and I'm ready for something new."

Milan suggested I was afraid of success.

I told him I feared continued failure.

Then he looked at me pointedly and told me what he'd seen over the past five years. "I've watched you win a conference championship off a few weeks of training. When you were a freshman, you were a fiery competitor. You lined up with purpose, with the mind-set to win. When you did that, you were very difficult to beat."

Milan said I'd had simply lost the spark. He said maybe I just needed a change of environment.

"Have you given running everything?" he asked. "Have you really given it everything you have?"

"Yes, yes," I said, emphatically.

But that night, I stared at the fake sunflowers on the coffee table, thinking about Milan's question. I had a deep respect for him. His words to me were carefully chosen, his speech was always intentional. So what did he mean by "everything"? And had I done it?

I'd shown up, I'd pushed my body as hard as I could. What else was there?

I had no idea how to answer that question. I didn't know why I had ever won or what had happened when I'd lost. I knew even less about professional running. Despite running most of my life, I realized I knew very little about the sport.

I was embarrassed by this, even sitting there by myself, and decided that before walking away from the sport, I wanted to know what I was walking away from. So the next day, I went to the library and read the latest editions of *Track & Field News*. It was June 1996, just before the Olympic Games in Atlanta, and nearly all the stories were about athletes preparing for the Games. A clear thread emerged: distance runners winning medals and championship titles trained in the high-altitude regions of Kenya and Ethiopia. And they trained in teams. Was this the "everything" Milan had been talking about?

I went into his office. "Is it the altitude, the teams, or did I have to be born in the Rift Valley to run well?" I asked. He smiled and scribbled a phone number on a piece of paper. "Call Coach Vigil," he said. "I did my graduate work with him. He's an excellent coach and an expert on altitude. He works with men, but he'll be able to give you some direction."

I'd first heard of Coach Joe Vigil six years earlier when I was a junior in high school competing at the World Cross-Country Championships in Aix-les-Bains, France. Coach Vigil was the men's coach on the professional side. Each day in the hotel dining room, a group of runners and coaches gathered around this older man. He had a stout, strong build, and he wore track pants and a USA T-shirt that revealed a faded Bugs Bunny tattoo on his left arm. Coach Vigil was animated when he talked. His face lit up and hands moved, as if they were part of the story, and he often chuckled at his own remarks. The dozen or so people around him all leaned in, listening, smiling. I couldn't make out what he was saying, but his strong, jovial voice carried across the room. I thought he seemed grand, though at sixteen, I mostly thought it was funny that a running expert could look more like a football coach.

Now, Coach Vigil was sixty-six and retired from Adams State

University in Alamosa, Colorado, where he'd coached for twenty-eight years. He had turned the school's fading cross-country program into a national powerhouse, had developed Olympians and national champions, and now he was coaching the only professional distance-running team in the United States.*

I put his phone number on the counter and ran the NCAA championships in Eugene, debating whether to call him. Back at home, I stood in the kitchen staring at the number. I decided I'd at least rehearse the conversation. "Good morning," I said out loud to the coffeepot. My voice cracked so I tried again. "Good morning. My name's Deena Drossin, and I got your number from Coach Donley. I'm considering pursuing professional running . . ." I poured more coffee, then, as if spontaneously, grabbed the phone and dialed.

"Hello."

He answered with the same strong voice I'd heard in France.

I introduced myself and Coach Vigil said he was expecting my call.

"What can I do for you?" he asked.

I told him I was debating turning pro, but I didn't know what it required. I shared my library discovery of altitude and teamwork, and that Milan directed me to him since he was an expert in both categories.

"Well," Coach Vigil said, "I can begin with altitude and tell you that while flatlanders argue the benefits, altitude-trained athletes will continue to earn medals."

He went on to say he thought Americans could benefit from working together. "Most of them run alone to protect their egos instead of seeing the challenge of teammates as a way to get faster and stronger," he said. "So to answer your question, yes altitude and teamwork are an essential part of the equation, but you've got to

---

* Today's top training groups, the Mammoth Track Club, Hansons' Distance Project, and the Oregon Project, were founded four years later.

be disciplined, and live an athlete's lifestyle every day to reach your goals. What are your goals?" Coach Vigil asked.

I thought quickly, making them up on the spot. "To break fifteen minutes in the 5K, make the Olympic team, and open a café." I added that last one in an effort to appear well-rounded.

"Well, you've only run 15:52. That's not particularly fast."

Not fast? For a second, I thought he might hang up. But he didn't, and the fact that Coach Vigil didn't think I was fast relieved me of thinking I had to be. My body relaxed and I tuned into Coach Vigil's voice with greater intrigue.

"You've got to structure your days around training and recovery, be committed, be patient," he was saying.

What I heard was that maybe I wasn't fast now, but with his program, there was a chance I could be.

"Is there a possibility I could join your group?" I asked, the question coming out of my mouth before I had time to stop it.

"Well, Alamosa isn't for everyone," he was quick to say. "The winters are harsh and we train outside year-round. Why don't you come for a visit and we'll talk."

We settled on dates and hung up.

I hadn't run since my last college race two weeks earlier. Now, feeling the bubbling of something, I rummaged through my closet to find my shoes, laced them up, and headed out. My usual loop went along the dairy farms on the outskirts of town. I had gotten into the habit of feeding the cows sugar cubes (not a good idea, I see now), so when they saw me coming, they rushed the fence. I waved my hands to show they were empty. The cows started running along the fence parallel to me, and I felt the vibrations of their hooves trampling the earth. I smiled their way and pushed the pace to drop them.

As I left the cows behind, the sound of my foot strikes became clear. Their rhythm seemed quicker than I remembered. I turned right onto Porter Road and took in the long stretch ahead of me. The fields that rolled on forever looked more green and lush under the climbing morning sun. The sun's rays were warm on my skin and the humidity, at times so annoying, felt comforting. I picked up the pace to catch a better breeze and stretched out my arms to mimic a bird soaring through the South's thick air. As I ran, I replayed the call in my mind. One of the more striking observations was that Coach Vigil never mentioned winning. He also talked a lot about traits, but not one of them was talent. This unraveled everything I thought about running. Coach Vigil showed me there were multiple aspects of the sport I'd never paid attention to. A buzz of opportunity swarmed around me. In one phone call, he'd suddenly made running new again.

I flipped around and headed back toward the dairy farms. The cows barely lifted their heads when I passed, sensing their sugar days were over. The hum of insects filled the sound between my foot strikes and I felt a resounding lightness. When I walked through the door of my apartment, I knew I wasn't going to visit Alamosa. I was going to move there.

You know that line in the movie *When Harry Met Sally* when Billy Crystal tells Meg Ryan that when you realize you want to spend the rest of your life with somebody, you want the rest of your life to start as soon as possible? That was how I felt as I stuffed my Jeep with my belongings and began the two-day drive to Alamosa.

Everything had fallen into place. I'd called one of Coach Vigil's athletes, Peter de la Cerda, who agreed to put me up until I found my own place. "Do you know of anyone who's hiring?" I asked. Peter was a manager at the local diner and said he'd put me on the schedule as a waitress. And just like that, I'd found a place to live and a job to keep me above water.

Crossing out of Arkansas into Oklahoma, I couldn't find a good radio station and thought my way through most of the miles. I imagined what Alamosa was like (big mountains), what training would be like (punishing), and if the food in the café would be good (fresh).

Mostly, I thought about running. I saw myself moving down the trails as a kid, fighting to keep the lead in a race, feeling the high of winning and the low of defeat. But I saw that these feelings had always been at the whim of my talent, an immovable trait, out of my control, and I had let it define me.

I've relied on you too much, I whispered. *I'm sorry. I'll take over now.*

And with that I let my talent go. In that moment, I felt potential fill the large space within me. Wanting to savor the moment, I pulled off the highway to fish in the Illinois River. As I walked upstream to find a good casting spot, I noticed a little boy sitting on a rock with an elderly man. The boy was using a stick for a fishing pole. His cheek rested on his hand, suggesting he wasn't too happy with his setup. I found a place where the river was wide and enjoyed the meditative act of casting and reeling without catching anything. On the way back to my Jeep, I handed the boy my fishing pole. His eyes lit up and I smiled. I told him maybe he'd have better luck with my pole than I had.

Back on the road, I committed to giving running four years, an Olympic cycle, and decided my goal would be to open myself to learning what it took to reach my potential.

Somewhere in Texas, I found a budget motel, and the next morning, while drinking bad coffee from a Styrofoam cup, I studied a large atlas map, plotting the route to Alamosa. The sun scorched Texas, then New Mexico, and as I crossed into Colorado, I waited for the desert landscape to turn more lush. I'd imagined Alamosa like the Colorado of postcards: green meadows, rushing rivers, deer leaping through forests. But the town sat on the vast, dry plateau of the San Luis Valley—a high-desert plain at roughly 7,500 feet. When I drove over the bridge into town, a tumbleweed blew in front of my Jeep, leaving a dusty trail in its wake. The San Juan range rose high in the west, the Sangre de Cristo in the east. The mountains seemed to shelter the area, closing it off from the rest of the world. It felt like I was sliding off the radar into a place where there was nothing but space and time. It seemed like the perfect place to grow.

PART II
Grow

4

GETTING SCHOOLED
IN RUNNING

Alamosa, Colorado, 1996

We are what we repeatedly do. Excellence, then,
is not an act, but a habit.

—WILL DURANT ON ARISTOTLE

"I heard you moved here."

Coach Vigil sat behind a large wooden desk, holding a cup of coffee in his hands. He resembled the man I'd seen on that trip to France in high school, barrel-chested, and in track pants and a T-shirt. Close up, I could see the sun had deepened his Hispanic coloring and that he had the strong hands of someone who had worked hard his entire life. His look was direct, but not unkind, more curious.

"I was really inspired by you during our phone call," I said, sitting up a little taller to make a good impression. "I really want to work with you, so I moved here to show my commitment."

Coach Vigil nodded. He asked me how I liked Alamosa and where I'd run. I told him Peter had shown me the dyke along the Rio Grande and that we'd looped around the backside of the golf course. I'd seen my first porcupine there. He smiled and nodded.

"We have a lot to cover," he began, putting his coffee mug on the table. "If I recall, you want to make the Olympic team and break fifteen minutes in the 5K." I nodded. "Those are big goals, requiring time and patience and living the athlete's lifestyle," he said.

I told him he'd mentioned that on our call.

"Repetitio mater studiorum est," he replied, leaning forward in his chair and pronouncing each syllable with precision. "That's Latin for 'repetition is the mother of learning.' You'll see it applies to every aspect of training."

He sat back and began detailing what he meant by the athlete's lifestyle. Training only took up a couple of hours a day, but the rest of the day was just as critical, he said. How you spent the time between workouts and how well you took care of yourself directly affected performance. He added that I needed to eat an abundance of good food and nap every day.

Coach Vigil was big on sleep. When you sleep, the body stops producing the stress hormone cortisol and releases growth hormones that repair and build muscles. Only by getting enough rest can you adapt to the training load.

"Do you sleep well?" he asked.

Yes, I did.

"Good. It means you have a clean conscience." Meaning worry about finances or family wasn't disrupting my sleep, and therefore my training and recovery.

Everything he said was new and fascinating. I never would have thought relationships and money had anything to do with performance.

Coach Vigil took time to explain the structure and purpose of training, how different workouts stimulate the body's various metabolic systems, and that together they enable us to run longer and faster. Every now and then he punctuated his speech with scientific terms—mesocycles, metabolic substrate, energy stores—and leaned forward in his chair. "Are you with me?" he'd ask, to make sure I was following along.

"How many miles a week have you been running?"

"Forty-five."

"That's not much. You'll need time to acclimatize to the altitude here. I'll start you off with an easy seventy miles a week for three weeks. We'll see how you feel before adding workouts."

Wanting to clarify if I was joining the team or if he was just agreeing to help me out, I asked if I'd be running with the men.

"Yes," he said. "I'm going to develop you as an athlete, not as a girl."

I sensed the meeting was coming to a close, but as I gathered my things, Coach Vigil asked, in an offhand manner, "What is your philosophy?"

Philosophy? I probably looked a little dumbstruck as I waited for more explanation, but he didn't elaborate. I tried coming up with a connection between running and philosophy and, finding none, said, "My philosophy is that I want to make the Olympic team."

"Shhhiiiit," Coach Vigil said, amused. "That's a goal," he explained. "I want to know the backbone of what makes you operate, the values you bounce your decisions off."

Values? Did he mean family? The backbone of what makes me operate? That seemed bigger than running, it seemed like life. *Man,* I thought, *I'm just here to run.*

"All right," he said, letting me off the hook. "The team meets tomorrow at seven thirty at Cole Park. See you then, and bring a good attitude."

The next morning, Peter and I ran to meet the team at Cole Park, a wide, green expanse dotted with cottonwood trees. Coach stood outside his pickup truck with about eight men dressed in running clothes. "This is Deena," Coach said to the group when Peter and I arrived. We nodded to each other. Most of the men had run under Coach at Adams State and would come and go over the years, but three were regulars. Peter, whom I was staying with, was twenty-four, had short black hair and big ears. Phil Castillo, twenty-three, was a

Native American from the Acoma tribe, and had a gentle nature I liked immediately. Both men were now pursuing the marathon, but had run on Coach's 1992 team that had stunned collegiate athletics when they'd earned a perfect score at cross-country nationals.

The third, Marco Ochoa, was thirty-two, short, with a dark complexion and a lean build. He was one of the top US marathoners at the time. Marco had come into the Campus Café the day before, my first day on the job, and was reading *Atlas Shrugged* when I delivered his food. "Coach recommended it," he said, "it's deep."

"You've got mile repeats today," Coach said to the men. "Take Deena with you on your warm-up and get acquainted. She'll continue running after that."

The men and I headed across the park and climbed a few strides to the dirt path along the Rio Grande, heading north toward the golf course. The vibe was relaxed, comfortable, and we made small talk. The men asked me how I got into running, about my time at Arkansas. I asked about their running history and goals. They ribbed one another. Phil gave Peter a hard time about his unshaven face, something Coach discouraged. Peter talked smack about eating his Wheaties in order to kick everyone's ass that morning.

Ten minutes out, we crossed the State Street Bridge and returned on the other side of the river. The conversation shifted. The men began discussing the workout pace and developing a strategy for switching leads. I listened. Each seemed to have a personal commitment to the work, so unlike the obligation to run I felt in college. It gave the group a focused feel.

The men peeled off toward Coach. I continued, doing loops around the park so I could watch. After a few drills and strides, the men gathered around Coach and I stopped to listen. "What a perfect day being handed to you," he said to the men, noting the warm air and clear sky. "Take advantage of it. You have five times a mile with three minutes' recovery. Any questions?" Coach paused, scanning their faces. "Okay, then, let's go."

I heard the scratch of feet on pavement as the men took off down the path. They ran in a tight pack and nearly disappeared from sight as they made the turn at the park's far end. Coming around, a few of the men fell back. Without losing stride, Peter reached his hand behind him as if in a relay waiting for the baton, a caring gesture to encourage his fading teammates. The camaraderie moved me.

The men crossed the finish together, jogging into their recovery. A few minutes later, they were off again. I finished my run and joined Coach under the cottonwood tree. The men charged toward us, crossing the mile mark in quick succession. After their penultimate repeat, one of the guys complained about a blister. "Good thing it's four feet from your heart," Coach said to him. Then he turned to me. "He needs to run with his heart, not his feet," he said. I listened, thinking that for a coach with a doctorate in physiology, he sure seemed philosophical.

I liked the men. I liked their commitment to Coach and one another and felt lucky to have joined such a caring team. I assumed they all had philosophies. They spoke Coach's language. "A step closer to excellence," Marco had said at the end of the workout.

We ran together daily, putting in miles along the river and the golf course. Sometimes we ran along the county roads, wide stretches of dirt paralleling potato fields and ranches, stringing together as much road as we needed for the morning's mileage. Each day, I noticed Coach sent us off with a positive comment. "It's a great day to work together toward our goals," he'd say after we'd gathered for the workout. On a particularly windy day, it would be: "What a great day to challenge and shape our perseverance." Sometimes his words were simple—"Okay, let's go"—and it was his upbeat, let's-get-it-done inflection that set the tone for the workout.

On some Wednesdays, Coach drove us to Forbes Ranch, a sprawling nature preserve east of Alamosa, where seeing herds of deer or elk was almost guaranteed. There, the men and I rolled along the undulating dirt roads while Coach drove beside us handing us fluids. Once, early on, Coach leaned out the window smiling wide and said, "Deena! Welcome to my office." He stretched out his arm, gesturing to the desert sage and pine. I looked around, letting it settle in that this beautiful setting was my office, too.

I had to press ever so slightly to keep up with the men's easy pace. The conversation was light, the prevailing tone sarcastic, and the subject matter often juvenile. If Marco showed up looking tired, the men prodded, "Are those bags under your eyes from too many miles, or did someone keep you up all night?" They talked about peeing blood after a long run, sexual positions, and the effects of a green-chili dinner on the following morning's bathroom visit. They folded me in. If I didn't understand a joke, one of the men quipped, "She is blond, after all."

Coach taught me how to properly execute drills like high knees and bounding. Push your feet into the ground to create the counterforce that'll drive your knees upward, he said. Ground contact time should be fast as possible. Use your arms to aid the motion. The men showed me how to blow snot rockets. You lean to one side, press a finger to close one nostril, and blow hard. There were factors to consider: wind direction, and location of teammates so you didn't spray them. Their instruction came with full demonstrations and encouragement for my technique.

After the run, Coach wrapped up the workout with a boost of enthusiasm. "Look how much you've accomplished and it's not even lunchtime yet." He smiled. "Now, go home and get some rest. There's still work to do."

Back at home, my focus turned to the rest of the day. I cooked omelets with extra vegetables. I drank pint after pint of water to stay hydrated. I waited for the closest spot in the grocery store parking lot so my tired legs wouldn't have to walk so far. Inside, my cart overflowed with produce, good cuts of meat, fresh fish, and pasta. I bought ice for ice baths and booked a weekly massage. Sleeping in the middle of the day seemed like a luxury, but was surprisingly necessary with the added mileage. I did evening runs along the river alone, though sometimes I met up with Peter, Marco, or Phil. A couple of times, I explored the valley and drove to the base of the Sangre de Cristo Mountains to run around Great Sand Dunes National Park or Zapata Falls. Afterward, I iced my legs in the falls' frigid water. After the training, stretching, eating, and sleeping were done, there was surprisingly little free time.

Colin "Pops" Bauer, the owner of the Campus Café, was a distant relative of American marathoner Buddy Edelen. Buddy held the marathon world record in 1963, and Pops had been hiring Coach's runners for nearly as long. Pops was tall and skinny. He never appeared without a chef's apron around his waist, and was almost always stoned. His snide comments about customers who sent a plate back to the kitchen were funny, but he always recooked their meal just to their liking.

I liked working the early morning shift, when the booths and tables were packed with ranchers, hunters, and fishermen. My regulars sat at a long Formica table in the middle of the room and I learned their preferences quickly. Linda wanted coffee when she sat down and needed it refilled a minute later. She wolfed down two pieces of house-made toast, heavily buttered and grilled on both sides, then she was off to tend her cattle. Allan lingered over a big ranch-style breakfast with crispy bacon, thick toast, and eggs smothered in green chili. Paul and Margaret sat long after their oatmeal was gone, sharing the latest about calving season, restricted water rights, and broken-down machinery. Red was the quiet one, eating in a corner booth with his mail-order bride—at least, that's what Pops called her.

Coach usually walked in shortly after the doors opened. He took a seat at the table of regulars. "Deena! Top of the morning to you!"

he shouted across the café as soon as he saw me. With his coffee, he had the Vigil Special, a tortilla folded around a fried egg and a Hatch green chili, a meal Pops made special for him. Everyone knew Coach. The ranchers referred to him as the mayor. He'd sit for two hours, outlasting Paul and Margaret as he offered advice and perspective to the locals who rotated through. If a rancher complained about the lowering price of hay, Coach would say, well, if there's a problem, then there's a solution. "Can you diversify your crop so you're not so dependent on alfalfa sales?" he'd offer, in the same stern, let's-figure-it-out tone he used with us.

When the morning rush died down, and the regulars had all moved on to work, Coach would rise, grab the paper he'd brought, and say, "See you at practice, Deena, and bring a good attitude."

Coach kept emphasizing a good attitude. I saw that it might make me nicer to be around, but I didn't understand why he kept saying it or how it would affect my running until I went to lunch at his house one afternoon. Coach lived on Carroll Street, a pretty, tree-lined avenue a few miles from Cole Park. I walked into his ranch-style home and into a kitchen filled with sunlight. Coach stood over a steaming pot of stew. Little bowls of diced tomatoes, hominy, and cilantro lined the counter next to him. I took a chair at the counter with his wife, Caroline, a petite and well-coiffed woman who matched her husband in strength of personality.

As he cooked, Coach told stories about the early days of running in Alamosa, when athletes like the famed miler Jim Ryun and steeplechaser Conrad Nightingale trained there. Ryun, the first high schooler to break the four-minute mile, clocked two world records after stints in Alamosa. "Everyone wanted to come here after that," Coach said. He and others in the community persuaded the Amateur Athletic Union to let them host the United States' first Olympic marathon trials in 1968 in Alamosa when the Games would be in Mexico City at elevation. Along with participants in the trials, runners, race walkers, and physiologists flooded into town. "We had 169 marathoners training here, top researchers, everyone," he said. "It really opened my eyes to what was possible. I got my Ph.D. after that."

As I was leaving, Coach handed me his book, *Road to the Top*. "It'll give you a better understanding of my training methodology," he said. Back at Peter's I opened it to the first chapter and laughed— the title was "Philosophy." The opening paragraphs were about how our values guide our behavior no matter our goals. He listed expected attributes like perseverance and discipline, but also creativity, intelligence, and patience. He wrote about love of knowledge and how important it was to be a student of the sport. The chapter summed up a phrase Coach had shared: the same qualities that build a better person also build a better athlete.

This was a beautiful and foreign connection to me. Though exactly how it would affect running was unclear. The "good attitude" Coach encouraged seemed like the "good sportsmanship" that Bill and Lance had advocated. It was tangible, and so I made it my place to start.

The next day at Cole Park, I arrived with the intention to consciously work at being cheerful and enthusiastic. We had a 15-mile run and as we headed out on the roads, I clapped my hands and said, "Let's go." The route took us out through farmland and as we looped back, I began to struggle, and noticed some of the men were, too. I typically said "good job" at the end of the workout. Now I patted Phil on the back and told Peter he looked strong. As I fell back, I noticed the men had nodded, seeming to appreciate the gesture, and that thinking about how to be encouraging actually took my mind off my own fatigue and sore legs. Being conscious about attitude seemed to lessen the strain of running for us all.

Intrigued by this subtle effect, I experimented with my perspective on the way to work. I often walked to the café dwelling on the fact that I'd be on my feet for the next four hours. Now I found myself acknowledging that the job was paying the rent, and I arrived grateful to be there.

All this prompted me to start paying more attention, not just to attitude, but to the details of training and recovery. I asked Coach more questions about stretching, training at altitude, and the purpose of each workout. I researched specific nutrients ideal for athletes, and the timing of meals, and made them part of my routine.

The combination of running, rest, and attention was proving effective. The weight I'd gained senior year in college was slipping off. I was less exhausted by the 70-mile weeks, and felt my endurance building each time I ran with the men. Coach must have seen the progress I was feeling, because when I climbed into the van for practice one morning a month after arriving in Alamosa, he asked, "How do you feel?" Good, I replied. And with that I'd be joining the men for the notorious Rock Creek climb.

Rock Creek was the main fire road up the San Juan Mountains to the pass between Windy and Sheep Peaks. The route started at 8,500 feet, topping out at 11,500, with the elevation gain extending over 8 miles. The workout was a stamina builder, and now, with me in the mix, Coach also made it an equalizer. The men would start at the base, and Coach would drive me up a mile where I'd begin. The men were to try to catch me. I was to avoid capture.

The mountains grew larger as Coach drove west toward the San Juans. We left the farm crops behind and began a long, gradual climb into forest. The road turned to dirt and we passed a few primitive campsites before Coach pulled off to the side and the men jumped out. "We're coming to get you," they teased before taking off. Coach started driving. I sat in the front seat, banging on the dashboard. "C'mon, drive a little faster." Coach grinned and pressed the gas.

At the mile, I jumped out, asking how fast I should run. "Just don't let them catch you," he said.

So I ran. I went hard, storming the dirt road as if off the line at a race. In an instant, I was sucking air. People had warned me about how hard running at altitude would be, but putting in easy miles had felt fine. Now the taste of blood rose in the back of my throat. I knew exactly what was happening. Oxygen wasn't getting to my lungs and limbs in this hypoxic environment. I'd read about it in Coach's book. This little bit of knowledge opened me to the pain of the workout, and I pressed on. I looked over my shoulder to see if I could see the men. No sign.

The road paralleled the creek, and the sound of water traveling down the mountain came through the pine trees. I started studying the tangents, looking for the shortest distance and hoping that each step I saved added up to the time I needed to beat the men.

Coach pulled up beside me a few miles into the run and handed me a water bottle. "Don't let them catch you," he said. I drank, handed the bottle back, and he disappeared back down the road. I imagined him handing bottles to the men, saying, "Don't let a girl beat you," or "Dammit, catch the girl."

The forest thinned and the slope turned to sand, shrubs, and grass. The pines were gone, replaced by long lines of aspen along the creek. Behind me, the men were gaining ground. They were close enough for me to make out their features. Peter's cropped hair. Phil's broad shoulders. Marco's forward lean.

Elevation hurt. It hurt more than any race I'd run, yet I had to run farther. But I pushed. I pushed because I had never run this hard for this long in my life, and with each step the need to know I could do it grew. I wanted to tough it out. I wanted to prove to myself I was strong. I was going to beat the guys up this damn hill.

Clouds formed over the peaks and the sky grew dark. Soon, hail began pelting my body. *Good Lord, what are we doing out here?* I heard the van coming from behind, and when Coach pulled up I expected him to say, "Get inside." Instead, he shouted, "See you at the top!" and pulled away.

I was suffering in a way I never had before. Altitude robbed my body of oxygen, creating a burn that felt like acid running through my veins. My lungs and legs were on fire, but the strain reached into new places—shoulders, back. The pain was silent, but if it spoke, it would have been screaming. But I pushed on. The guys were heckling now. "We're coming for you!" "You can run but you can't hide!"

The temperature dropped drastically above 10,000 feet. My skin was cold, but my insides still burned. Coach drove up the final sets of switchbacks and I watched the van zigzag back and forth, waiting for the flash of red brake lights to mark the finish. I kept my eyes on the van, and, finally, lights appeared. *Oh, thank God.*

Coach stood at the road's end, mountains rising behind him. It was dark, cloudy, and cold as the men and I battled the final meters. Pushing through, I reached the van ten steps ahead of them.

I couldn't speak. Neither could any of the men. We all bent over, put our hands on our knees, and gasped. Coach walked around patting us on the back. "Good job," he said, "good job."

It was too cold to linger. We pulled on our sweats and piled into the van. Inside, it was so warm my cold wrists ached from the contrast. Coach maneuvered the van off the pass and headed down the switchbacks at the frightening speed of someone who knew the road. He was chatty, turning his head around to talk to us, and we warned him of upcoming turns. It was the scariest drive of my life. But I couldn't stop thinking that I had done it. I had finished the hardest run of my life. It had been just 52 minutes. But it revealed a toughness in myself I'd never known existed, telling me I could do this, that I had it in me to be a professional runner.

Down the mountain, Coach pulled the van up to the Campus Café and we took over the long center table. Our battle was visible. Marco had dried salt streaks on his face. Peter looked pale. Phil's calf spasmed. I had big red blotches around my eyes from overexertion. We shoveled forkfuls of food into our mouths, too hungry and tired for conversation. Pops picked up the tab as he always did, and Coach told us go home and get some rest. He didn't have to tell me twice. Back at Peter's, I slept for four hours.

The weeks built. I ran with the team, we ate at the café, and I went home to nap. The cycle repeated itself in the afternoon. I ran along the river, now with my dog, Aspen, a chocolate lab I'd gotten at the pound when I was fraught with indecision at the end of college. My parents had kept her until I found my own place, which I now had. I was renting a small house three blocks from the café and six blocks from Cole Park. My roommate, Carl, was a plumber in his thirties, with feathered hair straight out of the '80s. We lived opposite lives: He was out late, playing drums in a Christian rock band. I was in bed by eight and sometimes woke at four thirty for the morning shift at the café.

Each day, I paid attention to Coach's words, allowing them to shape my perspective. Once, I jumped out of the van before a Rock Creek workout and said I'd try to fend off the men. "There is no try, Deena, only do," he said, loosely quoting Yoda. *Try*, I realized, was a soft word. I needed to *execute*. When I said I hated running in the wind, Coach looked at me and said: "Dammit, Deena, get tough." *Okay*, I thought, *rise to the challenge, be tougher than the wind, be tough enough to do it*. Sometimes Coach saw the I-don't-think-so look on my face before the last mile repeat and said, *"Repetitio mater studiorum est"*—repetition is the mother of learning. Repetition of speed built power. Repetition of miles built endurance. So I launched into the repeat with that perspective, running hard, and finishing the mile a few seconds faster than the week before.

One afternoon, Coach picked me up in his truck and we drove around the valley. He pointed out the alligator farm, the potato ranches, and the schools where some of his athletes were now teachers. He told me he grew up nearby in Antonito, a small, working-class town about twenty miles south. His father died when he was three months old and his mom remarried. Money was tight. To supplement his stepdad's job as a butcher and his mom's earnings at a department store, Coach started working young. He shoveled snow in middle school and worked the fields in high school, learning, he said, the value of hard work.

Coach told me he once aspired to be a football coach and I recalled my first impression of him as a man who looked like he belonged on the sideline of the gridiron. He played defensive guard in college, and after a stint in the navy, landed an assistant coaching position at Alamosa High School. It was his dream job, he said. But at one point, football practice coincided with the first day of track and only three kids showed up to run, so the head coach threatened to cancel the program. Coach couldn't bear the look on the boys' faces and volunteered to work with them. He didn't know much about running then but he built up their fitness, told them to run their best. At the end of the season, all three placed in the state meet.

"I was hooked," Coach said, telling me how the experience launched a lifelong quest to uncover the practices that built an athlete. He told me about returning to school for his masters degrees, about his travels to Kenya and Peru to study the world's best runners, and about his observations of the elites who trained in Alamosa. They worked hard, Coach said, more than he thought possible, but they could do it because they balanced the work with rest. "That's when I understood there is no such thing as overtraining," he said, "just underresting."

Later, Coach told me he'd never forget a conversation that took place between Jim Ryun and the Olympic coach Ted Haydon before the 1968 Games in Mexico City at altitude. Jim, Haydon said to Ryun in the training room, nobody's going to run faster than 3:40 in the 1,500. Ryun was astute, Coach said. He'd run the world record in the 1,500 in 3:33 the year before, and at altitude, 3:40 seemed reasonable, so he trained for 3:40. In Mexico City, Ryun's main rival was Kip Keino of Kenya, whom he'd beaten many times. No one, though, Coach said smiling, told Kip about the 3:40 limitation. Ryun ran a perfectly paced race, but it wasn't enough to catch Kip, who ran 3:34 without that mental governor. Ryun misjudged the race and took second. "That's the amazing thing about the mind," Coach said, "once you develop a mental level of expectation, it stays with you."

Like all of Coach's runners, I was the recipient of the knowledge he'd gained over the years. He'd taken his lessons and applied them to each athlete. Three years after the 1968 Olympics, Coach led Adams State to its first national title. Over the next two decades, he brought them eighteen more. He coached eighty-seven college runners to individual titles in track and cross-country, and guided professional runner Pat Porter to the Olympic Games and wins in eight national cross-country championships.

I saw how Coach was an example of everything he taught. He had developed himself through persistence and curiosity and was still learning. He read scientific journals and called research colleagues around the world to discuss ideas. Whatever he learned, he shared readily with everyone around him. I was touched by this. I felt privileged to be receiving all that he had worked so hard for. Each time we met and with every story he told, my belief in Coach, and my commitment to the process, deepened.

The brutal climb up Rock Creek became my favorite workout. Fending off the men made me feel strong and capable. They never caught me, and the satisfaction felt like something close to a win. That reward was present in Cole Park, too. I ran behind Phil, Peter, and the others, working to maintain some sort of contact with the pack, feeling gritty and tough, invested and professional. As a kid, I thrived on the rush of racing. Now, each victory up Rock Creek, each faster split and stronger mile in training, was a thrill.

What amazed me most was that Coach's program worked. After just three months in Alamosa, I was fitter and faster than I had ever been. Every choice to shift a perspective and push through a workout built strength. Eating healthier made me feel better in the moment and in my next workout. Napping left me more energized for the evening run. These bullet points of lifestyle were profound to me. I had relied on talent for so long that it had seemed the only things propelling my running were the genes I was born with. Now I felt part of the process. I was participating in the work, driving and directing it with the choices I made. Sometimes I was so giddy about it that when I climbed into bed for a nap I shouted out loud, "This is my job!" and fell back into a deep slumber.

5

ASSEMBLING AN ATHLETE

Alamosa, Colorado, 1996

Some people think design means how it looks. But of course,
if you dig deeper, it's really how it works.
—STEVE JOBS

After my first lunch at Coach's house, I went back two or three times a week. Coach would be dicing vegetables, I'd join Caroline at the counter, and another story would begin. Coach was prone to parables, though there was no mistaking the message. He was teaching, yes, but his goal was to motivate, to light a fire in your spirit. With each story, he revealed another layer of the qualities necessary to reach our potential, building his own vision of a super-athlete.

Three cowboys had been riding the range since early morning, Coach began. One was a member of the Navajo Nation. The sun was setting and the men had not eaten all day. As they rode toward home, two of the cowboys fantasized about all they would eat, deepening the agony of hunger. The Navajo shrugged, claiming he wasn't hungry. The other two continued talking of food in vivid detail. Arriving at the homestead, they all sat down to a steak dinner. The Navajo ate with the most gusto. His friend interrupted, pointing out that he had not been hungry less than an hour before. "It was not wise to be hungry then," he said. "No food." Coach then talked about delayed gratification, the timing of our desires. Don't think of the reward, he said, when there is still much ground to cover.

At the core of many of his stories was a distinction between success and excellence. Success was "having": money, awards, status. Excellence was "being": living your values, having them guide your daily life. Pursue excellence, Coach would say, and success will follow.

Excellence was behind Coach's preference for infrequent racing. He believed you trained for a goal and too many races in a season disrupted the training. Traveling and racing lowered weekly mileage, took you out of your routine, expended valuable energy, and directed your focus away from your goal.

When I first arrived, Coach and I had set my goal as the US National Cross-Country Championships at Stanford University that year and now it was just six weeks away. But when Peter and Phil told me they were heading to Kearney, Nebraska, for a 10K, I jumped at the chance for a road trip. "Go, have fun," Coach said when I asked, and I hopped in the car with my teammates.

Kearney was the seat of Buffalo County, a town of about 6,400 with a vibrant running community. The race was small, only a couple hundred runners, but there was prize money, so it attracted aspiring elites, including a handful of East Africans. I had no expectations for this race and lined up with the women just to compete and see what happened.

The gun fired, and I formed a lead pack with the Kenyans and Ethiopians. I'd never run this close to the smooth and efficient strides of an elite field before, and it felt like a privilege to be with them. We moved in a tight pack down the centerline of the road, twisting and turning through neighborhoods and alongside parks. Women fell off the pack as the miles passed, and eventually, it was down to three of us. My breathing seemed calmer than that of the two Africans, though this time, I realized it was a reflection of my training at altitude rather than a signal to surge. Altitude prompts the body to create more red blood cells to meet the oxygen demands. At sea level, the added blood cells deliver more oxygen to working muscles, making your effort feel easier. I thought for sure my altitude-trained body would be able to outkick the two Africans in the final stretch and I easily stayed with the women as we made our way past antique stores and restaurants back into historic downtown. But in the last few hundred meters, I struggled to get my legs to turn over faster. One of the women pulled ahead and I fought to keep my lead over the other, taking second place.

The finish, to my surprise, landed me my first paycheck, $500. I called my dad, who'd been as skeptical about professional running as he had been about baking. "Wow," he said, "you're making almost $100 a mile!" Then we calculated in all the training time and laughed, realizing it was more like five cents a mile.

Back in Alamosa, I told Coach my lungs and legs seemed out of sync. My lungs wanted to charge ahead, but I couldn't get my legs to run any faster.

"Speed is hard to develop at altitude," Coach said, explaining that training with less oxygen strengthened the cardiovascular system at the expense of the neuromuscular system. At altitude, I couldn't reach top speed, so I wasn't developing turnover.

Coach had a solution. Out at Forbes Ranch in the middle of a 10-mile run, he had me run a handful of 100-meter downhill sprints. Gravity would enable me to run at speeds unachievable on the flats, Coach said. It would activate my fast-twitch muscle fibers. He called it running at 110-percent speed, or overspeed.

The sprints were awkward at first. Running fast downhill felt out of control, like I was going to trip over myself. Coach stood at the base of the hill, citing his mantra: *"Repetitio mater studiorum est."*

Once my stride smoothed out a few weeks later, Coach began nitpicking my form. Tuck your elbows in. Lean forward a little so you're not breaking your stride. That's right. Now, pop your feet off the ground.

I repeated his words in my mind, thinking, *pop, pop, pop* every time my foot landed.

We switched to uphill sprints to increase power. "Pump your arms more," Coach shouted as I ran by. "Drive with your knees."

Drive, drive, drive.

One of the stories Coach told was about Italian marathoner Gelindo Bordin, who trained in Alamosa in the late 1980s. While Gelindo was running a 15-mile tempo run, Coach stood at one of the miles shouting his time as Gelindo passed. "You're wrong!" Gelindo shouted back. Coach looked at his watch. There was no doubt about the time, so later that day, he pulled out his survey wheel and measured the mile. Sure enough, it was off by seven meters. Precision was part of Gelindo's gift, Coach said. The details of pace, time, and distance were not arbitrary; they mattered. That's how I viewed perfecting my stride. Focusing on the individual parts—the turnover, the knee drive, the pop off the ground—were the specifics of excellence.

I got faster each week. Heading into the national cross-country championships, I set the goal of placing in the top five. I knew the competition would be tough. Lynn Jennings, an eight-time national cross-country champion and a three-time world champion, was competing. Top names I recognized from my collegiate years were also on the start list. My goal, though, was inspired by the fact that I had been runner-up at NCAAs, yet after a short time with Coach I felt worlds ahead of that version of myself.

I flew out to Palo Alto with Coach, Peter, Marco, and Phil, and we met my family at the race. Northern California in December delivered perfect conditions: sunny, a little crisp, though the course was nothing to be excited about. It was 6K on Stanford University's golf course, with one major hill we'd take at a slant. On the starting line, I was aware of feeling true confidence for the first time. Whenever I'd connected to the word "confidence" as a kid, it was because I thought I'd be the most talented runner in the race. The word now linked me to the work of the last four months and I thought of the great Tanzanian marathoner Juma Ikangaa. To Coach, Juma was an example of "unparalleled preparation." He'd once driven Juma to the New Mexico border when he was in Alamosa training for the 1990 Boston Marathon so he could run the 35 miles back into town. I had not put in a 35-mile run, but I had, like Juma, focused on training, and for the first time in my life felt the confidence born of preparation.

The gun fired and off the line, I was not with the leaders. The pack of about 15 women surged ahead, and I noticed the group included competitors whose names I didn't know.

Who are these girls? I thought. *How can they be beating me?*

I ran on, chasing the women across the field. *C'mon, just work to catch them.* I targeted a tree ahead and willed myself toward it. The pack, though, reached the landmark well before me. So I put my focus on the hill. I reminded myself hills had been my strength since youth and were even more so now that I lived in the mountains. If I could catch the leaders on the hill, I could draft off them.

Pushing on the climb, my body felt strong. There was power in my drive and energy in my execution. But I wasn't gaining any ground. This confused me. *I feel strong and fast right now, how can I be this far back?*

I crested the hill and let myself run out of control on the descent. Yet still, runners passed me. I tried going with them, tried forcing myself into a faster pace. *Why can't I get up there?* In the last half mile, women began their finishing kick. I wasn't capable of giving anything more, and realized that even if I could pass a few more women, I wasn't going to place in the top five. I was instantly defeated and in my mind, heard the screeching of brakes, the abrupt end of progress, and gave up. *What's the point? I'm missing my goal. Why keep pushing?*

I ran the flat stretch with my head down and crossed the finish line in twentieth place. As in college, my self-judgment was quick and damning. *Even after all this work, I guess I'm not that good.*

My parents, Lesley, and Coach stood near the end of the chute and I shrugged at them as if to say, *I don't know what happened out there.* Good job, Coach assured. Good job, my dad echoed. You did great, my sister said. You'll be fine, from my mom.

Back at the hotel, I sobbed into a towel, confused at how I could go from confident to crushed in the span of thirty minutes. My family came to my room. "Don't be disappointed," my dad said, "You did great out there, you should be proud."

I tried adopting this attitude, but forcing it didn't resolve my feelings.

Coach knocked on the door and I answered. "Listen," he said standing in the doorway, "I know you're disappointed, but I'm glad for it."

Glad for it?

"It shows you're invested. It shows you care."

It struck me that Coach wasn't trying to change my feelings. He was, in my mind, giving me permission to be disappointed. I'd always thought negative emotions were a sign of weakness and I'd linked them to failure and self-judgment. Coach's comment, though, showed me negative feelings could have a positive reasoning: My disappointment was rooted in a desire to be better. My place wasn't what mattered to Coach. What mattered was my commitment.

Understanding this, I began moving away from thinking *this is as good as I am*, a limiting, judgmental perspective that left me powerless, to *this is as good as I am today*, a statement that allowed for growth and returned my power.

It was my first lesson in resilience, emboldened again by Juma's example. Off the line in the Boston Marathon, Juma went out hard. He ran much of the race on world-record pace, pushing his way toward victory. On Heartbreak Hill, the twenty-mile mark, his bold pace proved too much. His legs lost power and his body lost steam. Partway up the climb, Italy's Gelindo Bordin passed him and went on to win in 2:08, with Juma placing second. At the press conference, Juma showed no regret. When a reporter asked why he had gone out so aggressively, he answered with a question, "How fast would you have gone out if you were trying to break a world record?" He was chasing a goal, reaching to see what he could do. Juma didn't let defeat define him. He didn't own his place or time. Instead, he focused on being proud of the risk he'd taken and the courage he'd displayed.

On the plane home, I thought of all that I was proud of: the move to Alamosa, giving running a chance, the workouts I'd endured, the lessons I'd already learned. These thoughts filled me with drive and the desire to get better, and I turned my attention right back to where it belonged—to the pursuit of progress.

6

WHAT ARE YOU THINKING?

Alamosa, Colorado, 1997

Be careful how you are talking to yourself,
because you are listening.

—LISA M. HAYES

Coach had been right: Alamosa winters were harsh. The men and I ran along the river and county roads bundled against subzero temperatures. The snowfall was light, but the wind cut deep. Sometimes we were so exposed, the wind froze our breath to our faces, frosting the men's eyelashes and the peach fuzz on my cheeks.

Few things were better afterward than sitting at Coach's kitchen counter while he made posole, a spicy Mexican stew that warmed you through to your bones. As Coach moved from the stove to the sink, he asked, "Do you know who Jim Fixx is?" Before I could answer, he disappeared into his office and returned with a hard copy of *The Complete Book of Running*, featuring a man's muscular legs mid-stride, wearing red ASICS Tiger shoes against a red cover. The book had been published in 1977 during the early stages of the first running boom. By then, the New York City Marathon, the Falmouth Road Race, the Peachtree Road Race, and other races had started pulling more people into the sport. In *The Complete Book of Running,* Fixx wrote about how running transformed him from an overweight, two-packs-a-day smoker into a healthier and happier person. His everyman story and practical advice was credited with helping the running boom explode.

I skimmed it. I wasn't interested in reading about training, gear, or injuries. Feeling the positive energy that came with approaching practice with a good attitude had given me a window into the power of the mind. Coach's lesson in resilience had popped it wide open. I trusted that Coach Vigil would guide my physical training, but my mind was my own. It felt young, undiscovered, and I sensed there was potential within it to unlock. So I asked Coach for self-help books, the only term for mental training I knew at the time.

Coach loaded me up with a large stack, and in between running and shifts at the café, I curled up with a cup of coffee and read. *The Celestine Prophecy* spoke about our relationship with nature. I thought about how trees and mountains inspired me, how nature was uplifting, and that if we moved among it consciously, we could feel its strength.

Power vs. Force by David R. Hawkins was about the nature of power. Hawkins explained that true power was subtle. It rose from meaning and purpose and required no flaunting, no explanation, no claim of power. Power simply was and its strength emanated. Force, on the other hand, was always met with a counterforce. It had opposition, another force pushing back, and that can lead to collision and damage. It made me think of running in college. I'd forced myself to train against the needs of my body and the willingness of my mind and had ended up injured and burned out. To train powerfully, I needed to give myself the time to adapt, not force the fitness, but build it.

I was fascinated by these books. I wanted to dive deeper into the study of the mind. I wanted to dog-ear pages, highlight passages, and write in the margins, so I handed Coach back his books and bought my own. *The Way of the Peaceful Warrior*, *The Closing of the American Mind*, and *The Power of Positive Thinking* all pointed to the same thing: the power of thought, attitude, and perspective. All these books confirmed for me that the mind was essential in performance. Our thoughts can either stifle or draw out our physical potential.

My practical application began in earnest after reading *The Power of Positive Thinking* by Norman Vincent Peale. Peale was a pastor in New York City who often sprinkled his sermons with ideas on perspective. Most of the literature on positive thinking at the time—1952—was academic. Peale's book offered real-life anecdotes and practical tools, helping to popularize positive thinking. His advice on staying focused on "today"—the moment right in front of us—reinforced Coach's refrain of giving one task your full attention. Peale wrote about the effects of word choice on our perception, which encouraged me to look at words that frequented my vocabulary: "hard," "cold," and "tired." Replacing those words with "challenging," "tough," and "adapting" provided a greater feeling of strength and purpose.

As I read, a passage jumped out: "Our happiness depends on the habit of mind we cultivate." I highlighted the sentence and put three exclamation points in its margin. I saw so clearly that Coach had the habit of a positive attitude. In repeatedly telling me to bring a good attitude to practice, he was trying to instill the same in me. Habits are developed through repetition, so instead of focusing on my attitude periodically, I set out to make thinking positively a practice.

The next morning, I noted that I usually woke thinking about how heavy my body felt and slogged through the kitchen making coffee half asleep. I only woke up mentally after taking Aspen outside. So the following morning, I replaced thoughts of fatigue with *Let's take Aspen out*. My energy shifted right away. By pulling my attention away from sleepiness and onto a task, I was already more alert. Outside, instead of standing on the porch with my arms crossed waiting for Aspen, I noticed the crispness of the morning and the light coming up. Back inside, I was alert in the kitchen. I added a dash of cinnamon to the coffee grounds, enjoying the process and pleased at having turned a previously mundane task into something pleasurable.

In practice, I began consciously experimenting with my thoughts and their effect on the workout. My hamstrings tended to fatigue, which annoyed me. It took me a moment to become aware of the irritation, but when I did, I asked myself how else I could view it. *I'm gaining strength where I need it.* Good, I thought, and ran on, emboldened by the idea of getting stronger.

Every Thursday we had repeats at Cole Park. When I lost contact with the men, I noticed my mind drew a quick conclusion: *I'll never be able to hang on.* This surprised me because I actually liked the workout. I flipped the thought to *I'm a little closer to Phil today*, and again felt an immediate energy shift. The negative thought had been weighing down my stride with doubt and disappointment. The positive thought had created lightness, and the confidence and desire to keep pushing.

I'd gotten a sense of this interplay as a kid. When people said I was a "phenom," I felt a buzz. When someone referred to my win as a fluke or said I'd burn out quickly, I felt slighted and sad. I'd experienced the feelings connected to these comments when I was young. But only after experimenting with positive thoughts as a professional did I realize how the nature of my thinking influenced the quality of my running. Each time I shifted my attention away from something negative and put it on something positive, I felt my body loosen, my stride open up, and my confidence rise.

I began making connections beyond training. I noticed how an argument on the phone with my mom was followed by a bad workout. A fast mile-repeat session came on the heels of exciting news about a friend getting married. Perfecting my cinnamon-roll recipe on Friday had me running light on my feet on Saturday.

Suddenly, I noticed all sorts of small moments in my life when negativity popped up. At the café, when one of the regulars, Wade, walked in, I reacted with *Oh no, not Wade*. Wade was grumpy and unfriendly. He never looked up from his paper, even when I came to take his order, which he then barked at me. I walked over to his table bracing myself for his assault and carefully asked if he would like coffee. Now, I realized I'd let him condition me into approaching the situation with dread. So the next time he came in, I walked over and said good morning. He grumbled and ordered pancakes. When Pops rang the bell, I ran to the back and drew a big whipped cream smiley face on top of his pancakes. I walked the plate over to Wade and placed it in front of him. I got a crooked grin.

I left the café that day lighter, feeling good about having made the effort to be kind. I started my workout in a more positive and up-beat mood, and when the tough part came—frustration at fatigue, disappointment at a slower mile—I found a positive perspective to get me through it. *I am pushing my limits. I am stronger than I was yesterday.*

It wasn't just workouts that improved. The positive shifts built on one another. The whole day became more productive and enjoyable and I moved through it with greater ease. So I kept experimenting. When someone snagged the parking spot I had my eye on at the grocery store, I dispelled my irritation with: *The next spot will be closer.* Or, *maybe I'm supposed to walk the lactic acid out of my legs.* Whining about being too tired to cook dinner became *It's a good night for takeout.* An achy calf turned into an appreciation for rest. If a foreigner didn't leave me a tip at the café, I reminded myself tipping wasn't customary in their culture, and walked over and poured Wade more coffee.

Ironically, practicing positivity showed me just how negative I could be. Sometimes snide and cynical thoughts streamed through my head. They were often directed at myself, but sometimes at others. I observed how irritable I could be around my roommates. Carl and I had filled a third bedroom with a rotating set of characters, and the current occupant, who played standup bass in a bluegrass band, practiced at night. *Jerk! Didn't he know I was trying to sleep?* I also noted how often in practice I cut myself down—*You're worthless, what a dummy*—similar to how I had treated myself in college.

It took tremendous effort to control those thoughts. My brain easily slipped back into negativity, and I found I had to stay on top of my thinking in the same way I had to remain conscious and diligent about my pace in a workout. *Oh, you're doing it again*, I said to myself when I became aware of negativity, being careful not to rebuke myself and therefore wind up being negative about being negative. I told myself: *Find a thought that serves you better.*

The more tired I got, the easier it was to be negative, and the more relentless I had to be. Often it seemed I could redirect my thinking hundreds of times during a workout.

I was, though, becoming more skilled at recognizing negative thoughts. I even started interrupting them midstream.

Negativity: *Why can't you stay on pace here?*

Me: *I don't need criticism right now, I need help!*

Then I found the words to encourage myself: *Focus on the next mile. Keep going.*

Coach continued to shape my thinking. Despite my efforts, I could still show up at practice thinking about fatigue. "Good morning," Coach would say, "You look nice and rested," which redirected my mind to the work ahead. On a particularly cold day, I'd be protesting in silence, *This sucks*, and the next thing I knew Coach would be beside me in the van shouting, "Deena, you're doing great!" I'd barely be holding on in mile repeats and he'd say, "Perfect, Deena, you've got another one in you." And there it was: the perspective that improved my execution.

One morning in early February, a few weeks before I was scheduled to compete in Houston at the US cross-country trials, the race that would determine the US team for the world championships, I set a goal to run a personal best in a mile-repeat workout. Conditions weren't ideal. It was cold and a little windy. So for inspiration, I thought about two great athletes who had run the Cole Park loop in under 4 minutes: Olympian Pat Porter, and New Zealand miler Martin Johns. As I ran, I imagined my legs turning over in the same long and powerful ways as these men. It worked for two of five repeats. During the third, my temples throbbed and my glutes ached. *Let the pain signal that you're building endurance and speed.* I waited for the positive interpretation to give me a boost, and was surprised when it did not. So I switched my focus to my arms. I watched them fly in front of my face. I admired how quickly and strongly they moved. With each stride, I was so preoccupied with my fast-moving biceps and fists that the headache and muscle fatigue no longer registered, and my strength flowed through. I nailed the last two repeats in record time (5:05).

The workout offered an important lesson: positivity wasn't a one-thought-fixes-all tool. I had to cycle through different approaches to find the right tool for the moment. For example, my arms pulled me out of the physical effort of mile repeats, but that same focus didn't work when I tried it during a long run. I was 12 miles into a 15-mile workout and everything felt overextended, legs, arms, and lungs, and my stomach was ready to lose the eggs and toast I'd eaten hours earlier. I tried focusing on evening out my breathing, to no avail. Turning my mind to the rhythm of my feet, then to my fists, didn't do the trick either.

I started feeling anxious. I was fumbling through the tools I had and none were working. Training would always take me to a place of discomfort, and I saw it was my job to push past it, so I focused on the rhythm of my feet, trying to open myself to the effort. North River Road bent to the east and when I made the turn, the stunning granite face of Mount Blanca came into view, the defining peak of the Sangre de Cristo range. I absorbed that vision, taking in the dramatic way the stark gray mountain pierced the blue sky. I sensed why that peak was sacred to the Navajo, for it also offered me great inspiration.

Nature was what I needed in that moment. A distraction, something to pull me out of my body. I learned that some days it took scenery, music, or musing about dinner to get through a workout. Other days, I needed to think myself through the tough parts. *Only one more mile. You've got this.* Turning my attention inward, to my breathing, stride, or arms, worked in other situations. My job was simply to uncover the tool necessary for the moment. Often I found it on the first or second attempt. Sometimes, it took several tries. But each time, a shift in perspective got me through the crux of a workout, and built more endurance, more speed, and greater confidence.

The effects of positivity didn't surprise me. What surprised me was that they worked *all the time.* Frustration and irritation didn't disappear. Rather, they became a signal to pause and consider a different perspective, which dispelled the negative emotions.

Even when changing my thinking didn't drastically transform my mood, it kept me from spiraling into a negative space. I hated running in the wind, and no matter how often I told myself the added resistance would make me stronger, or that air currents were joyrides for birds, I still despised the wind. But I no longer let frustration take over the workout. I thought about lunch, an upcoming race, or a quiet afternoon of reading ahead. By controlling these thoughts, the wind became a simple fact of the run rather than its principal opponent.

In one of my final workouts before the trials, winter delivered one of its coldest days to date. The temperature dipped below zero and the wind was brutal. We had an 8-mile tempo run to the barn and back, and the minute Coach sent us off, gusts took my breath away and nearly made me trip over myself. *Just adjust. Prepare for the gusts.* We turned right and wind smacked my face and belted my quads. I focused on slowing my breathing to give my mouth and nose time to warm the air before it entered my lungs, and I imagined my lungs happier for my effort.

I ran on, turning away from thoughts that the run would leave me half frozen by being glad I'd worn soft gloves, better for the constant wiping of snot. I thought it'd be better after the turnaround, when the wind was at our backs. But the wind must've been coming from the side all along because we took its punishment the whole way back. Its driving force numbed my quads. *Numb is good; numb is not feeling.* My mind became a mediator between the wind and the wrath it was inflicting on my body. Mile after mile I stayed focused on the positive things I could do to keep going, one warm breath, one snot wipe at a time. What could have ended in massive irritation concluded as an accumulation of successes—countless moments of resilience throughout the run—that made me feel tough. After that, I knew I could handle any and all race conditions.

Mid-February, I flew to Houston for the national cross-country trials and met my parents there. None of the men were competing, so Coach stayed back to work with them. At the trials, I was going up against the same girls who had defeated me at nationals in December, and it allowed me to set a clear goal of improving my place. I'd finished twentieth at nationals but I wanted to make the US team for worlds, which meant I needed to place in the top six at the trials. The leap from twentieth to sixth wasn't on my mind. Coach had taught me that high expectations were good. The mistake I'd made was attaching my self-worth to whether I reached them. So I linked my *actions* to aiming high—my stride, my effort—rather than the outcome.

Race morning I slipped into my new yellow, blue, and white racing singlet and shorts. I lingered a little too long in front of the mirror wondering if the uniform made me look fast, meaning I wondered whether I was fast. *Make it fast; go make that uniform fly.*

Houston's Buffalo Bayou Park was a long expanse of green tucked in between two heavily traveled roads. Monsoon rains had flooded the fields, turning the course into a slick loop of mud, water, and grass. I dug through my bag, worried I'd forgotten to pack the large spikes that screwed into the bottom of my shoes for better traction. Anything can throw off your race, fretting about weather, wondering if you're fast enough, freaking out about gear. My anxious moment passed once I found my spikes, but my thoughts jumped right to wondering whether I was good at running in the mud.

Where did that thought come from? I loved running in the mud. I excelled at running in the mud. The doubt came from that little bit of fear before a race that you won't run well, or that everything will fall apart. So as I walked to the start, I reflected on my first national championships when I was twelve. I had stomped through the mud and puddles as if on the playground. I put that playful approach in my mind and got on the line.

The gun fired and I shot forward, feeling my spikes grip the grass, affirming my trust in them. I landed at the back of the lead pack, this time running with girls who two months earlier were out of reach. I made matching their rhythm a game, picturing my stride equally long as theirs and hearing the simultaneous sound of our shoes slapping the mud. The pack seemed to move like a swarm of bees and I was entranced by its steadiness. When one of the women slipped or tripped, it threatened to throw off my own rhythm. *Don't let it affect you, just gain a step on her.* That thought pushed me closer to the mud-splattered butt and braids in front of me. During the last mile, I counted the girls ahead and realized I was in sixth, the final spot on the world team.

My reaction: *Oh no, how many girls are on my heels waiting to pounce?*

Then: *No, don't go there, focus ahead.*

I put my attention on the leaders, working to catch them. One competitor, Elva Dryer, made a left turn and I counted until I reached the same spot. Six seconds. I pushed to narrow the gap between us and checked my progress against a tree. Four seconds. The numbers game continued and I kept my place, crossing the line in sixth.

My first thought: *I'm tired.*

No, wait a minute, how about: *Hot damn, I'm going to worlds.*

Phil and I flew around Cole Park, a dusting of snow coming down to cover the path. I had a little over a month to prepare for worlds, and Phil had offered to pace me. He pulled me through mile repeats, then to the barn and back during tempo runs, then it was back to the grass for lappers. Phil's effort helped free my mind a little from pushing, allowing me to put more mental energy into keeping pace with him. My trust in Coach's program did the same. I never had to debate if I should do 400s or 800s that day, or what pace was ideal for a tempo effort. I was free to focus on the mental side, pay close attention to where I put my mind.

Worlds was in Torino, Italy, and on the flight over, I got to know my US teammates, most of whom I'd met at nationals or in college. Amy Rudolph was an Olympian. Tall, with shoulder-length brown hair, she ran with a gazelle-like rhythm, a fast beat, which I learned matched her taste in house music. Elva Dryer had short dark hair, a warm smile, and a tight, compact stride. She trained in Gunnison, Colorado, just north of Alamosa, home to Adams State's biggest rival, Western State. I teased her, saying we could be friends only when Coach wasn't around. At thirty-two, Olympian Gwyn Coogan was like our team mother. Short and petite and the most experienced at worlds, she'd guide us on the ground. I knew most runners by their stride, and Kristin Beaney's was quick and sharp. Nnenna Lynch, the final member, was tall and slender, with Diana Ross hair. She'd been a Rhodes Scholar and was now a professional runner and model—the perfect blend, I thought, of brains and brawn.

We were punchy, hungry, and jet-lagged when we landed. We all stood weary-eyed at the baggage carousel. One by one the girls grabbed their suitcases. The carousel stopped before mine came.

You've got to be kidding me.

Then: *There's nothing you can do about the bag.*

Luckily, I had my racing spikes and my running shoes in my backpack, so I let it go. Amy offered to lend me some running clothes, and I used the missing luggage as an excuse to buy a cute Italian outfit (suede dress pants, a blouse, and flats, which I wore to dinner and again the next day).

World cross-country to me was the Olympics of distance running. It was the toughest foot race, the epitome of the sport. All distance runners competed, runners who specialized in the mile, the 3,000, the steeplechase, the 5K, the 10K, on up to the marathon. They were all there on one big stage in a race that required a particular combination of strength, speed, endurance, and grit. I loved it.

We'd arrived three days before race day, enough time to adjust to the time zone and, hopefully, scout out the course. US coaches were trying to get us access to the race site at Parco del Valentino, a city landmark on the Po River. Meanwhile, we took to the streets. Torino was a classic European city set at the base of the Alps. We ran in the heart of it, down cobblestone streets and on the sidewalks, passing magnificent Baroque buildings, elegant churches, and art galleries. Nattily dressed people sat at the outdoor cafés, smoking and talking.

I had competed in the junior race at worlds twice in high school, traveling to France and Belgium. What I remembered most was the aggressiveness. I thought I was an assertive, hard-hitting competitor. But at points in the race when I'd typically catch my breath, the other girls had surged, showing me there was a higher-level aggression to aspire to, one that I now understood required more physical quickness and mental fortitude. At my first worlds as a professional,

I had two objectives: learn what I could from the best in the world and improve my place on the US team. I'd taken sixth at the trials, so I was aiming for a higher place in Torino.

We gained access to the park the day before the race. Teams from Kenya, Ethiopia, Japan, Morocco—seventy-two nations were competing in total—were jogging in warm-ups, amid work crews assembling the grandstand. The course was 6.6K, which we'd cover in two loops, a bonus because it condensed the crowd, creating more hype and energy. We jogged to get a sense of the terrain. It was grassy but not very hilly, so organizers had added hay bales. There was a muddy section, which men were in the midst of hosing down to make it as nasty as possible.

Race morning was cool enough that we could see our breath. We warmed up on the roads surrounding the park and, once back on the grass, did a few strides. The race was a gated start, like a horse race, and each country's stall was marked with a sign.

The United States's was to the right. Before filing in, we put our hands in and shouted, "U-S-A!"

The stalls were just wide enough for two athletes, and as I took my place at the front with Amy, a memory of getting demolished at worlds in high school came to mind. I exhaled, leaned forward, and took in the scene. Britain's star runner, Paula Radcliffe, was a few runners over. Ethiopia's Derartu Tulu and Gete Wami were on the line. Ireland's greatest female distance runner, Sonia O'Sullivan, wore her signature killer pre-race stare. *You can be intimidated. Or you can find a thought that serves you.* I settled on: *I'm part of this big, top, talented field.*

The rope across the stalls dropped and I readied myself. I put my right foot to the line, brought my left arm to the front, and bent it. Once the gun fired, that arm would be my pendulum, swung back with great force to push my body forward. I locked my eyes on the line of grass ahead and let out a long, steady exhale. *"Pronto!"* the announcer said. Then: *Bang!*

Amy and I got out strong, and with runners coming at us from both sides, merged into the field in about twentieth place. I spent most of the race from that vantage point, with Amy strides ahead, delighted to be close enough to watch the lead women's tactics. I marveled at how they surged into the hay bales, flew over them, and surged again upon landing. I had to work to get my rhythm back.

A Japanese runner passed me. *Shit, am I slowing down?*

Don't panic. Try to stay with her, let her pull you.

But I couldn't stay with her. So instead I worked to latch onto the girl ahead of me and got on her heels. *Enjoy the ride.* I took in the sound of spectators shouting *"Andiamo!"* (Let's go!) and ringing cowbells. Closer and more subtle was the sound of our spikes tearing up the wet grass. On the first loop, the course smelled like a freshly cut lawn. On the second, after we'd trampled all over it, it smelled like mud.

I felt someone on my shoulder and a moment later, girls from Italy and Russia tried to pass. *Not today.* I pressed the pace to fend them off. Other women, though, were passing me. I tried chasing them and in doing so, reeled in the Japanese runner who'd passed me earlier. *Gotcha.*

Amy was ahead and I crossed the finish in twenty-ninth place, three places behind her. In the race within the race, though, Amy was first and I was second, a trajectory that felt like a victory. In less than a year, I'd traveled from quitting running to twentieth at nationals, then to sixth, and now, second among the Americans at worlds. It seemed as though when my mind talked, my body listened, opening me to progress. My plan was to keep making more.

7

A WELL OF STRENGTH

A grateful mind is not only the greatest of virtues,
but the parent of all others.
—MARCUS TULLIUS CICERO

I never tired of time with Coach. Whether at practice, at the café, or in his kitchen, listening to his stories enthralled me. I liked the people he brought to life and the lessons he shared. One afternoon in his kitchen, he told me he hadn't been sure I'd stay after the harsh winter, but that he was glad I had. "Remember when you first called?" he said, smiling. "I tried to discourage you from coming."

"Discourage?" I exclaimed. "That phone call was the most inspiring moment of my life!"

Coach dished out the salad he had been making and we planned my summer. The goal was a podium finish in the 10,000 meters on the track at US outdoor nationals in June. We set up my season to include races in the 1,500, 3,000, and 5,000 meters, which would develop my speed and aggressive tactics for a top-three finish in the 10,000. Coach polished the plan with an uptick in mileage to 80 a week.

Sometimes after lunch, Coach would take a nap and I'd sit in the sunroom with Caroline. Caroline's hair and makeup were always perfectly done, even when she was wearing a coach's wife's attire of track pants and a T-shirt. She was full of wit and humor, delivered with such dignity and properness that I often thought she was born too late. I pictured her appearing in a Jane Austen novel, fitted in a bustled dress, gently balancing a cup of tea in her gloved hand while nodding in agreement at the gossip going around, her smirk telling you she'd rather be home reading a good book. After a conversation with Caroline, I sometimes went home and looked up words she'd used—"assiduous," "impetus," "winsome"—and put them into sentences the next day.

A former English teacher, Caroline loved discussing books. After reading one of her favorites, *Watership Down* by Richard Adams, I read her a passage I'd highlighted: "You know how you let yourself think that everything will be all right if you can only get to a certain place or do a certain thing. But when you get there you find it's not that simple." It launched a discussion on the danger of expectations and how they can lead to disappointment. I told her I'd fallen victim to that way of thinking, detailing my experiences at Kinney and cross-country nationals. "The mind and ego can get tangled up," she said. "But defeat can wake us, refocus us if we allow it to work in our favor."

Caroline suggested we read *The Artist's Way* by Julia Cameron, a self-help guide for creative people. The book prescribed morning pages—journaling when you first wake up—and we found our writing went deeper each week. Mine evolved from to-do lists into ramblings and rants, and eventually into more thoughtful entries on topics like belief, and choosing the people you surround yourself with. Journaling became crucial, because for me running was not time to reflect. I was focused on getting faster, building strength, and when I ran, my thoughts centered on those goals. Journaling opened me to understanding more about my thoughts and feelings and how they affected running and my life.

Every now and then Caroline assigned topics to guide our reflections: family, the San Luis Valley, teamwork. We wrote separately, but later talked about what came of our writing. Once, our topic was gratitude. My pages overflowed with how cherished I'd felt as an adopted child. My parents told me all the time that they chose me, making me feel special and loved. Caroline wrote about growing up on a turquoise mine and the lively and rich childhood it provided. The topic evoked such powerful feelings of love and warmth in both of us, that we agreed to write a gratitude list each night for a few weeks. Ten items, every night.

It was easy at first. An extra-hot cappuccino. A new pair of running shoes. Reading before napping. Lemonade after a 15-mile run. Aspen's eagerness to see me when I got home. Pops feeding me at the café. Writing the list made me smile and I went to bed happy.

Caroline made a rule we couldn't duplicate items, so instead of thinking about gratitude at night, I began looking for things for my list throughout the day. I watched Aspen run along the Rio Grande among the cattails and dense stands of willow and thought how grateful I was for her company. I smelled fertilizer in the fields while running and sent thanks to the farmers for the food they grew. After a spring rainstorm, I acknowledged Mother Nature for packing down the trails for my second run.

The more I looked, the more there was to be grateful for: Driving my Jeep with the top down. Crisp white wine on a summer evening. The tree across the street when the leaves caught a breeze. I appreciated small realities, like the fact that I had the money to buy the cappuccino, and big things, like the conversation with Milan that led me to Coach. The simple act of writing Milan's name made me so deeply grateful for his guidance, tears swelled.

Constantly scanning the world for goodness, I ran with greater lightness, infused with a deep appreciation for Coach, everyone around me, the opportunities before me, and my body itself. Positive thoughts came more quickly now, without a conscious shift. Traffic, wind, feeling tired, or being confronted with a broken washing machine paled in comparison to sunshine, kindness, and the skills of a handyman. The more I focused on the brighter parts of the day, the experiences that drained me retreated to the background, and a greater vitality rushed forth. I was happier, more content, and optimistic.

One afternoon, out for my second run, I felt overly tired. Aspen and I were running along the river, so I looked around. The air was calm and on the cusp of cooling for the day. I admired the fiery red sun, which cast a glow on Mount Blanca's still snowcapped peak. Aspen jumped into the river to swim after a beaver and I laughed from the trail. I ran on and noticed an undercurrent of energy pumping through my body, coming from an unknown source, a well inside I'd never noticed before. It was such a stark contrast to the fatigue at the start of the run that it clicked: practicing gratitude had opened a whole new channel of energy within me.

My world exploded and expanded after that. Nothing around me changed, only I did. Or rather, my mind changed; it became a place of constant positivity. I no longer had to keep intense vigilance over my thoughts. Gratitude relieved my mind of that duty. I was, however, more aware and conscious of my thinking, and I noticed a subtle yet profound tonal change in my head. I would be running and *I'm so slow today* might come to mind, but as a fact, not a judgment, and I'd spend a little time considering how I could rest better to prepare for tomorrow's workout.

Living without the toxins and tension of regular negativity gave way to greater feelings of health. My body felt more fluid when I ran, lighter, and stronger. My senses were heightened. I saw beauty in ordinary things. A still rocking chair. Dew on a leaf. The creaky floorboards of an old house. Lemonade was more tart and refreshing, and the look of adoration on Aspen's face touched me more deeply. Reading seemed more relaxing. I experienced a sense of synchronicity with everything around me. The mountains and the trees, but also the men, Coach and Caroline, the regulars at the café. Items on my gratitude list—drinking a cappuccino, reading a book on the porch—evolved to become sacred moments in the day, rather than routine.

Running remained physically challenging, but there was a mental ease as I ran through the wind, up a hill, or around the track. The ease carried over into racing. While running the 10,000 at Mt. SAC in California to earn a qualifying time for track nationals, the sounds of competition—crowds, breathing, foot strike—had a new vividness. As I moved around the track, I was more immersed in the pack, more emotionally involved. A competitor pulled up beside me in lane 2 and I made room for her to move in. Then I picked up the pace to push us both. I took an elbow and got the wind knocked out of me. My mind automatically interpreted the moment humorously—*what were the hard-elbow tactics of cross-country doing on the track?*—allowing me to smile at the girl who glanced back, sharing a split-second moment of positive energy. Near the end, when I passed a competitor, I encouraged her: "Come with me."

In the 5,000 at the Twilight Series, a three-week event at Northeastern University, in Dedham, Massachusetts, I attached myself to the heels of Amy Rudolph, the American record holder in the 5,000. My goal was to stay with her stride for stride. When I began to fade physically or mentally, gratitude was my answer. I inhaled the sound of the crowds and exhaled appreciation. I watched her back-kick and thanked her quick turnover for the assistance. I concentrated so intently on her rhythm, her cadence became mine.

The pace was fast, yet running with the intention of gratitude opened my legs, limbs, and heart, powering my stride. I felt it in the 3,000 later that week and again in the 1,500. I finished the series dumbfounded. I had run personal bests in all of my races: 15:43 in the 5,000; 9:10 in the 3,000; 4:20 in the 1,500; and 32:47 in the 10,000, where I'd shaved off a remarkable 83 seconds from my time. This was it, I thought. This was my competitive edge: the athlete's life, positivity, and gratitude—the mental choices that elevate training.

My streak of personal bests in racing carried over into practice and had me running mile repeats in under 5 minutes. I was actually right there on the back end of the guys, able to run close enough to step on their long shadows. Easy days were the opposite: joyous, easy jaunts. Once, during a run around the golf course, I took off my shoes and felt the warm grass on my feet. The guys followed suit, and on the sixth green we did barefoot strides, rejoicing in summer.

Heading to Indianapolis for the 10,000, I felt like a finely tuned athlete. Conditions were hot and humid, so I let go of any thoughts of clocking another personal record and focused solely on putting myself in a position to get on the podium. From the gun, I inserted myself behind the best in the pack, running close on the heels of cross-country great Lynn Jennings and Olympian Annette Peters.

I listened for the sound of their cadence and blended my foot strikes with theirs. I felt like I was riding a train, me a cart linked to these powerful engines. Smooth, powerful, hypnotic, I pushed on, the rest of the field strung out behind us. Immersed in the ride, my awareness was of feeling grateful for the crowds and the two women dragging me toward my goal. As the laps counted down, competitors fell off pace behind us and the pack grew steadily lighter. Lynn and Annette began pulling ahead and I held fast to them. Despite a gap opening between us, I kept my eyes on Annette's back-kick and didn't feel the heat of the day and the sweat dripping off me until I crossed the finish line in third.

On the podium, I felt the race was a beautiful expression of all the goodness in the world. Competitors can know your times and places. They can learn and guess at your race tactics. But your inner strength is where you gain a real advantage. And I felt mine growing.

8

STRATEGIC JOY

Alamosa, Summer 1997

Look closely at the present you are constructing. It should
look like the future you are dreaming.

—ATTRIBUTED TO ALICE WALKER

Something magical happens when you take control of your thoughts. You realize you are your own creation. Moment to moment, who do you want to be?

I wanted to be an athlete. I wanted to become the strongest and fastest version of myself possible. I was creating that runner every time I arrived at a tough spot in a workout and used my thoughts and perspective to power through it. But why wait? I didn't have to limit myself to being an interpreter in the moment. I could be the creator of that moment, even before it arrived.

So I looked for weak spots in training and began to set the stage for success.

I started with my bread-and-butter workout: mile repeats. Mile repeats were the perfect balance of speed and stamina. They gave me a clear indication of my fitness and progress. My goal was to hit each mile in 5:00 or under. But my times in the last two repeats often slipped by 5 to 10 seconds. I knew a problem spot was the small hill on the backside of Cole Park. I hated that hill. I approached it with irritation and resistance even before stepping foot on it, killing my momentum and losing time. So I decided to approach the hill playfully. *Hill*, I thought as I jogged to Cole Park for the workout, *today, you're mine*.

I warmed up with the men, launched into the oval, went through the trees, past the rec center, north along the river, and arced onto the backside. I grinned as the hill came into view. When I arrived at its base, I mouthed, *Charge!* and pushed into the climb, accelerating all the way to the top.

The playfulness allowed me to enjoy the effort and made cresting the hill feel like a victory. I repeated the game every repeat, and over time, the hill became my own private cheering section, shouting *Go! Do it!* as I approached.

I continued to analyze the workout and noticed that I was fried during the last two repeats, and losing a little time there, too. So after the hill, as I approached the last quarter of the repeat, I took deep, energizing breaths. I imagined the oxygen relieving the fatigue and gave the finishing stretch more effort. I crossed the line and looked at my watch—4:57. Right on pace.

Tempo runs were transformed in similar fashion. On Saturday, we had a 6-mile hard effort toward the barn and back. I'd been trying to hit the workout in under 35:00, but hadn't been able to. I got off to a good start, but in the second half, fatigue set in and I just wanted to be done. Thinking about it, I realized I went into the run with a long list of excuses: I was tired from mile repeats; tired from the cumulative weekly mileage; the wind was a factor; the mile markers were off.

So I began by getting rid of the excuses and committing to giving the miles my greatest attention. Next, I made the workout fun. Dressing for practice, I put on my favorite running outfit, a blue and green matching tank top and race shorts that coordinated with my shoes. I pulled my hair back into what was surely a more aerodynamic ponytail and jogged to practice with my goal on my mind.

The men and I warmed up along the river, toed the start on State

Street, and Coach sent us off. I ran with an advantage from the start. The outfit made me feel good, professional; and the excuses, which used to be tucked into the back of my mind, were replaced with focus on executing the pace. We ran into a headwind and I celebrated the fact that we'd have a tailwind on the way back. The barn in sight, I made it to the halfway mark in 17:15, ahead of pace, and flipped for the return.

In previous attempts, I'd turn around and run the second half waiting for fatigue. This time, I used the success of being on pace to feed the return. As I ran, the momentum built and I felt the wind at my back and thought how fun it was to have Mother Nature pushing me from behind. When I began to struggle, I noticed the sound of my foot strikes created a rhythm that matched the bouncing of my ponytail, and focused on maintaining the same cadence as my ponytail. In the final mile, I thought about how nice it was to have a slightly closer view of the men.

Coach stood in the middle of the road with his stopwatch and clocked me at 34:35, faster than my goal. "If Deena continues to progress like that," Coach said to the men, "she'll be kicking your asses in no time." I smiled, but I have no idea how the men reacted. I was bent over, sucking wind, and seeing stars.

Improving the long run took more thought. I just didn't enjoy the workout the way I did mile repeats and tempo runs, where the satisfaction of nailing a split was a built-in reward. I also knew those faster workouts were lifting me to greater fitness. Theoretically, long runs were developing endurance, but in trying to keep up with the men, I fatigued quickly and woke every Sunday already feeling defeated by the workout. Each week I worked to hold on longer by using positive thoughts to get me through the final miles, but the run left me depleted mentally, physically, and emotionally for the remainder of the day.

No one wants to do something they don't enjoy. So how could I bring enjoyment to the long run?

I approached the day as a whole, creating a ritual centered on manufacturing pleasure and ease. Upon waking, I selected a French press from my growing collection, made strong, thick coffee, and baked cinnamon scones. Over the morning paper, I relished my breakfast. I paid attention to the crumbling texture of the scone and its delicate sweetness. As I scanned the headlines on the paper spread out before me, I cupped my coffee mug close to my lips and felt the steam warm my face.

When you put yourself into a mind-set of enjoyment, the cycle unfolds. Out the door I had more energy. On the run I immersed myself in the conversation with the men, and when they strung out ahead, I let them go and maintained some sort of rhythm. The run was still physically challenging, but it was no longer emotionally draining. I went home tired but not depleted and could enjoy an afternoon of reading. With no second run, Sundays began to feel so leisurely that it quickly became my favorite day of the week.

Eventually I broadened the application of strategic joy to the entire cycle of training, because no matter my perspective, the day-in, day-out repetitive nature of professional running could be a grind. To address the monotony, I added small details to enhance the enjoyment of the process. I bought pretty water glasses and kept fresh lemon water in the fridge to make hydrating more appealing. I placed lavender from the garden inside my shoes to freshen them up. I set out my favorite pajamas to wear for my nap. These simple additions made the sometimes-tedious work of training and recovery pleasurable, and discipline became secondary.

There was a spiraling effect to strategic joy: One enjoyable task propelled me into the next one. A delicious breakfast led to a good mood heading into the workout. A better mood resulted in a stronger workout. A stronger workout provided motivation for recovery. Better recovery made it easier to get out the door for my second run (even if Aspen sometimes barked at the door to nudge me along). It kept going. The afternoon run became a practice in reveling in nature—the waterfowl on the Rio Grande, the sound of frogs I'd never see, the grandness of the surrounding mountains in summer.

The goodness of those feelings carried me into the evening. My mind would be free from stress, allowing me to focus on whatever activity I was doing that night, usually reading and cooking. Falling asleep relaxed, I slept soundly and woke ready to do it all over again in the morning.

Coach talked a lot about character. The stories he told reinforced the qualities he believed were important to success. The discipline of Juma Ikangaa. The perseverance of Olympian Billy Mills, a Native American who pushed on despite encountering prejudice on and off the track. The elegant stride of the Tarahumara, Native American distance runners from Mexico's Copper Canyon, whose grace was to Coach an act of love and devotion.

Coach had said the qualities that build the person build the athlete. I saw now that the details of developing myself as a runner—the work, the discipline, the quality of thought—were also building my character. The practice of those traits, though, went toward the singular goal of building an athlete. It made me wonder, who was I besides a runner trying to get faster?

Similar to piecing together running traits, I sought to piece together the rest of me in a way that felt authentic and whole. I explored what I admired in others to gain a greater understanding of myself and my values.

Caroline was as fiercely independent as she was a committed wife. She sometimes traveled abroad with Coach and nurtured his athletes with a motherly instinct. The Vigils hosted team dinners over the holidays, and Caroline would throw open the doors of the sunroom, telling us to sit and get off our feet as she crossed to the side table and poured us drinks. She was compassionate and empathetic toward everyone around her, including herself. She could spend an afternoon reading classic literature and contemplating. She took online courses to broaden her education and inspire herself. A need to reconnect with her creative side was what had prompted us to dive into *The Artist's Way* and write gratitude lists. Sometimes she chose to stay home while Coach traveled, prioritizing her own schedule and needs. Her independence reassured me. My singular focus scared me sometimes. It made me worry that sharing my life with someone was not part of my future. Caroline's ability to balance independence and devotion, though, showed me it could be achieved.

Linda was a regular at the café who had become a friend. She was a rancher with a beautiful combination of femininity and grit. In her fifties, she had highlighted hair fresh out of rollers and dirt under her fingernails. In the early hours of the morning, she fed her cattle by the light of her truck, then swung by the café for toast and coffee before heading off to her day job as a construction company's office manager. Whenever Aspen and I went to her house for dinner, we'd pull in to her gravel driveway just as Linda was shutting the pasture gates behind her. She'd greet me with a hug, then stomp the cow manure off her boots before we headed inside to a meal that was already on the stove. Linda taught me to make strawberry jam and tamales. She hosted cookie exchanges during the holidays and sold freshly cut flowers at the farmers' market. Once, we birthed a calf together, taking turns holding the mother in place, and pulled the breech calf out. The work over, we washed up and Linda pulled together a mean meal of carnitas enchiladas, Spanish rice, and cumin-scented black beans, served on dishes warmed in the oven.

These women showed me I could define myself in more than one way, and I loved them because they were authentically themselves.

Once, during a visit with Caroline, we were gossiping about people in the community, which led to a discussion on the character traits we valued and detested in others. The list of qualities we liked included compassion, kindness, humor, and optimism. Traits we cringed at: prejudice, dishonesty, arrogance, laziness. Later, I went home and considered my own traits. I'd become resilient and disciplined through running, was proud of my attention and toughness, and was truly valuing my growing confidence. But confidence often fits into a silo, not penetrating other areas of our lives. I didn't know myself well enough then to be confident outside of running. The traits that came to mind immediately were negative: dramatic, self-conscious, reclusive. I could stand in front of the mirror and find more to dislike. My ribs stuck out farther than my chest. My shoulders were too square. My legs too skinny.

It took some time, but I eventually found qualities outside of running I admired in myself: I was creative, curious, generous. I liked how I experimented with ingredients in the kitchen and was good at voicing my appreciation for others. I admired that I read books on a variety of subjects and always studied the places I was traveling to. Acknowledging these good qualities felt like a kind gesture toward myself, a means of nurturing. Had I stood in front of the mirror in that moment, I would have seen a powerful set of lungs, shoulders that drove my stride, and legs that carried me to my goals. Seeing this side of myself was its own kind of progress, one that a stopwatch might never reveal.

One night in late summer, I was standing in the living room of the house I was renting, admiring the crab apple tree across the street. I loved that tree. I loved how it caught the breeze just before a thunderstorm rolled in. I loved that nothing seemed to bother the tree—rain, sun, wind, snow, the occasional dog lifting its leg. It was raining that night, but I felt an overwhelming urge to let the tree know how much I appreciated it. So I pushed open the screen door, walked across the road in my slippers, and kissed the trunk. The bark was smoother than I imagined, not grainy or rough. I turned to go back to the house and, looking around, suddenly felt self-conscious. I shuffled quickly across the road, glad for the cover of darkness.

Back inside, the tree caught my attention again. It had been fulfilling to let something know how I felt about it. So I changed my mind and decided I didn't feel silly at all.

9

SEEING IS BELIEVING

Alamosa, Colorado, Fall 1997

As he thinks, so he is; as he continues to think, so he remains.

—JAMES ALLEN

It's pouring. The grass is slick and unforgiving. I dig my spikes into the dirt for better traction, keep my head forward.

I'm leading the national cross-country championships. A handful of competitors nip at my heels. Olympian and American record holder in the 5,000 meters Amy Rudolph is practically on top of me. She's a strong competitor, with a long, beautiful stride, and close enough that I can feel the strength of her quick turnover as she surges past, her back-kick flinging mud in my face. I wipe it away with my glove and cover her move easily.

Annette Peters is trying to work her way onto my shoulder. An Olympian, she uses her wicked track speed to try to gain an edge. I surge, cutting off her effort, and work the terrain to shake these women for good. I power up a small hill and cannonball down the backside. Lynn Jennings, the defending champion, refuses to be dropped. She's a hard-charging bull, strong and powerful, her drive clear and apparent in her stride.

I'm ready for her. We run stride for stride in a grassy stretch that turns to mud. As she cuts a tight turn, her elbow smacks my rib cage. I suck for air and she takes the lead. It doesn't faze me. I use the adrenaline to run harder, surging into and out of the next turn, gaining an inch with each step. The battle intensifies. I kick up my turnover and am on her shoulder. When I pass, she can't stay with me, and I open a small gap between us. I take advantage of the moment, surging before she can recover, and increase my lead. I know Lynn won't catch me. Still, I run hard and fast toward the finish, crossing the line as the new national cross-country champion.

The race over, I opened my eyes. The bedroom ceiling came into view.

I smiled at the mental victory I'd just earned. After savoring it briefly, I pulled myself up off the bed to make coffee before my afternoon run.

It was October. The mornings and evenings had begun to cool. Dry leaves blew across Cole Park and the river moved more slowly. At the café, the regulars started predicting when the first frost would arrive. Linda came in with news about the calf auction and the barn repairs that would ready her for winter. The divots in the grass at Cole Park became more plentiful as Coach, the men, and I returned to lappers on the field. I had started thinking about the national cross-country championships during track season. I'd placed third in the 10,000 at nationals and was second among US runners at the world cross-country championships. I was almost there. So I told Coach I wanted to win cross-country nationals this year. "That's a great goal," he said. "It's going to take every bit of who you are."

I'd found strength in positivity, gratitude, and enjoyment. But I wanted to use everything available to further my mental preparation. So I turned to practices I'd been introduced to in high school: positive affirmations and visualization.

I'd gone to a running camp at the Olympic Training Center in Colorado Springs one year. In a session with a sports psychologist, we wrote our goals or desires as statements in the present tense.

These, the psychologist said, are positive affirmations. They confirm who you're striving to be.

The most famous comes from the great Muhammad Ali, when he was a brash young fighter still climbing his way to the top. Before he went up against the world heavyweight champion, Sonny Liston, in February 1964, he proclaimed to a group of reporters, "I am the greatest!" It wasn't just in-the-moment bravado. He had written a poem the year before about the "most beautiful fighter," ending it with the sentiment on being the greatest. Ali perhaps wasn't consciously working on his mental side, but there's no doubt he was steeping himself in belief.

The affirmations I wrote in high school were *I am fast* and *I am elite*. Back then, it was just a camp exercise. Now, I wrote I AM THE NATIONAL CHAMPION on a Post-it note in black marker and stuck it to the bathroom mirror. There, I'd see it multiple times a day, allowing the idea to work its way into my mind.

Affirmations reminded me of visualizations, another practice I'd learned in high school with Dr. Jonathan Brower, a psychologist and the father of one of my high school teammates. Junior year, he offered to lead the team in a visualization exercise and my parents volunteered our living room. About twenty of us, the boys' and the girls' teams, lay on the living-room floor, eyes closed, and Dr. Brower began. *You're at a trailhead. Anywhere in the mountains, anywhere you want to be.* I immediately saw the rocky, familiar contours of the Santa Monica Mountains. *The skies are clear, the sun is high. Now, bend down and retie your shoes, looping one lace through the other. Pull it tightly so you don't have to retie mid-run. Stand up, start your watch, and begin running.* Running, in my mind, created a nice breeze and I imagined feeling it move across my face and arms. I ran by the mustard plants I loved, heard a rattlesnake, and looked up to see craggy oak trees. *The sun is hot and there are no trees*, Dr. Brower said, and so the oaks disappeared. *The sun is beating down and there's a big hill ahead. A few more steps and you're at its base, beginning the climb.*

It's getting harder and hotter. You're starting to sweat and your heart is beating faster. Thump, thump, thump.

My heart was beating faster! I actually felt warm!

Dr. Brower had us crest the hill, barrel down the back, and return to the trailhead. He asked afterward what we'd experienced. I piped up. "I was actually sweating!" I said, still surprised that my mind could have such an effect on my body. Dr. Brower told us the mind doesn't distinguish between fact and fiction. What the mind sees and thinks, the body feels, and what the body feels, the mind, or at least the subconscious, learns.

I was so taken with the experience that my parents hired Dr. Brower to give me private sessions. As I lay on the living-room floor, he took me through similar trail runs, encouraging me not only to see the scenery, but feel and hear the experience. The sound of the creek gurgling. The relief in stopping to splash cool water on my flushed face. The more senses you bring to the imagery, he said, the greater the effect it will have on the mind and body.

I practiced on my own at home. At first, any noise or slight movement broke my concentration. With time, though, I could run through a dozen virtual miles, spending time with the deer and squirrels out in the golden hills while my parents watched reruns of *M*A*S*H* and *The Cosby Show*. As a teenager, visualization was a way to spend time in the hills I loved. Now, I saw it as an untapped mental tool I could use to help me win nationals.

Every afternoon for three months before the championships, I ran through a race scenario. I put "Jóga" by Björk on the stereo, lay on my bed, and closed my eyes. The moment I heard the slow and dramatic instrumental opening, the heightened feel of the race came to me. I watched myself pin on my bib number and tie my shoes. I did a few strides off the starting line and noticed the other women strung out across the start. I knew that Lynn would be the toughest to beat, but everyone was a threat. I lined up at the front. Right toes on the line, knee bent, left arm cocked in front, the gun fired and I flew.

Each visualization unfolded organically. I didn't plot it out or overthink it. I followed along as the terrain and competitors came at me. Sometimes I was in a pack, steadily moving to the front. Other times I led the race and pressed to stay in the lead. In some editions, it was hot. Other times it was raining. My hair was in a ponytail. The next day it was tucked into a hat.

The only common denominator was that the competition was fierce and I was fiercer. I outmaneuvered Annette. I blew past Gwyn. The next day, I fended off a hard-charging Amy. I saw each woman at her best. Amy's speed had never been sharper. Annette's stride was more powerful than I remembered. Lynn was never more aggressive than she was in my mind. She put up the nastiest fights. We stomped side by side through puddles, chased each other up hills. She tried breaking me with flying elbows and such aggressive surges that the two of us might as well have been in the ring.

Behind closed eyes I pictured their aggression drawing out the best in me. A competitor from behind pushed me to run harder. Lynn's attempts to break me strengthened my composure and grit. Never had I run with such force as the day Amy and I ran stride for stride down the grass toward the finish. No matter the situation, I matched it with my own strength—faster reactions, quicker recoveries, a stronger push. Race after race, I won. Sometimes by as little as 2 seconds. Other times, by a 2-minute margin. But every time, I won. I didn't want my subconscious to think that losing was possible.

"Jóga" played throughout each visualization. The dramatic violin riffs and her melodic voice struck an emotional chord, uplifting me, and amplifying the intensity of the visualization. The song put me in such a powerful state that I started playing it in the morning while I got ready for practice. When it came on, I was immediately connected to the powerful emotions of racing, linking the workout to my goal.

As I dressed, Björk's voice, an instrument itself, entered the song and the day's workout came to mind. I saw myself running lappers in fast-forward to get more speed out of them. I pictured myself able to stay with the men in mile repeats or running powerfully side by side with them on long runs. The heightened emotion from the song and workout went with me to the bathroom, where I saw the note on the mirror: I AM THE NATIONAL CHAMPION. I repeated the words in my head as I brushed my teeth and Björk wailed in the background. Sometimes I got so psyched up, I spat toothpaste into the sink as if I were spitting at the feet of Lynn herself. (Something I would never actually do!)

Seeing myself as a champion prompted me to think, and therefore act, more like one. I was already living an athlete's life and giving my all in each workout. Affirmations, visualization, and musical associations were for me layers of reinforcement in my self-belief. That belief expressed itself in a subtle but important way in practice. I held myself in a new regard. As I ran, I did so with the confidence of a champion. A greater level of belief and determination mixed with the physical adaptations led to greater speed. In November, a month before nationals, my times dropped in most workouts: lappers, mile repeats, and tempos.

The progress on my watch made me take more risks during visualizations. I purposefully cut off a competitor, took sharp turns recklessly, surged when I was tired. The confidence from the mental moves prompted me to run faster in workouts, and my speed and strength continued to climb.

Seventeen days out, while Marco and Peter did repeats in Cole Park, Coach had me run a time trial: a 2K, 1K, 1K all-out effort to sharpen my fitness. Phil, who had been encouraging me throughout training, offered to pace me. We headed out on State Street as snow fell. Phil ran fast and a stride ahead to pull me as we crossed the bridge and passed the golf course. When I started to fade, he reached his hand back to rally me. I reeled him in, slapped his hand, and said thank you on the exhale. During the last repeat, Phil shouted, "Pretend I'm Lynn!" I smiled, dug down, and passed him. I ran my fastest times to date.

The last week before the championships, my visualizations intensified. Lynn, Annette, and the rest of the field were rowdier, the weather nastier. I fell flat on my face. A competitor's spikes sliced my heel. The sun beat down in unseasonable warmth. We ran in sleet and high winds. I even responded to moves I didn't see coming, a hard trick to play on yourself when you're the one doing the imagining. I felt so strong, like such a badass, that when I finished these visualizations, I may not have shouted, "I am the greatest!" but something like it was flying around in my head.

In the end, I got a stormy day.

Cross-Country Nationals were in Portland that year at Blue Lake Park on the Columbia River. Coach and I pulled up race morning in a downpour. Freezing rain pelted the car and wind whipped the pennant flags marking the course. The only people out were officials checking the course for downed branches and runners needing to warm up. Everyone else took shelter in their cars.

Despite the conditions, I was calm inside. I headed out into the rain, did my warm-up, and climbed back in the car Coach had kept warm. I shimmied out of my wet warm-ups and slipped "Jóga" into my Walkman. I'd listened to the song during more than 100 visualizations by now, and Björk's voice was to me the sound of winning. She sang as I put on dry socks and my spikes, and all the physical and mental training I'd done rushed to the forefront of my mind, putting me in a state of readiness.

"Go get 'em," Coach said when I pulled off my headphones and opened the door.

I did a couple of strides off the starting line and was one of the first to line up. I was aware of the other women, but also internal. I didn't want to break the focused spell Björk's voice had put me in.

The gun fired and we launched into the first of two 2.5-mile loops around the park. I was in the lead immediately. Lynn, who was going for her tenth title, and Kathy Franey, a top-ranked 3,000 meter runner, were on my heels. I'd pictured this, I'd seen them right there in my mind, and I was confident I could cover any move because I'd seen myself do it.

I pushed into the driving rain and at the first mile had a small lead over Lynn and Kathy. I didn't, though, think of myself as pulling them. They were pushing me. I kicked it up. Kathy fell back and by mile 2, Lynn was also trailing. I imagined she had the same desperate face of my last race episode.

Leading the race was in one way easier than any visualization because no one was challenging me. I had conditioned myself to fight every step of the way and without the competitive shoving and jostling, heading into the second loop, I got creative and began playing with the terrain and weather. Puddles were waves I rode to the finish. The wind was a pack of competitors I elbowed my way through. I tried matching the force of the driving rain as it beat against me. At one point, I saw my family on the sidelines and heard my sister shout, "Go Dee!" I grabbed her love and ran with it.

In the final mile, spectators shouted out the length of my lead over Lynn. Twenty-five meters! One hundred meters! But in my mind, a competitor had to be right there, because in my visualizations, one always was. So I pushed with every step. I wanted to finish the race knowing every stride had been my strongest.

The finish line appeared. *Charge!* I thought, sprinting down the final stretch, lifting my arms to break the tape. I turned to see Lynn making her way down the homestretch. She still had a way to go, which was satisfying. When you win by a big margin, the win feels bigger in some way.

Coach stood just outside the chute wearing a heavy rain jacket and a wide smile. I threw my arms around him. "We did it!" I said. Over the cowbells, I heard him say, "Baby, I'm not going to pat you on the back until you can run with the best in the world."

My parents and the media came over and the moment moved on. But as I was talking to reporters, my mind was turning. What was Coach saying? I had just won the most prestigious cross-country race in the United States, crushing the long-dominant queen Lynn Jennings. I was officially on top.

Then it came to me: Coach didn't see me on top. He saw me climbing. His words told me that this win didn't define me any more than a previous loss had. You keep going. You think bigger. With his simple statement, Coach had elevated the excitement of a national win into a vision for the future. I'd caught the nation. Now I set out to catch the world.

After nationals, my name went around the country. *Drossin Top Finisher,* the Associated Press announced in its story. The headline in *Track & Field News*: *Drossin Shocks,* which made me smile. Reebok signed me to a $12,000 per-year contract, which allowed me to quit the café and focus solely on running. The win also secured my spot on the US team headed to the world cross-country championships in Morocco.

I felt like a woman on fire. I was running well, yet I also knew there was so much more to pull out of myself. The feelings of confidence and possibility were so big within me, they seemed like two tectonic plates pushing me upward.

With worlds at the end of March, three months away, I resumed training. I headed out with the men feeling more grown-up, in the way that finally being able to pay your own car insurance can do. The winter was cold that year, but whenever the sun was out, there was a blinding whiteness to the land that was beautiful. The cold was numbing and unbearable at times, yet it also suited my internal focus. I returned to reading. I picked up Deepak Chopra's *Ageless Body, Timeless Mind* and Daniel Goleman's *Emotional Intelligence,* books that reinforced the powerful interplay of mind, body, and emotions I was immersed in.

I studied Spanish and noted the acuity of mind that came from trying to think in a foreign language. Sometimes I sat quietly at home and listened to nothing but the ice in my glass to see how well I could pay attention. Stepping out of the shower, I stood and felt the water from my hair dripping down my back. By improving my ability to notice and record information, I would allow nothing in a race to pass me by.

At the end of March, I flew to Morocco and woke in the warm, dry climate of Marrakesh. The sound of the muezzin's call to prayer came through the windows. The call had a deep, soulful resonance that gave me chills.

Most of my teammates preferred to rest at our luxurious hotel, which USATF athletes and coaches had taken over for the week. But I had never been to Africa and was intrigued by the place. I headed to the souk, the central marketplace, and strolled among the outdoor stalls taking in the colors and exotic smells. I bartered for spices and bought camel leather stools as Abdul, the Moroccan gentleman serving as my police escort (US athletes were required to have one outside the hotel) looked on. A little boy kept putting a monkey on my shoulder and I kept giving it back. This went on for a while until my escort flashed his badge.

I came upon a group of tables circling a man cooking. He wore the traditional djellaba and stood over large steaming pots. I asked him to feed me his specialty. Within seconds, a large plate of couscous and a stew of lentils with tender pieces of goat meat were set before me. Seeing no utensils, I watched the locals rip pieces of the msemen flatbread and scoop the food into their mouths. I followed their lead, closing my eyes to relish the sophistication of flavors. When I opened them, there was a cold Coca-Cola bottle in front of me. I looked up and the cook winked.

Two days later, I was on the starting line with the world's top runners: Ireland's Sonia O'Sullivan, Kenya's Sally Barsosio, Gete Wami of Ethiopia, and Britain's star athlete, Paula Radcliffe. Last year in

Torino, I'd watched these women from far back in the chase pack. This year my goal was to run with the leaders long enough to get a sense of what it took to stay up there. So, off the line, I put myself out front. We were running 8K on a 2K circuit on what seemed like a makeshift course in the desert. The ground was parched, save for patches of half-dead grass. Officials had added hay bales, a mud pit, and one small fabricated hill that resembled, appropriately, a camel's hump. Potted palm trees decorated the center, where ornately dressed Berber men sat on camelback under the hot noontime sun.

There was a powerful rush to leading a pack of Olympic medalists and world champions. I sensed a maturity in their confidence, slightly different from the newness of my own. There was strain and delight in my stride that contrasted with the antsy feel of the rest of the pack. Paula made the first push. The pack stretched a bit, like an accordion, then regrouped when she settled. I held on up toward the front. Gete made the next surge and the pack expanded again, regrouping this time without me.

At most races, the pace was more or less constant until someone made a definitive move to the finish line. What I learned was that on the world stage, surging was a temporary acceleration to drop competitors. Understanding this made the pack feel less intimidating. It also made it more unpredictable, confirming for me that the more skilled I became at sensing mood and absorbing details, the better.

In the final lap, I questioned if I had the energy to finish. But I was the leader among the US team, which was incentive to keep pushing. Each racer ahead became a target to chase and I pressed, jumping the hay bales, zipping past the Berber men, and crossed the finish in twentieth place. I was exhausted, mud-splattered, and sunburnt. It took me a moment to be able to stand straight without effort.

Walking down the finishing chute catching my breath, I felt a kinship with the women ahead of me. I had been *with them,* and even though I was dropped, I had been there. I'd learned the physical language of the pack, understood how it worked, and gained appreciation for the aggression required to lead. I'd moved from twenty-ninth to twentieth place on the world stage. With another year and another season of physical and mental growth, I knew I could put myself back in with the leaders, and hang on even longer.

10

POSITIVITY HAS A PASSPORT

Heinola, Finland, Summer 1998

I am the master of my fate, I am the captain of my soul.
—WILLIAM ERNEST HENLEY

Here's something I learned about the mind: It forgets.

I was jet-lagged as I sat slouched on my overstuffed bag in the Helsinki airport. My phone didn't work internationally, so I sat wondering if Kimmo remembered I was arriving that day. Kimmo was an aspiring Finnish runner who had trained in Alamosa the summer before. He was twentysomething, and had the blond-white hair and fresh face common among Scandinavians. As a favor, he was coordinating my stay in Finland, where I'd be training and competing for the next six weeks.

Distance runners from around the world descended on the United States for our vibrant road-racing scene, but when it came to track racing, Europe was the place to be. Each summer, hundreds of international athletes went from race to race in cities like Rome, Paris, Monte Carlo, and Stockholm, training in between. The best athletes competed in what were then known as Grand Prix and Golden League events, A-list meets reserved for the top fifteen to seventeen competitors in each discipline. B-level meets catered to nationally ranked athletes like me working to move into the world rankings. I'd skipped the European circuit the previous year because Alamosa was more suited to my growth. Now, in order to build the speed that would enable me to challenge the world, I would challenge myself against international runners week in and week out.

I looked up and spotted Kimmo bounding down the terminal, his flip-flops slapping the concrete floor. "I'm sorry," he said when he reached me, wearing the serious expression I remembered. "I was warning your host family of your arrival." *Warning?* I hoped his translation was off.

We sped out of the city toward Heinola, a town in the country-side about ninety minutes north. Kimmo had arranged for me to stay with Matti and Anna-Marja Martilla, a young couple he knew through running. Kimmo explained we'd be spending some time with the Martillas at their vacation cabin on one of the surround-ing lakes. "It's beautiful and relaxing," he said. I was anxious to get training, so a vacation at the lake didn't appeal to me. "Lovely," I said in an effort to be flexible.

Matti and Anna-Marja were standing outside their small wooden cabin when we pulled up. Anna-Marja folded me in a hug. She was tall, in her thirties, with warm, soft features. Matti was her opposite. Short and angular, a recreational runner thinned by an obsession with miles and pace.

We spent the day fishing and swimming, and Matti and Kimmo took me on an easy run through the woods, with Kimmo serving as translator. In the evening, we had a traditional dinner of makkara, or Finnish sausage, and afterward, Anna-Marja introduced me to the sauna, the Finnish bathing ritual. She led me to a small wooden building a hundred paces from the cabin that reminded me of an outhouse. Behind partitions, Anna-Marja stripped down. I hesitated. I was the girl in the locker room who changed with a towel around her. I looked around, but not wanting to draw greater attention to my modesty, I slowly unclipped my bra, pulled off my pants, and what the hell, my underwear, too. Inside, it was warm and smelled of cedar. Anna-Marja, bare-breasted, poured a ladle of water over hot coals. Steam sucked the air out of the room. I closed my eyes and took a few deep breaths.

WHACK.

A sting traveled across my back and, suppressing an angry scream, I turned to see Anna-Marja's warm face smiling widely. She held a bundle of birch leaves, a *vasta*. "Good circulation," she said in her limited English. With that, she proceeded to smack my body from neck to legs. I jerked and jolted, taking the strange beating for the sake of foreign relations. When she was done, I repaid the favor. She asked for harder.

We sat on the front porch shooing away mosquitoes well into the night. I was surprised by how bright it was. I knew about Finland's white nights, but the reality of near-daylight at midnight was startling. I missed Alamosa's starry sky.

It was past one in the morning by the time I asked where I'd be sleeping. I tossed and turned on the couch, restless from the strange effect of extended light. I woke at 4:00 a.m. to the sound of Kimmo crunching on an apple. The day passed in a fog of exhaustion, and I was grateful when, a few days later, Anna-Marja announced we were heading home a bit early. Finally, I'd get into a good routine of sleep and workouts.

The Martillas lived outside of town down a labyrinth of dirt roads that twisted through dense forest. Their traditional two-story farmhouse sat in a clearing in the woods, a sauna and a small garden on the side.

Inside, the rooms were small and tidy. I followed Matti up a narrow staircase to the attic, a sparse room with a slanted ceiling and a twin bed pushed against the wall. I don't remember what we ate that night, only that I could've eaten all three portions. Once in bed, I couldn't sleep. Midsummer sun streamed through the curtainless window, spilling onto the bed, which would have been lovely had it not been after midnight. I tried appreciating the novelty of white nights, but mostly, I wished for dark curtains. I dug a sock out of my bag and placed it over my eyes. I slept—until the sock slipped off and I had to retrieve it again, a game that lasted through the night.

I woke to the faint smell of coffee. Downstairs, Anna-Marja had already left for work at a factory. Matti pointed to a container of instant coffee. *"Kahvi?"* I nodded and sat down. He had laid out breakfast: a small piece of buttered bread topped with a slice of ham and cheese. We ate in silence, smiling, nodding, and sipping coffee. Before leaving for work, he pointed to the number 8 on the clock and said, "Kimmo," indicating he was coming at that time. Then he left for work. I waited by the front window, and at 8:15 began wondering what happened. Kimmo arrived at nine. The wait was frustrating, but I was dependent on him, so I didn't say anything. We went for a short run on the forest trails around the house. With no transportation options, I asked Kimmo if he could drive me to the nearby track at Vierumäki, Finland's national sport institute, later that day. We headed over after he got off work.

I thought we'd see other elite athletes at the center, but the place was deserted when we arrived. I followed Kimmo into the forest of spruce and pine to warm up. "Is it always this quiet?" I asked. He indicated yes, unless there was a camp in session. Most Finnish runners, he added, train on their own. Kimmo finished his run in the woods while I did a solo workout on the track.

I began to tally up my reality. Vierumäki was not a training hub for international or even national competitors. Kimmo's club, whom I thought we'd be working out with sometimes, was an organizing body for racing, not a training group. I was in a farmhouse in the woods with no house phone, and no cellphone. The $1,500 in cash I'd brought with me to Finland had been stolen at the airport, and without an ATM card, I was left with only a credit card. Plus, without a car, I couldn't get to the track or a race or even a grocery store without assistance.

Having little control over my environment made me tense. Anna-Marja told me not to worry about shopping. She was happy to do it on her way home from work and take care of the cooking, too. It was kind, but the meals were never quite enough. She didn't stock the fridge or cook portions large enough for the appetite of an elite distance runner, and I was constantly hungry.

The week leading up to my first race passed slowly. I waited on Kimmo and ran irritated. I ran alone on the trails that crisscrossed through the woods around the Martillas' house, stopping at junctions to draw arrows with the heels of my shoes so I wouldn't get lost, and wishing I were with my team on familiar roads. Nights in the attic were restless and the long hours confined to the farmhouse were isolating. Hungry, I nibbled on the cloudberries and lingonberries in the woods as I ran, and got into Anna-Marja's pulla bread that always sat on the counter. I was careful to cut thin slices so my hosts wouldn't notice.

I felt silly. Why hadn't I researched this better? I should have known there were no training groups in the area. I should have learned I needed an ATM card, and considered that transportation would be necessary. Most runners have agents who coordinate travel and racing. I'd been spoiled by USATF, who put us up in fancy hotels and fed us lavish meals. I didn't think I needed an agent. The lack of foresight was stressing both Kimmo and me out. On the three-hour drive to my first race in Turku, Finland's largest city, Kimmo and I spent much of the time working through logistics. I'd be competing every four to five days throughout my stay, and he couldn't keep taking time off from work to drive me. Another complication: Kimmo hadn't been able to confirm what distance I'd be competing in that day, which made heading into the race stressful. I was unable to time my meals and nap and couldn't mentally prepare for either a short and fast 1,500 or a longer push for the 5,000. The race was frustrating before we'd even arrived.

Turku was built at the mouth of the Aura River, where it enters the Archipelago Sea. It was historic, home to a medieval castle, a thirteenth-century cathedral, and the Paavo Nurmi Games, the meet I was competing in. The games were founded in 1957 and named for Finland's greatest distance runner, known around the world as the

Flying Finn. At the peak of his career in the 1920s, Nurmi won nine gold medals in the Olympics and set twenty-two world records in distances between 1,500 meters and 20 kilometers.

Neither the Paavo Nurmi Stadium nor the games themselves matched the runner's stature, at least to me. The stadium was small, with only one set of metal bleachers on the homestretch, and while athletes from Japan, the United States, Britain, and Kenya were competing, the atmosphere was understated. I'd heard about the hype of the European circuit—big venues, loud music, crazy fans—and thought robust racing would be part of the international environment that would elevate my fitness. So when I walked into the small stadium to find few fans in the stands, the subdued vibe was another mark against Finland.

Kimmo learned at the last minute that I was competing in the 5,000. I had just enough time to head out for a quick warm-up, which I did in irritation. What I needed in that moment was for Coach to shout out as I ran off, "When you come back, Deena, bring a good attitude!" Instead, I returned annoyed and full of self-pity. I must have run inside or at least near the pack because I placed fifth, but I have no memory of it. I ran disengaged, without paying attention.

Shortly after crossing the finish line, my body became hot and prickly. Small red welts emerged on my stomach and forearms, then my legs. The hives spread over my body and my eyes and throat began to close. I walked, a little scared, across the track to the medical tent. Breathing was hard and I kept swallowing to make sure there was still space to breathe. Medics quickly swept clear a table, lay me down, and placed a cool cloth on my forehead. They gave me a shot of Benadryl to calm my system and rested an Epi-Pen on the table next to me. I lay there trying to relax, just wanting to go home. Luckily, the Benadryl kicked in and the swelling and itching subsided.

On the car ride home, Kimmo joked, "Deena, maybe you are

allergic to Finland?" I gave a weak smile. *Couldn't have said it better myself.*

Back in Heinola, I worried something was wrong with me. The other foreign athletes in the race, and others across Europe I assumed, seemed to be handling training abroad with no problem, while I was struggling. I worried I couldn't handle it, which deepened my frustration. Every direction I looked I saw it negatively. I took Kimmo's tardiness personally, and once past my waiting limit of an hour, I fumed when I headed out on my own. On days I couldn't get to Vierumäki for a track workout, I did mile repeats by time on the trails, running 5 minutes hard, 3 minutes easy. But without clear confirmation of progress on my watch, I assumed my fitness was fading. I ran through the woods seeing the clear-cut sections as loss of animal habitat instead of their importance for the local economy. The quiet farmhouse to myself? Lonely.

One Saturday, a few days before I was scheduled to leave on a five-day trip around Finland to race, Kimmo dropped me off at Vierumäki for a track workout. It was empty, as usual, and I dropped my bag in the outside lane and warmed up on the trails for 10 minutes, half my usual time. Back on the track, I toed the line and made myself run on the grippy, ruby-red surface. I finished a lap, hit my watch, recovered, then headed off for another 400. Coach had ten repeats on the schedule. I stopped at five. *What's the point?* I thought. *I'm not progressing here.*

After the Paavo Nurmi Games, I told myself I just needed an adjustment period, but after another fruitless and demoralizing week, I went on the five-day trip eager to get the races over with. Kimmo dropped me off in Valkeakoski, a few hours north of Heinola, and I ran the 1,500. Standing on the infield afterward, a tall, tan guy with cropped blond hair and big white teeth came up. "Deena, I'm your ride to Lohja," he said. He picked up my race bag and started walking off the field with a jovial, bouncy step. Surprised, I said, "Um, thank you," and hustled to follow.

Ilpo was a runner in Kimmo's club. That night at the hotel bar, he strolled in wearing a USA tank top with shorts, a cowboy hat, and dress shoes. He chewed on a toothpick as he showed me nine rolls of photos from his trip to the Hoover Dam and the Grand Canyon. The next morning, we met for a run and his stories continued. I picked up the pace until it was too difficult for him to form sentences.

Over the next three days, as we traveled south to Helsinki and over to Lohja for a running camp and another race, Ilpo talked and I listened. He told me about his love of the United States, his deep interest in karaoke, and about Finland's geologic history (heat was pushed into the region and melted the ice). Ilpo said that sometimes instead of running on easy days, he went for a walk in the forest. He said his coach had told him that training didn't matter so much, what mattered was that you believed. "You, Deena," he said. "The way you run, you should be a world champion. Maybe you don't believe." I rolled my eyes from the passenger seat. "Of course you have to train hard," I said. *Hard work, good sleep, proper nutrition was exactly why I needed to go home.*

I arrived back at the Martillas' late at night after the trip. Matti and Anna-Marja were on the couch watching the final match of the World Cup. I had run a slow time (16:11) in the 5000 and wondered how athletes did this every summer. I didn't feel well and I kept sighing and yawning, like I couldn't take a deep breath. I wondered if it had anything to do with my allergic reaction in Turku, which I'd never figured out. France scored two goals against Brazil in the first half. I said good night and went to bed.

In the attic, the sun poured through the window. I grabbed a sock and lay down with it over my eyes. I felt anxious, so I closed my eyes and ran through a relaxation technique, telling my toes to relax, then my calves and knees. I worked my way up my body to my thighs, hips, and stomach. Once my attention was at my chest, I noticed my heart was racing and I was beginning to sweat. I got up to open the window. It was fastened shut. I felt panicky.

Calm down, I told myself. *Lie back down and take some deep breaths.* I climbed under the covers and adjusted the sock. Feeling claustrophobic and hot, I switched to lying on top of the covers, letting my body sink into the cushy down comforter. The room felt sterile and I suddenly felt exposed. I flipped the end of the comforter onto my chest and held it close. My right arm began to tingle. I couldn't remember which arm indicated you were having a heart attack, and I thought I might be dying. I tried mindful relaxation again, but thoughts of death kept interrupting my attempts, and soon I became convinced I was going to die in that airless room in Finland. Worse were thoughts of the aftermath. My parents would never find me because I had not given them my address here. Matti and Anna-Marja would panic at discovering my body. Not knowing what to do, they would bury me in the backyard. Unless . . . unless they were the ones trying to kill me! They'd been poisoning the food. I'd read enough Stephen King to think this plausible.

I didn't understand I was having a panic attack. I was afraid to sleep, but eventually, fell into a dark slumber.

When I woke, I waited for Matti to leave for work before heading downstairs. I rolled open the heavy wooden door of the Martillas' garage and pulled out a rusted single-speed bike. I was scheduled to call Coach in two days, but I couldn't wait that long to get home. I began riding on the dirt road toward town and pedaled urgently, until I saw an opening in the woods and a phone booth outside a general store. I leaned the bike against the metal frame and stepped inside. The minute Coach accepted the collect call, I launched in. "I'm miserable here," I said. "You have to let me come home. I'm losing fitness, there's no one to train with, the races are dull—"

Coach cut me off. "That's not a big deal," he said. "You made a commitment. We're not going to change horses midstream."

Stunned, I begged, gradually becoming aware of the desperation in my voice. Coach didn't relent. "Deena," he said sternly, "you need to find a way to make it work." I hung up on him.

As if on cue, lightning cracked, thunder rolled, and it began to rain hard. I swung open the door, grabbed the bike, and started riding back to the farmhouse. I pedaled with hard strokes, reminiscent of the wicked witch in *The Wizard of Oz*. As I rode, I imagined someone driving by, looking over, and seeing an angry, indignant girl riding an old bike in a downpour. I pictured the car splashing mud up on her, the situation getting worse. The image was so pitiful it made me laugh. The laughter felt good, like a jolt to the system. *Find a way to make it work.*

Coach's words reminded me that the responsibility was on me. I couldn't change my environment, but I could change my perspective.

Of course!

I knew this, but I'd been so fixated on needing others and strong races to progress, and so rigid in my routine, that I'd forgotten to check my attitude and manage my thoughts—the things that were, in fact, blocking my progress and within my control.

Back at the house, I set out to get them back. I put the bike away and went into the bathroom. I looked in the mirror and heard Coach's voice: *Get tough.* I made a funny face as I towel-dried my hair, then put on techno music and danced around the living room, a strategy to lighten my mood.

That afternoon on my run, I didn't stop to dig arrows in the dirt. Why not get lost? Why not run longer? I went farther down the trail, climbing a small peak to see views of dense forest. The next day I made a wider loop, extending into new territory. I stopped asking Kimmo for rides to Vierumäki and ran there and back on a trail, adding 10K to the workout.

If I couldn't train with Coach and the team, I could bring the challenge of our workouts to Finland. On the track, I set a goal of breaking 70 seconds in each 400 repetition. Coach, in my mind, stood trackside holding a stopwatch, and I ran hard to hit the time. For tempo runs, I ran out and back on the trails, working to beat my time on the return, chasing the clock instead of the men. Lining up to race, I pictured Coach standing next to his fax machine waiting for the results to come in. I played with tactics, challenging myself to see how fast I could run the middle laps. Sometimes, as the calm, low-key meet took place around me, I imagined the stands full and the crowd rowdy. I ran around the track, hearing fans pound their feet and cheer, the steady pump of techno music thumping as I raced.

The days began to take on a steady rhythm. I ran, slept, and read at the kitchen table, reminding myself to relish the quiet and solitude of the farmhouse. Progress returned quickly. At my next race, I ran a personal best in the 3,000, winning that race in 9:04. My weekly mileage jumped from 76 to 90. The following week, I logged my first 100 miles. I felt good and strong—and relieved. The summer wasn't going to be a failure.

It amused me to realize one night as I wrote a gratitude list that the items on the page—the farmhouse, the trails, Kimmo—were the same things that bothered me in the weeks prior. I flipped back through the pages in my journal, scanning the words, and was caught short when I read my note about Ilpo's comment on belief. I'd noted that maybe he needed to take training more seriously. But it was I who had been dismissive. I'd twisted his words to support the victim story in my head. He was right. I needed to believe that I could train anywhere, on my own, propelling my own progress.

Kimmo picked me up for a race in Lahti, forty-five minutes away. As he pulled out of the driveway, he looked at me with bright eyes. "You are running DN Galan," he announced. I was stunned. DN Galan was one of the world's premiere Grand Prix meets in Stockholm, Sweden, two weeks away. Athletes were typically invited to compete based on previous track races, and I didn't have the times necessary for an invitation. It turned out that the race's athlete coordinator was a friend of Coach's and he had asked him for a favor.

My first thoughts were filled with fear. I could get clobbered. I could finish last. Worse, I could embarrass Coach. But I turned it around. *This is what you wanted. This is what the summer was for.* At the race in Lahti, I went out in the 800 at a bold pace, running all-out and hitting the first 400 in a fast 66 seconds. While I faded in the end, the speed of the first lap gave me confidence that I had the turnover to compete in Sweden.

The Martillas took me to my last race, not far from Heinola. We were all feeling sentimental about me leaving. Sitting in the stands, Matti handed me a water bottle. Anna-Marja gently massaged my shoulders. I brought my hands up to hers and gave them a squeeze, hoping I'd hid my meltdown in the early weeks well. I won the 3,000 and gave my victory bouquet to Anna-Marja. It was luck that cornflowers and daisies happened to be her favorite flowers.

A few days later, I stood on the deck of the overnight ferry to Stockholm watching the city recede and reflecting on the summer. Had I gone home early, I might have concluded I couldn't train on my own, or couldn't handle traveling abroad. Instead, I stood there feeling heroic. With a simple shift in perspective, I had changed the outcome of the summer, and myself. I was stronger, more enduring, flexible, and independent. And I knew now that whatever I needed I had within me.

DN Galan was held at Stockholm's historic stadium, a brick, castle-like structure built for the 1912 Olympic Games. An imposing building, it turned a race into an event, an athlete into a competitor. Multiple world records had been set within its walls. Warming up on the dirt path surrounding the stadium, there was finally the buzz of racing. I ran with Amy Rudolph and Cheri Goddard Kenah, a middle-distance runner with a fierce kick. It was dusk. The girls laughed when I told them about my Finland struggles. You need to get an agent, they said.

Amy, Cheri, and I went to the staging area in the trackside tunnel. Women were adjusting their spikes, tying their shoes, shaking out their legs. The premiere athletes were there: Britain's Paula Radcliffe, Kenya's Sally Barsosio, Morocco's Zahra Ouaziz. I felt a flutter in my stomach as I tied my laces. The fact that they'd been invited and I had a favor done for me weighed heavily on my mind.

You don't belong here.

Coach must have believed you belong here, so believe it.

"Ladies, take to the track."

I walked out of the tunnel and into the lights alongside Amy. We were assigned our starting positions based on our times. She went to an inside lane, and I took my place in the far lane.

If you run poorly you might not get invited back.

So, this is your shot then. Get it right.

The stadium was packed. Fans cheered. Some tried to get a wave going. I leaned forward slightly and put my eye on the first turn, creating the sight line I'd run to get into a good position.

"Runners set."

My mind piped up with a bunch of clichés to bolster me: *It's now or never! Here goes nothing! Ready or not, here I come!*

The gun fired and I shot off the line, falling in behind Paula, Zahra, and two Kenyans, Tegla Loroupe and Leah Malot. The women all had personal bests almost a minute faster than my own and by 200 meters, the pace was already hot, much faster than I'd ever run.

Hang on as long as you can.

The thought opened me to the women's speed. I didn't so much get on their rhythm as insist on it, pushing myself through the first lap, then the next.

We ran single file, each girl nearly on top of the other. I was right on Leah's heels, near the front, and hugging the inside lane. *Hang on, hang on.* We finished four laps, then five. Each time we came through the lap and the counter flipped, I was amazed I was still there.

We pushed on, the steady thump of feet on track. The crowds seemed to fall in line with our rhythm, stomping on the stadium floor to the tempo of our pace. It felt crazy to me. Drafting off the runner in front saves energy, so I told myself to stay connected to

Leah. She had a long, graceful back-kick that seemed to go on for-ever, as if in slow motion, and I watched it closely, using it to help me hold pace. With four laps to go, Leah began to struggle. Her knees caved a bit, her arms swung wide, and she began losing contact with the woman ahead of her. I watched to see if she'd close the gap, but it lengthened. *Pass her.* I pulled to the second lane, shot past Leah, and reconnected with the leaders.

A camera moved across the infield, following my foot strikes, and I wondered if Kimmo, Matti, and Anna-Marja were watching from home on Eurosport. I pushed in an effort to show my thanks.

The leaders kicked up the pace. I thought of my 800 race in Fin-land. *You have the turnover. Go with them.* The pace increased again, and as much as I willed my body forward, I couldn't cover the move. Two girls passed me in the final stretch and I crossed the line in sixth place, having run 15:07, a 34-second personal record. The time would rank as the fastest of any American woman that year.

II

LOVE MAKES YOU STRONGER

Alamosa, Colorado, 1998, 1999

We cannot think of being acceptable to others until we have
first proven acceptable to ourselves.

—MALCOLM X

The men called me Big-Time when I got back. We were at Cole Park.
I'd run over, happy and relieved to be home. Peter saw me as I approached the group and said, "Oh, here comes Big-Time." I thought
I detected an edge to his voice. Marco and Phil and the other men
joined the banter: Oh, how was your summer, Big-Time?

"It was really hard," I said.

"How hard could it have been since you hit such a huge PR?"
Peter said.

His tone was clearly sharp, and I ignored it, saying I'd brought
pulla for everyone to enjoy after practice.

The tension with the men continued and I grew quieter at practice, but stayed focused on my training. I continued running 100-
mile weeks and my fitness showed. I was now only a few strides
behind the men in mile repeats, close enough to hear their breathing,
and my ability to hang on to them during long runs nearly doubled.

Cross-country nationals had been moved from December to February, freeing me up to explore my new fitness in fall road races. I found one in early September that looked good. The US 10K Classic outside Atlanta was a festival of races that offered prize money, which meant it attracted top international talent, including the dominant East Africans. I picked up the phone and called the race director.

"No, sorry, registration has been closed for weeks," he said.

"Oh, okay, thanks."

Ten minutes later, the race director called me back. He must have confirmed my time at DN Galan because now he was offering me a bib, hotel, and plane ticket.

Georgia in September was muggy and gorgeous. About 800 runners packed the start. I lined up at the front with an international field of roughly thirty other elite men and women. I stood next to two Kenyan women who had never-ending legs and hid competitive stares behind Oakley sunglasses. One was world-ranked Catherine Ndereba, the other, rising star Lornah Kiplagat. At world cross-country in Morocco, I'd dabbled with being in the pack. At DN Galan, I'd run with the leaders until the final kick. In Georgia, I believed I could hold my own against these women. The confidence showed in my posture: if there were a split screen of those two races, you'd see me on the starting line at DN Galan wide-eyed and holding my body back from the line, while in Atlanta, I stood with a forward lean and the soft, relaxed face of a confident competitor.

The gun fired and we followed the elite men out of the mall parking lot to the road. The course was point-to-point, mostly along a long stretch of highway from the town of Cumberland north to Marietta. As we climbed the course's only hill to a bridge, I felt the refreshing breeze and took a moment to enjoy it before descending on the hot and humid highway.

The women's field narrowed in the first mile to me, Lornah, and Catherine. The summer's gains in fitness and confidence allowed me to be in the pack without strain and with full awareness of the competition. Lornah and Catherine had steady, strong strides and I ran trying to read the emotion emanating from their effort. Was Lornah straining or determined? Was Catherine hanging on or waiting to pounce? It was hard to tell with these two. They ran cool and steady, never losing their game face.

The rhythm of Lornah's foot slaps shifted and I wondered if she was fatiguing or preparing to make a move. Catherine's right shoulder dropped a bit. Had it always been this way, or was that her tell?

Was I doing those things? I tried smoothing out my stride, aiming for an equal sound in my footfalls and an upright posture.

My breathing stayed comfortable as we moved into the fifth mile. I still felt strong, which surprised me. The 10K had always felt long to me, like a grind by this point. My 100-mile weeks had made the distance feel shorter, a perception based on the physical feel and greater mental endurance.

We exited Cobb Parkway onto city streets toward the finish. A girl on the sidelines shouted, "Go Catherine!" Catherine was the defending champion, but I absorbed the energy of her enthusiasm as support for me, too. Lornah fell back a couple of strides. Simultaneously, Catherine and I hastened our turnover. I felt a thrill at having reacted similarly to Catherine upon signs of Lornah's fatigue. My brief celebration at having outlasted one Kenyan was replaced with an urgency to keep contact with the other. I pushed into the pace and held on until the final 100 meters when Catherine's speed easily overpowered mine. She won in 33:06. I followed 4 seconds later, with Lornah taking third.

Preventing the powerful Kenyans from sweeping the top spots sent me home with a strong sense of belonging on the world stage, but also a clear understanding of how much more there was to learn about the nuances of competing at this level.

At practice, we had an easy run and Coach asked us which direction we wanted to run on the river. "I don't know," Peter said. "Ask Big-Time." A brief pause. "I mean, ladies' choice."

The snipes had become a thing and I just kept deflecting them.

"If it's my choice, we're going to the Campus Café for cinnamon rolls."

I didn't like what was happening between me and the men. But my career was progressing and I stayed focused on moving it forward, which included finding an agent. Agents coordinate travel and racing, and crucially, they help you build a career. If I wanted to compete at higher levels and earn a living, I needed someone to help get me there. So I hired Ray Flynn. Ray was Amy Rudolph's agent. An Irishman long based out of Johnson City, Tennessee, Ray had one of the strongest reputations in the business. He was a logistical genius and a fierce negotiator with a clear understanding of the demands and needs of being a professional athlete. Ray had competed for Ireland for over a decade and was twice an Olympian. He still held his country's record in the 1,500 meters and had also run the mile in under 4 minutes a total of eighty-nine times, in an era when running sub-4 dubbed you king of the distance.

Ray made things happen right away. He secured me invitations to two fall road races with paid travel and appearance fees. The first was the North American Challenge 5K in Riverside, California. On the plane, I pinched myself. I was a professional runner being paid to do what I loved to do: race. If there was a word in the English language to express amazement at living your dream, I would have had it tattooed on my forearm right when I landed in California.

I won the 5K in 15:21, a course record, and flew next to Hartford, Connecticut, for the Manchester Road Race, one of the nation's longest-running turkey trots. Past winners included Olympians Eamonn Coghlan, Lynn Jennings, and Amy Rudolph, who was the defending champion. I was proud to add my name to that list with a win.

Back in Alamosa, winter had set in and I left the house bundled up, my racing flats in hand for mile repeats at Cole Park. Coach was out of town to give a clinic, so the men and I were on our own. I arrived first and stood in the morning chill, doing leg swings to stay warm. I jogged around a bit and when the men still weren't there, I started my warm-up, wondering what'd happened to the guys. I ran through the trees and onto the river dyke. As I arced north, I saw the men coming toward me. Phil, Marco, and Peter were there, but also newer members, Jeff, Teddy, and Bryan Dameworth, my friend and former teammate from high school who'd joined about six months ago. When we reached one another, we all stopped.

"Hey, what happened? Why did you start without me?" I asked.

"We changed practice time," Peter said.

"Why didn't someone tell me?"

"Because we don't like you."

Peter said this with no hesitation. I waited for someone to laugh, indicating it was a joke. When no one did, I asked why they didn't like me.

"We just don't," he said. "We never have."

I looked at the others, trying to assess if Peter was speaking for the group. The men looked away.

I didn't know what to say. The men walked past me and took off down the path.

I stood there stunned. I abandoned the workout and ran home, sobbing into Aspen's fur until she smelled like a wet dog. I quickly scanned the last few months of workouts and café breakfasts. What had I done? Did they really not like me? None of them, ever?

I was angry, sad, and hurt. I spent the next three days running on my own and trying to figure it out, to trace their dislike back to something I did, or something I could apologize for or change. All I could come up with were good times—hard workouts, red beans and rice on Friday nights, gripping our seats on the drive down from Rock Creek. I felt ridiculous for thinking they were my friends, while the whole time, they hadn't liked me. Caroline said they were just jealous of my success. I wasn't so sure. Maybe I'd disrupted the male team dynamic. I was close with Coach, a man they loved, too.

What confused and upset me the most was that I believed I was at my best. While I had been becoming a stronger athlete, I thought I was also becoming a better person, teammate, and friend. Their words made me question who I was and the path that I was on.

When Coach returned, I ran over to Cole Park wanting to get back to work. I knew the men would be kind with Coach around. We all acted as if nothing had happened, knocking out the workout and going our separate ways. Caroline must've told Coach because Peter showed up at my door later and stumbled through an apology that sounded as if Coach had put him up to it. I mumbled something about it being okay, that we all must have been having a bad day.

Had we been more mature, the men and I might have talked about the incident and learned something about ourselves and one another. But they never brought it up and neither did I. We showed up at practice, ran, and kept the conversation light. None of the men teased me or called me cute names anymore. I replaced my upbeat attitude with a businesslike approach, aware that my cheerfulness was something that might have bothered the men. I was actually afraid to speak, fearful that they'd use it against me.

I had cross-country nationals coming up and in order to focus on the workout, I stopped thinking of the men as friends and teammates and saw them simply as tools for progress. I ran soaking in the scenery as I always had and they blended into the landscape. It was a form of protection, but it replaced sadness with a feeling of control over my environment.

In February, I traveled to Tacoma, Washington, for the national cross-country championships. The previous year, I'd wanted to win for a host of reasons: for Coach, for the team, to prove myself. This year, I wanted to win for me. I knew I had the training and strength to defend my title and I wanted to show myself that no matter what was going on, I could get the job done. There was also a little spite. It wasn't so much an F-you to the men, more of a demonstration that they had not broken me.

The championships were on the weekend of my twenty-sixth birthday, and my family flew up for it. At breakfast before the race, my sister said, "I bet there are a thousand things you'd rather be doing on your birthday than this."

"No," I said, "actually, being here with you and racing is exactly what I want to be doing."

I led a field of forty-one athletes running stride for stride with Lynn Jennings again. The skies were clear and the temperature was an ideal 48 degrees. The 8K course was mostly flat and I dropped Lynn around 3K, holding the lead for the rest of the race. As I approached the finish, the announcer said: "On the weekend of her twenty-sixth birthday, Deena Drossin will capture her second US title. Let's bring her in, folks." I held my hands high as I broke the tape, making my third world team.

I returned home feeling stronger. The performance helped quiet the questions. It was for me a testament to who I was becoming.

I also returned feeling a void and sadness at the loss of the men's friendships and decided to be more of a friend to myself. I started with dinner at a small, upscale restaurant. I'd never taken myself out to a nice dinner before; it had always seemed like an unnecessary extravagance. I found a table in the corner and thought, for a moment, that everyone must be wondering why I was alone on a Friday night. Was I too weird to have friends? The waitress was chatty and I wondered if she pitied me and was trying to help. I wrote in my journal to give the impression that I was doing something important. After a while, though, I realized nobody cared what I was doing, so I set aside the journal and just enjoyed the live music and the food.

I went back most weeks. Sometimes I grabbed a napkin and jotted down the beginning of a poem: "The smell of patchouli and grain, like rain, in this café." I made dream lists: "Plant a garden. Buy a house. Run sub-15 min in 5K (71 seconds per quarter)." I included the pace to make the goal real and firm in my mind.

I started viewing simple walks down Main Street as dates with myself. I bought fancy lotion, the kind you'd usually only buy for a friend on her birthday. I took myself off-roading in my Jeep past Great Sand Dunes National Park with Aspen. When the weather warmed, I went camping in Creede, near the headwaters of the Rio Grande.

These dates felt like nurturing. I was giving myself time and space to do what I enjoyed, and it evolved into conscious acts of self-care. I lit candles in the evening and made elaborate meals for one. Sometimes I put on opera music and baked cookies. My favorite nights were reading on the couch with a glass of wine. None of these actions was really new. Only my intention had shifted. Up until that point, self-care had been about performance—I wanted to feel better so I could run better. Now these actions were acts of kindness toward myself. I was deserving of such care whether I'd run a hard 10 miles or not.

Worlds that year were in Belfast, Northern Ireland. We landed in March 1999 when the tension between Catholics and Protestants was intense. I'd expected a bustling and vibrant city, but it was quiet, with very few people on the streets. Even the colors—browns and grays—seemed muted. I took myself out to a pub for fish and chips one night. The bartender and locals discussed football, and as I ate, I listened to their thick accents and the passion in their conversation as if they were music for the meal. Another day, I walked through Queen's University, the race site, just to enjoy the gardens and culture.

We couldn't get onto the course early, so the women's team ran the city streets. Passing Belfast's grand historic buildings and modern skyscrapers, I thought mostly about the religious conflict and its contrast to sports. How could religion be at war and sports be getting it right? Competitors from all over the world were converging on the city to engage in a tough battle. We'd fight our fight, then get along. I had a peace inside me that rested right alongside a fierce competitiveness. The two could coexist. In fact, they nurtured each other.

I ran with the pack amid familiar faces and new ones. Gete from Ethiopia. Paula from Great Britain, plus a few Kenyans I hadn't yet met. I was close to Leah for parts of it, the Kenyan whose long back-kick helped tie me to the pack at DN Galan. We pushed each other over the flat, muddy fields of Queen's University. I'd outkicked her on the track. She beat me this time. I followed her to an eighth-place finish, my highest to date at worlds.

I felt like a stronger version of myself. Previously, I'd competed to figure out what was in me. In Belfast, I'd raced to express the strength I knew was inside. That was how I approached a string of spring races. In April I ran the 10,000 at Mt. SAC and won in a personal best of 32:17 on the track. In May, I ran the Bolder Boulder 10K in Colorado, finishing fourth, first American, while also blowing away the US altitude record for the distance. In the 10,000 at the US outdoor championships that June, I led for most of the twenty-five laps. I felt strong and confident of winning. In the last kilometer, Libbie Hickman and Anne Marie Lauck outkicked me. I held on for third, meeting my secondary goal: making my first world team on the track.

Back home, I felt a stirring, the need to create a more nurturing place for myself. I'd done the best I could with a rental shared with roommates, but now I wanted a place of my own. I wanted to paint walls, redecorate, grow wildflowers, and let my personality spread out. So I started looking at real estate. In the afternoons, Aspen and I ran up and down Alamosa's streets looking for FOR SALE signs. We slowed to get a longer look at some of the houses. I noted changes I'd make: a more welcoming front door, more color in the landscaping, two rocking chairs on the front porch so friends would know they were welcome. I never went to the open houses, though. Prices hovered around $70,000. I didn't have that in the bank.

That summer, I moved through the European circuit thinking about those houses. I read home-decorating magazines on the plane and at hotels between races. Traveling was nearly flawless that year, thanks to Ray's organization. He sent me off with a printout of hotel addresses, race directors' contact information, a race schedule, and flight information, and he was on hand at most races to manage anything that came up.

Ray also rented a room at the Friends Mathildenhöhe, a bed-and-breakfast in Darmstadt, Germany, for me to share with Amy Rudolph and Jen Rhines. Jen and I knew each other from college racing, when she'd been a three-time NCAA champion in the 5,000. The three of us ate, ran, and sometimes traveled to races together, and over the span of the summer, grew close. Amy was the one who got us fired up for workouts and out the door for drinks after races. Jen was quiet, the girlfriend you could rely on to let you know that the tapered jeans you were wearing were out of fashion. She was also an expert at adjusting to travel. She put herself right into her routine: stretch at eight thirty, run at nine, hot green tea at three, Leno at night. Jen was giving herself what she needed. So I followed Jen's example and created my own sense of place away from home. I went to a farmers' market and bought a basil plant to put on the desk behind my rollaway bed. I propped up a photo of Aspen there, too. I woke early and went downstairs to give myself alone time. The breakfast room was silent, save for the sound of my petite coffee cup landing back on its saucer. I relaxed and dreamed. Flipping through home-design magazines in whatever language I found them in, I dog-eared pages with fabrics and color schemes I liked, writing notes in the empty spaces of the ads, piecing together what my own place would look like.

My racing goal for the summer was speed. Specifically, I wanted to work on my finishing kick for the world track championships. Getting passed at the end at nationals revealed a weakness, and a string of 1,500-, 3,000- and 5,000-meter races provided the opportunity to work on my turnover in the final stretch.

I competed in the 1,500 in Belgium and ran a personal best in the 3,000 in Nice. At DN Galan for the 5,000, I toed the line feeling a little uneasy. I'd had such a breakthrough the year before, after my long Finland summer, and it created an expectation to live up to that performance. I worked through the worry by thinking of the strong performances I'd just run. *The strength is there. Go reveal it.*

Off the line, I was in the top three, running with the tiny and powerful Tegla Loroupe of Kenya and Fernanda Ribeiro of Portugal. The three of us separated ourselves from the field in the first mile. It was exhilarating to lead such a high-energy event. Instead of being dragged along, I felt like I was pulling my own weight, and it was fun. I hammered every stride of that 5,000, crossing the line in third place. My time was 14:56—the sub-15-minute 5,000 I'd told Coach I wanted to reach in our first phone conversation. Such a lofty goal had seemed out of reach then, not far from fantasy. What amazed me wasn't so much that I'd reached the time, but that I believed I could surpass it. With all that I'd learned and applied, the milestone had become a stepping-stone.

The rest of the summer was long and good. Jen, Amy, and I put in strong morning workouts followed by lazy afternoons. Worlds on the track wasn't my best day. I attached myself to the leaders, but couldn't find a rhythm and finished eleventh. The morning after the race, I met Coach, who'd flown in for the championships, in the hotel lobby where he was having coffee with John Godina, a US shot-putter who had won gold at a previous world championships. When I pulled up a chair, John was telling Coach that he was using his earnings to buy and flip houses. I mentioned I'd been looking. "You've got to get your own place," he said. I told him I wished I could, but that houses were seventy grand and I simply didn't have the money. "Deena," he said, giving me a surprised look. "You don't need the whole amount. All you need is a small down payment, and then it's like paying rent to yourself."

I couldn't believe I'd never really understood what a mortgage was. *Paying rent to yourself. Brilliant.* The whole way back to the States I thought about finding a place with a yard for Aspen, a bright kitchen, and enough bedrooms for my family to visit. A few months later, I walked into a small bungalow on Second Street, a block from

Cole Park. The kitchen was big, although it needed gutting. There was a sunroom with large windows to welcome the morning light. I could fence in the large yard for Aspen. The shag carpets would need to go, but underneath were beautiful wood floors. I knew immediately it was home.

Buying the house restored a sense of stability the incident with the men had shaken, and affirmed my commitment to Coach, Alamosa, and myself. Linda helped me find someone to refinish the floors and remodel the kitchen. I spent hours looking through the scrapbook I'd kept of images from the home and gardening magazines (my early version of Pinterest) and settled on colors. I painted the living room cappuccino, the kitchen white with a yellow wall, and the bedroom sage green and eggplant. My armoire became an entertainment center in the living room. In the bathroom, I laid small white hexagon tiles, touched up the claw-foot tub, and rolled new towels symmetrically to fit in the Shaker-style cabinets.

One night, I made myself an elaborate dinner. I baked salmon and wild mushrooms wrapped in phyllo dough and served it with a simple side salad and a generous glass of Pinot Noir. Tony Bennett played on the stereo. Aspen followed me to the dining-room table. I sat, and before taking my first bite, looked around, relishing the warmth of home. I ate slowly, and afterward sank into a hot bath. The warm water surrounded me and I closed my eyes. The stillness of the house felt peaceful. A thought came to mind: *I'm alone, but I'm not lonely. I like who I am. I like who I'm becoming.* I felt whole and good and content, and lay there letting the feeling soak in. When the water cooled, I grabbed a towel and climbed out of the tub, feeling like I had everything I needed to succeed.

PART III

Believe

12.

A FUNNY THING HAPPENED ON THE WAY TO OPTIMISM

Olympic Games, Sydney, Australia, 2000

Seeing the bigger picture opens your eyes to what is the truth.

—WADADA LEO SMITH

I was putting new dishes away in the built-in hutch, talking to my friend Sandy, when she mentioned Andrew Kastor, her teammate at Adams State. I'd seen Andrew running with the cross-country team along the river. He was one of the taller Grizzlies, with a bouncy stride and a long torso. "He's cute," I said. Sandy shot me a look. "He would die if he knew you'd said that."

Later that afternoon, I was walking from the kitchen into the living room when I noticed Andrew ride by on his BMX bike. That's funny, I thought, and left it at that. I took Aspen for a short walk and back inside, saw Andrew ride by again. Ten minutes later, there was a knock at the door. The floors in the entryway had just been refurbished, so I waved Andrew around to the back.

Hi.

Hey.

We sat across from each other on stools at my kitchen island. I poured two glasses of water and put the pitcher between us. Andrew had sandy blond hair, sage-green eyes, and wore a black North

Face fleece zipped all the way up, which accentuated his long neck. "Congratulations on Carlsbad," he said, referring to the 5K I'd recently won. He told me he'd grown up just north of Carlsbad, in Fountain Valley, California, and had run the race as a sophomore in high school. I told him I grew up in Agoura Hills, north of L.A. We swapped stories about going to the beach as kids. He'd ridden his BMX bike to Newport. I'd taken the school's "beach bus" to Malibu.

Andrew was easy to talk to. We realized we were both at the final soccer match of the 1984 Los Angeles Olympic Games. Neither of us could remember who won, but we both remembered that a guy streaked across the field with an American flag. We talked about our families. I liked that his parents were still together. My mom and dad didn't always see eye to eye, but their commitment to each other was strong. No topic was off-limits. We discussed religion and politics. He was a Ralph Nader supporter. I thought a third-party vote was a waste. He was raised Catholic. I came from a Jewish heritage. But both of us, we realized, were raised to have faith in people rather than an idea.

Five hours passed like nothing. He confessed Sandy had told him I'd said he was cute and that he'd ridden by the house multiple times before getting up the nerve to knock. I liked his honesty. He stood to go and asked for my number. I wrote it on a piece of paper and we said good night. When I closed the door, I felt that he would be in my life for a long time.

I was disappointed when he didn't call the next day. Or the day after that. *Hadn't we hit it off?* Apparently, I would find out later, he'd just seen the movie *Swingers* and Vince Vaughn's character said you should wait six days to call a girl. Andrew waited five because he misremembered the movie. My parents were visiting by then and I told him my sister and I would be at the Purple Pig Pub that night and to swing by if he was free.

Lesley and I were tucked into a booth with some friends when Andrew walked in. I scooted over and he sat down but seemed distracted. When I asked what was on his mind, he said, "I didn't come here to talk, I came here to dance." It was the cheesiest line I'd ever heard. I pushed him out of the booth, tugged at my sister's sleeve across the table, and we all hit the floor. Andrew's dance moves were so spastic, I thought he was going to hurt himself.

At the end of the night, Andrew walked Lesley and me home. He swung on the light poles, bringing himself nearly parallel to the ground, as if the wind were taking him away. We laughed at his antics and skipped along the sidewalk. Lesley and I said good night to Andrew and went inside. I felt light, giddy. "I love him," Lesley said. "My cheeks hurt from laughing so much." She went to get ready for bed while I went into the kitchen to get us water for our nightstands. As I was filling glasses, I saw someone coming to the back door. It was Andrew. "What are you doing?" I whispered, walking down the stairs. "I couldn't go without giving you a good-night kiss," he said.

Andrew was four years younger than me, but seemed more mature than most guys my age. He was graduating the following month with a degree in exercise physiology and planned to work as a personal trainer at his cousin's business in California. I liked that he had a plan, that he was driven and organized. After he kissed me and said good night, I woke the next morning wanting to see him. It surprised me. I'd dated but had never craved someone's company before. I preferred reading a book at home to sitting on someone else's couch watching a sporting event or a romantic comedy. I had worried I didn't have the capacity for romantic love, or maybe I was just too focused on running to share my time. Andrew made me want to share.

He called the next day and I told him my family was going to a Seder dinner that night and he was welcome to come. He met me outside the restaurant and we joined my family inside. About twenty people—friends of the neighbor who had invited us—sat at a long table set with the food that helped tell the story of Passover. Plates with a chicken bone, an egg, and parsley. Small bowls of saltwater. Multiple bottles of Manischewitz, and baskets of matzo crackers, each with a napkin over it. Despite being Jewish, none of us had been to a proper Seder before, and we were all intrigued. We went around the table taking turns reading from the Haggadah, the Passover guide, and drinking way too much Manischewitz. During dinner Andrew made everyone laugh with his Jim Carrey impersonations and we all busted up when, four hours into the service, my mom said, "All right already, let's eat."

After dinner, my family drove back to my house. Andrew and I decided to walk. We'd only made it next door to the Catholic church before stopping to make out.

We saw each other every day after that. I was training for the Olympic trials and Andrew had final exams coming up, so I made dinner while he studied at the kitchen table. When Coach and I were on the track at Adams State, Andrew walked over from his dorm to watch. I was training for both the 5,000 and the 10,000, though my emphasis at the trials in July would be on the 10,000. My body had adapted well to the higher mileage and my longer speed sessions showed Coach and me that my strength was in the longer distances.

At this point, I was training mostly alone in Alamosa. Coach had told the team that he would soon be moving to Green Valley, Arizona, to help Caroline care for her mother, and the men were making plans to move on from running. Marco was moving to California to pursue coaching. Phil was going into the army, and Peter was juggling running with family and a teaching job. Coach and I discussed whether it would be best for me to relocate to Arizona with him or stay in Alamosa and work together remotely. I tucked the options in the back of my mind for later in order to focus on my Olympic preparation: a few more weeks in Alamosa, followed by six weeks at the Olympic Training Center in Chula Vista, California. Assuming I made the team, I'd spend the summer on the European circuit to sharpen my fitness for Sydney.

As I ran around the Adams State track with Andrew and Coach on the sideline, something inside me expanded. I was hammering a 400 and came around the final turn to see these two men, one whom I loved like a father, the other whom I already loved in a way I'd never experienced before, and a big fat grin spread across my face. Just as I could sometimes still be surprised at my own strength as a runner, I was surprised at how love felt as if it overflowed from a bottomless place inside. Gratitude felt similar, but it had a peaceful, calm quality to it. Love was more hyper and youthful, filling me with the urge to do cartwheels or run through sprinklers or finish a 400 a little faster.

One night in my kitchen, I asked Andrew when his job in California started. "It's flexible," he said. So I asked if he wanted to join me at the Olympic Training Center, and go to the trials and—here it went—let's travel the European track circuit together. Andrew's jaw dropped. Then his eyes lit up. "Could we make that work?" I told him USATF would probably allow him to join me at the center, that we'd just figure it out. He smiled. "I'd be crazy not to go."

The Olympic Training Center in Chula Vista, California, was a sprawling complex of sports fields and buildings on the Otay Reservoir, set against the pale peaks of the San Ysidro Mountains. Entering the front gates put you in a place apart. Your world narrowed to one thing: the athlete's life. There was no need to grocery shop, run to the post office, tidy the house, or even do laundry. The daily tasks of living were taken care of so you could devote your entire day to maximizing your preparation. On hand to help were massage therapists, athletic trainers, sports psychologists, physical therapists, strength coaches, and medical staff. Such care went into everything—the housekeeper straightened out my row of running shoes and there were even heating pads in the training room to warm your hamstrings before workouts.

Alfredo, the driver, dropped Coach, Andrew, and me at the bronze cauldron at the entrance (lit only during the Games). I'd spent two weeks at the center earlier in the year before cross-country nationals. The atmosphere had been focused then, but this time it was a different magnitude; we were at the Olympic Training Center, focused on making an Olympic team. There was a saying on every glass door we went through: "It's not every four years, it's every day." That dedication hung in the air.

Coach settled into his room, and Andrew and I got situated in ours. Rooms were small and simple with high ceilings built, I assumed, with basketball players in mind. Andrew and I shared a small common area (an uncomfortable couch, a TV, and a small refrigerator) with Justine Van Houte, a US mogul skier who was rehabbing from knee surgery.

Coach, Andrew, and I met in the cafeteria and sat down to review the six-week program Coach had written. I'd be hitting 100 miles every week and doing the workouts that had been serving me well: 400s for speed, mile repeats for strength, and tempo and long runs for endurance. Most of our training would take place at the center, but we'd head to the nearby Bonita golf course for tempo runs. On Sundays we'd run long at Peñasquitos Canyon or on the horse trails at Rancho Santa Fe. As a 1,500-meter runner fit from a final season in college, Andrew would help pace me.

We spent the first few days running easy miles on the exposed trails around the center, careful to keep an eye out for rattlesnakes stretched across the sun-warmed dirt. Four other distance runners I knew were there. Jenny Crain was a diverse athlete who'd run the marathon trials and was now getting ready for both the 5,000 and 10,000 meters on the track. She lived and worked in Milwaukee in the insurance industry, grateful her job gave her the flexibility to pursue her Olympic dreams. Meb Keflezighi was born in Eritrea and had immigrated to San Diego with his family at age ten. He'd won four NCAA championships while at UCLA and was training for the trials 10,000. James Menon was from California, a recent Wisconsin grad with All-American honors, and competing in the 5,000. Phil Price was from the Midwest, an Arkansas grad, two years behind me, and also training for the 5,000.

I already knew them from being at the same races over the years. Now we fell into an easy rhythm together, seeing one another at meals and coordinating workouts, and friendships formed quickly. Coach drove us to the golf course for a tempo run and suggested structuring the workout as an equalizer. Everyone agreed. Jenny went out first, with Andrew and me following a minute later. I tried to catch her while the men chased from behind. Andrew was faster than me but lacked the stamina for sustained speed. He'd hold on as long as he could, then his breathing would become so exaggerated it seemed like he was faking distress. Five or six strides later, he'd be out the back door, walking in. We joked that he was the sacrificial lamb. I would catch Jenny, the men would catch me, then we'd head to In-N-Out Burger.

I loved these workouts. We were an impromptu team and it felt good to be running hard and fast and pushing one another. The whole scene was new to Andrew, and his excitement fed the group energy. On the track, Coach shouted, "Go!" and the two of us tore off the line. His stride was like a metronome, steady and strong. Depending on the workout, he ran a lap or two, rested for a lap, then jumped back in. In the final 200 meters he'd belt out "BOOM!" encouraging me to the finish.

The luxury of the Olympic Training Center was time. We lingered over meals in the dining hall. Andrew had majored in exercise physiology, and he and Coach discussed training cycles, periodization, and adaptation. Coach told Andrew the same stories he'd told me. Andrew was rapt, just as I had been. The other runners joined us most of the time and our lunches could extend to three hours. We talked about training and travel—Coach's stories were always prominent—and we shared our goals and aspirations. I wanted to go to Iceland and still fantasized about opening a café. Andrew liked helping people fulfill their potential and was entertaining going to massage school. Meb's main goal was to give back to his family. His parents had endured a harrowing journey to bring him and his nine siblings to the States, and he wanted to run well enough to support them. Coach was all about the Tarahumara, the renowned ultra-runners from Mexico's Copper Canyon. After watching them run, Coach wanted to hike the canyons and see their lifestyle. Fifteen years later, he finally would. James, who carried two cellphones while he ran, wanted to climb the ladder of the tech world. Phil said that, after running, he wanted to be a weatherman. Jenny, whose coffee cup was as tall as she was, said she was living her dream.

People are always talking about the loneliness of the long-distance runner, but these moments were why I never felt it. We were lone competitors pursuing our own dreams and yet our singular goal united us. The intensity of the pursuit and the doubts and miles we all pushed through connected us, and these conversations were to me not just the sharing of information but intimate moments of support.

As the weeks passed, my 5K time in tempo workouts came in faster than some of my 5K race times. It was the effect we were hoping for. The body recovers faster at sea level, and because you can run faster, you recruit more fast-twitch muscle fibers in workouts. That, plus the string of high-mileage weeks, had pushed my body to greater strength and speed.

In our final week, I headed out for a mile-repeat session. Coach shouted "Go!" and Andrew and I took off. He slipped off at the half mile and I held the rhythm he'd set. The first repeat was 4:47. I'd run faster, but the challenge came from consistently hitting the fast time in subsequent repeats. My second repeat was 4:45. Coach grinned. I launched into the final repeat aiming for the same time or faster and ran 4:45. On a good day, you feel as if you can run forever. This was one of those days.

When I'd told Coach on the phone four years earlier that I wanted to make the Olympic team, it was a lofty, farfetched goal. But I was stronger and fitter than I'd ever imagined and ready to aim higher: I wanted to push beyond making the team and win the trials outright. And the mile repeat workout told me I could do it using any race tactic.

This was my first Olympic trials and I wanted to experience the race from the inside, be part of it, not in front of it. Plus, my competitors knew I was a front-runner. Staying in the pack could throw them off and create tension. Particularly, I hoped, for Libbie Hickman. Libbie was a petite blonde who'd used her wicked kick to overtake me in the 10,000 at the US championships the year before. I suspected her plan was to do the same at the trials. An unexpected tactic from me could play with her mentally.

The women's 10,000 was held on Friday night—July 14, the first day of the nine-day Olympic track trials in Sacramento, California. The stands at Hornet Stadium at Sacramento State University were packed. Warming up under the lights on the practice field, I could hear the crowd's volume rise and fall as it watched the men's 10,000. I did some strides and felt the springy strength in my rested legs. *Ready to roll.*

I moved to the staging area with the other women and, hearing the crowd go wild, rushed to the chain-link fence. Meb had made a move in the bell lap. He was pulling ahead with a strong lead, but reigning 10,000-meter champion Alan Culpepper started his kick and was gaining fast. Both men fought. Alan was closing the gap with every quick stride while Meb lunged for the finish. From where I stood at the fence, I couldn't tell who won.

The scoreboard flashed their times. Meb ran 28:03.32. Alan finished in 28:03.35, three one-hundredths of a second behind. I exhaled, excited for Meb, but inspired by both of their efforts.

I walked onto the track with the twenty-three other competitors thinking about Meb. He ran boldly. When he took over the race, he did so with authority. Had he let himself settle at any point after surging, it would have been Alan's race to win. When I took over, it would be with Meb's conviction.

I did a stride down the straightaway to get a read of the track, feel my spikes grip the rubber surface. I spotted my mom, dad, and Lesley in the stands, sitting with various aunts and uncles and friends, all wearing matching shirts that read: GO DEENA. THE ROAD TO SYDNEY. I waved. Andrew was with them. Coach, I knew, was on the other side of the track, but most likely at the fence for a good view.

We took the line.

"Runners set."

The gun fired, and the pack swallowed me. It took the first two turns to get to the inside curve. I tucked myself behind a large group and began observing. *Kim's out front. She's going hard but not too hard. It's fine. Just watch.*

The pack spread out on the backstretch, with the leaders running single file. I sat in about seventeenth place. *Rachel and Kristin are going wide in lane 2. Hold 'em off, Jen. Good job.*

The pace slowed slightly and the lead women bunched up into a tighter pack. Elbows bumped. Shelly tripped in front of me.

Damn.

I windmilled my arms to stay on my feet. I heard a few girls stumble behind me and enjoyed the lighter weight of not having them in my draft.

Natalie took the lead after the first mile and surged slightly but settled. Kim took over again at mile 2. Natalie took it back a few laps later. *They're playing. But no one is making a move.* I stayed tight to the curve, in about eleventh place, feeling like a hawk. I began using the Jumbotron to study the women ahead of me. Libbie's face was soft and she was looking at the feet in front of her. *She's feeling fine.* Jen's and Annette's faces were strained, their eyes darting around. *They're fatiguing, or maybe worried. Interesting, Kim is fading, she's falling back to me.*

Mile 3 was where a 10,000 can start to feel long; you've still got half the race left. I was getting antsy, the feeling I normally have at the start. Annette Peters surged to the lead and the pace got hotter. Kim couldn't go. I surged past her, then another runner, into ninth place. Kim rallied from behind, passing a long line of girls, and took the lead again. *Of course she feels better out front.* I looked at the Jumbotron again. *Kim is leading, she'll fade. Jen is second and looks good now. Anne Marie. Annette. Libbie. Me.* Sylvia kicked by everyone and took the lead. *Is this the move? Is she breaking it open?*

No, they settled.

Positions changed. We were now a pack of nine. Then a pack of six, with me in the back. Annette took the lead again. She began to push and wasn't letting up. *This is it. Get up there.*

I swung out into lane 2 and passed Libbie, Sylvia, Jen, and Anne Marie and got on Annette's shoulder just as the lap counter dropped to four. I shot past Annette and took the lead. *Game time.* On the backstretch, the crowds chanted "Dee-na, Dee-na!" *Thanks, guys, thank you.*

On the Jumbotron, it was me, Anne Marie, Jen, and Libbie. *Four of us battling for three Olympic spots.* The girls behind me had good leg speed, any one of them could catch me, so I pressed. With every step I powered to get the lap behind me as fast as possible and into the next one. The bell rang for my final lap. I had a good lead, but Meb's lead had been quickly reduced by the speed of his competitor. With his relentless effort in my mind, I sprinted the last stretch, throwing my hands up as I crossed the line and winning in 31:51, a personal best and a trials record. Andrew clocked my last mile at 4:38.

I turned to watch Jen cross 7 seconds behind me, followed by Libbie. The three of us hugged, and we ran a victory lap wearing American flags like capes. We were going to Sydney.

The Games were the second half of September, which allowed time for a month on the summer track circuit. Andrew and I flew to Europe and met up with Jen and Amy in Stockholm, where I ran a personal best in the 5,000. In Belgium, we connected with Meb and US distance runner Nick Rogers. The three of us were competing in the KBC Night of Athletics, a small meet held on a track set in the trees. I was running the 1,500, a distance that doesn't usually get me fired up. But after a fast final mile at the trials, I was eager to see what I could do in the metric mile.

Andrew found a spot along the fence to watch the races, while I warmed up with a few drills on the track. One included a pawing motion, scraping your forefoot through the running stride. I was wearing spikes, which wasn't smart, and felt my hamstring flicker. I didn't think about it. I toed the line and, when the gun fired, I went all out, charging hard through the 3.75 laps. Flying around that track, it was as if I were powered by the full force of optimism itself. I had met the love of my life, won the trials, and was headed to the Olympics. The strength of my future seemed so strong that my body knew exactly how to express it. Andrew and I had been together 24/7 and yet I didn't crave alone time. He was kind and caring and already invested in my running. He went to the lobby for coffee when I needed to nap, grabbed groceries, and looked up flight information. Standing at the fence together after my race to cheer on Meb and Nick, I felt like I could stand with him forever.

My hamstring still felt a little twingey back at the hotel. My Achilles' tendons were also sore. I'd run the 1,500 fast, clocking a personal best of 4:07.82, so it was understandable. Andrew massaged my legs to flush them out and I went to bed thinking a good sleep was all they needed. My hamstring was fine the next morning, but my Achilles' were a bit stiff and swollen. They loosened up during an easy run and slipped out of my mind.

We had six days between the 1,500 and my next race, the 3,000, and we spent it in Zurich preparing me to run another personal best. My Achilles' ached before and after my runs, but after a warm-up, the run itself was fine, so I didn't worry about it. Andrew ran out for Advil and ice, and he massaged my calves at night. We spent one afternoon walking the city to celebrate Andrew's twenty-third birthday. We saw the largest clock face in Europe, took a boat cruise on Lake Zurich, and listened to techno music as we strolled the Street Parade.

The next day, my Achilles' were visibly thicker and red compared to the milky whiteness of my legs. I lay on the floor of our hotel room with my legs up against the wall to drain the inflammation. "Maybe you should take it easy for a couple of days," Andrew said. Today "easy" would mean lying on the couch with a book. Back then, "easy" meant running my 10 miles slower. Between ice, massage, and Advil—and now elevation—I believed I was managing the injury well and would continue to do so through the Olympic Games. When they were over, I would rest.

I was running the 3,000 at a meet called Weltklasse, which was equal to DN Galan in prestige. Zurich's Letzigrund Stadium lacked the beauty and boldness of Stockholm's historic stadium, but the meet itself was electric. So many of the world's best track and field athletes participated in Weltklasse that some called it the one-day Olympics. To ease the pressure on my Achilles', the day before the race, I ran on the practice field to take advantage of the grass cushioning. When Andrew and I arrived, the only runner on the field was Hicham El Guerrouj of Morocco, the world record holder in the 1,500, Andrew's event in college. Andrew gripped the fence and his eyes widened. He told me the story, in a rabid whisper, of having been in the stadium watching El Guerrouj fall at the previous Olympics, the 1996 Games in Atlanta. He was moving to challenge the leader, Noureddine Morceli of Algeria, when his foot clipped Morceli's heel and he tripped. By the time El Guerrouj got up, he was in last place. The disappointment in his first Olympic Games nearly crushed him. But now, he was back on top. At the meet the next day, El Guerrouj won the 1,500.

I lined up for the 3,000 with familiar competitors: Tegla Loroupe and Sally Barsosio from Kenya, Great Britain's Paula Radcliffe, Amy, and others. My Achilles' were tender, but the rest of me was sharp. I ran the seven and a half laps with full force, placing eleventh and running 8:42.59, another personal best.

I couldn't walk the next day without pain. The Olympics were forty-six days away, but to me, they were right around the corner. Another personal best was proof that I could manage the issue if

I could handle the pain. One night, Andrew went to massage my calves and said, "My God, Deena, your Achilles' are angry. I can feel heat coming off them." In Monte Carlo, my last race in Europe, I limped through runs. "I don't know how you're doing this," Andrew said. Yet even without full power, I ran another 3,000 only a few seconds off my personal best, a performance that suggested to me I could still pull off a fast time in Sydney.

That turned out to be foolish optimism. In the weeks before the Games, the pain was so intense I could barely walk. I received ultrasound and electric stimulation treatments; had acupuncture, laser therapy, and chiropractic care; and tried switching from spikes to racing flats. Nothing eased the pain. There wasn't a miracle cure because what I needed was rest.

I knew I had overdone it. I also knew I wasn't going to run well in Sydney. It was a huge disappointment, but when I thought about it, I realized I wouldn't do anything differently. The Games were part of a larger summer of progress. They were the goal that had driven me to an Olympic trials victory and a string of personal bests on the track, performances that told me I had a strong future.

In the moment, though, running twenty-five laps seemed unbearable, and I just hoped the hype of the Games would quiet the pain enough to make finishing the race possible.

"They're going to take us. Deena, they're going to take us."

My mom couldn't get over the fact that the captain of the RiverCat was going to make a special trip down the Parramatta River to Sydney Harbour so they didn't have to wait an hour. "Everyone is just so nice here," she said. At one point, I'd thought that I didn't want my family to come to the Games. Why make the trip across the world when we knew I wasn't going to race well? Now I couldn't imagine being there without them.

Andrew stayed with my family in a sprawling farmhouse tucked into the woods. I stayed at the Olympic Village, a small town built over wetlands to house over 10,000 of the world's best athletes. It was a lively place. Athletes hung flags off balconies and ethnic music streamed from open windows. There were coffee carts on street corners and golf carts shuttling athletes from their front doors to the dining hall or weight room. Houses were divided by sport. Inside our track and field home, athletes were packed three or four to a room. I use "room" loosely, because some athletes shared the garage and others slept in the incomplete kitchen. Jen, Amy, and I got lucky. We had a bedroom upstairs.

We were there two weeks before my race and I was able to hobble through easy runs with the team. Once while out with Amy and Jen, we stopped by NBC's broadcasting booth in Olympic Park and got on air with Katie Couric and Matt Lauer. The best pre-race moment, though, was when Muhammad Ali paid Team USA a visit in the village. We'd all been told he was coming, and when his black sedan rolled onto our street, athletes filed out of their houses. The great fighter stepped out of his car and addressed hundreds of US athletes and staff. Everyone was silent as he said there was no greater pride than representing your country and the communities you are from. It is worth fighting your greatest fight, here and now, he said.

The days followed a similar rhythm to my time at the Olympic Training Center. I got medical treatments in the village, napped, and spent long hours in the dining hall visiting with other US track athletes, feeling my Achilles' throb as I sat there.

Every few days, I took the RiverCat forty-five minutes east to downtown to meet my family and Andrew at the AT&T hospitality suite, a restaurant the US sponsor set up that allowed athletes an easy way to connect with family. I heard about their day—how stunning the skyline looked from the ferry, how the cockatoos on the farm had swept down from the trees to eat nuts from Lesley's palm. Once my mom gave me a stack of cards from friends and family back home.

I read them on my bunk, getting teary. A cousin said she couldn't believe she was related to an Olympian. Bill, my high school coach, wrote that that he'd seen the Olympian in me all along.

On September 27, the stadium was packed to watch the finals in the men's 800 and the women's 400. In between would be the two preliminary heats of the women's 10,000 meters. Jen ran first at 12:40 p.m. She was fit, but a recent bout of the flu caused her not to advance to the finals. I ran about forty minutes later and was flat and heavy off the line. I didn't take in the scene. I was a bit embarrassed not to be at my best on the world stage, so I kept my head down, thinking, like a kid, that if I didn't see anyone, no one would see me. The stadium cast a shadow across the field and we ran in and out of the light. I finished thirty-sixth out of forty-one total competitors.

Jen and I pulled our backpacks over sweaty uniforms and walked back to the village. She showered and headed off to meet her family. I was too physically and mentally drained to do anything but shower, nap, and, eventually, hobble to the corner for a cappuccino. A part of me still wanted to keep my head down. I wanted to bury the performance and pretend it never happened. The cappuccino was my attempt at cheering myself up, sparking some gratitude. Look at where I was. At a coffee cart in the Olympic Village in Australia. What a beautiful country. The other side of the experience had been full. I'd held a koala at the Crocodile Hunter Steve Irwin's animal sanctuary during training camp and given my family an Olympic vacation. The love of my life had been with me the whole time, and I'd built stronger friendships with Amy, Jen, Abdi Abdirahman, and Meb. I would be going home with plenty of goodness to hold on to.

My family, Andrew, and I sat in the living room of their host family's city apartment near the harbor to watch the closing ceremonies. There were more than a dozen of us gathered around the large television. Australia put on a great show, with performances by Men at

Work and Olivia Newton-John. The band Midnight Oil wore black T-shirts with the word SORRY in white, a reference to the tension between the white settlers and the indigenous community.

Watching Midnight Oil onstage, I found myself thinking about Cathy Freeman, the 400-meter runner and indigenous Australian who many hoped would win gold in Sydney and help heal the country's racial divide. She had the added pressure of lighting the Olympic torch in the opening ceremonies under a global spotlight. When I think about these Games, I see Cathy holding a torch over a pool of water and igniting a ring of fire. I see her dominant stride on the track and the fluid way she carried that through the finish, winning gold. I admired how she carried out her role as both athlete and ambassador with grace. She'd pulled it off. She had a Games like no other.

As the ceremonies ended, a fighter jet flew low over the stadium. Just as it reached the Olympic torch, the flame extinguished and the jet put on its afterburners, giving the illusion of carrying the flame away. The jet was headed downriver from the Olympic Park toward the harbor, and realizing this, Andrew, Lesley, and I ran out to the waterfront. Fireworks exploded from barges all along the river when the jet passed. When it reached the harbor, the bridge seemed to explode in fireworks, lighting up the black sky in Olympic colors— red, yellow, green, and blue, chosen because every country's flag has at least one of those colors. It was a remarkable end to the Games. Watching with Andrew and Lesley, with my parents close, the fireworks were for me a celebration not just of the Olympic Games, but of the beauty, challenge, joy, and success of the entire summer.

13

GOING THE DISTANCE

Progress lies not in enhancing what is,
but in advancing toward what will be.

—KHALIL GIBRAN

There's a trail through Sycamore Canyon in the Santa Monica Mountains. It starts in the suburbs not far from my parents' house and slips west, dropping through forest and field before coming to an abrupt end at the Pacific Ocean. I'd thought about running that trail over the years whenever I was home, and the idea occurred to me again when I was visiting my parents a few months after the Olympics. I was home helping look after my mom following surgery. She'd been diagnosed with breast cancer and had the tumor removed. I sat with her during a follow-up appointment at the hospital. The doctor pulled a drainage tube out of the side of her breast, and at the sight of it, I fainted. When I woke drenched in sweat in the chair next to her bed, she smiled and thanked me for my support.

I didn't run the trail that visit. It was 18 miles long. The farthest I'd run at that point was 15 miles, and those workouts exhausted me. Four months later, though, in April 2001, I returned to California to be with my parents again. My mom was going through chemotherapy and radiation treatments and I wanted to help them manage the appointments and the house. My mom was a worrier and hypochondriac. She'd handled surgery surprisingly well, but I worried she'd struggle with the intensity of chemo.

To our relief, she was fine. She played mah-jongg with friends and went out for sushi with my dad. When her hair began falling out, a half dozen of her girlfriends came over and shaved her head. My dad followed with the vacuum, suctioning the hair before it hit the ground. It was touching to see that everyone brought hats and head scarves for her. Through it all, she never missed a manicure. There's a moment in Lance Armstrong's book *It's Not About the Bike* when he speaks to cancer and says, "When you looked around for a body to try to live in, you made a big mistake when you chose mine." I saw that conviction in my mom. She treated cancer like it was a common cold and went about her life. It made my fear of surviving an 18-mile run insignificant. I headed to the canyon.

The trail began at the fence just off a dirt parking lot. I stepped out of the car, hit my watch, and headed into the hills. The first few miles passed through tall grass and oak, then dropped into the canyon. I ran easy, wary of the length of the run, and took in the muted tones of green and browns. Large oaks and sycamore shaded the trail and squirrels darted about. The terrain was comfort food, bringing me back to the running of my childhood, and I had to resist the urge to veer off course and explore the side trails.

Out of the trees, the sun cooked the canyon and the pungent smells of sycamore, anise, and sage filled the air. Birds scurrying in the chaparral made the mountains seem alive, and the sound of my shoes on the gravel was part of the pulse. The descent to the ocean was gentle, and I hoped the climb back would feel equally mild.

Peaks rose to my left and right as I got deeper into the canyon and the air turned moist and salty. I was getting close. The dirt gave way to asphalt. I passed a campground and emerged onto Pacific Coast Highway in Malibu. I crossed the road, bent down, picked up a handful of sand, and let it fall through my fingers.

When I turned around, the Santa Monica Mountains looked massive. I wondered briefly if I should find a phone and call my dad to pick me up. I shrugged off the thought and started back. Over the highway, I slipped back in between the peaks, following the canyon floor. The trail climbed gently, and I quickly found a rhythm. I waited for the usual fatigue to set in, for the pace to feel as desperate as it had with the men. But as I moved, I felt good. I picked up my rhythm, surprised at my body's strength. I hit the steepest pitch of the return, a few miles from the trailhead, thinking that I had to be beyond the 15-mile mark at this point. I got competitive with a mountain biker and chased him, passing before the top. Cresting the hill, I kept pushing, gaining momentum as I held out my arms to brush the tops of the tall grasses. I couldn't believe it. I was getting faster and going longer. I thought of my mom and couldn't help but think we are all so much more capable than we give ourselves credit for.

Back at the trailhead, I called Coach and told him I wanted to run a marathon. "I've been waiting to hear those words come out of your mouth for a long time," he said. I could practically see him grinning on the other side of the line.

Up until that moment, the image that had kept me from running the marathon was of Gabriela Andersen-Schiess of Switzerland struggling to stand at the end of the 1984 Olympic Marathon. She staggered across the lanes of the L.A. coliseum, her body contorted by heat and distance, and after crossing the finish line, was carried off the field. *A race that causes that much distress can't be good for you,* I'd thought.

Those 18 miles changed my mind. Most distance runners waited until their speed on the track dwindled to take on the marathon. Coach, though, had a different view. The greatest distance runners improved on the track after running the marathon, he said. That was my objective: I wanted to use the marathon as a training tool to gain strength for track and cross-country.

Coach and I discussed my options. Boston was historic. Chicago was fast. I thought of the L.A. Marathon because my dad and I had watched it on television when I was a kid. Coach suggested New York City. "The course requires cross-country grit," he said. It sounded like my kind of race and we settled on it.

The marathon was in the fall and I tucked it in the back of mind while focusing on track season. With Coach in Arizona, training could've been tough. But Andrew and I formed a team of two in Alamosa. He ran with me on easy runs and rode the bike next to me during long runs, carrying the water bottles. He was goofy. During mile repeats at Cole Park, I'd come around the bend and Andrew would be cheering from up in a tree. On tempo runs, he'd lean out the car window and in his best Coach voice shout, "Get tough!"

One afternoon midsummer, Coach called. "I just received an interesting call from Basil Honikman," he began. Basil was the executive director of Running USA, a nonprofit that promoted US distance running. He wanted to know if Coach was interested in creating a professional team modeled after the East Africans' high-altitude camps. The idea was a direct response to the United States' poor showing in the 2000 Olympic Games, including my own. We fielded only one athlete in the men's and women's marathon. Running USA was out to change that. Its goal was to return US distance running to its previous heights, when athletes like Jim Ryun, Billy Mills, Bill Rodgers, Frank Shorter, and Joan Benoit Samuelson dominated the sport. Coach had talked with Bob Larsen, Meb's coach, about leading the team together. "We're thinking of Mammoth Lakes, California," Coach said. I was immediately excited, remembering the fun of going to Mammoth for high school running camp.

"I want to get Amy, Elva, and Jen up there," he said. "Maybe we can convince Alan [Culpepper], Abdi [Abdirahman], and Dan Browne, too. What do you think?"

I couldn't think of anything better. The idea contained everything I believed in: altitude, teams, and most important, Coach. Andrew was on board. He also had fond memories of running in Mammoth during junior college.

On the summer circuit, Jen, Amy, Elva, and I talked a lot about Team Running USA. The girls were already committed and I talked up Mammoth, telling them it was a small but vibrant ski town with trails snaking in every direction. There were waterfalls and hot springs and stunning views. "Yeah, but what about altitude?" Amy asked. She and Jen had never trained at elevation. "You just need to hydrate and get your rest," I said. "Coach will talk a lot about the benefits of altitude, but once you get to a race, you'll actually feel it."

Coach and I were the first to arrive in Mammoth. Andrew was in massage school five hours away in Thousand Oaks, living with my parents, and would join me later. When the team arrived from points around the country, Coach gathered us in his condo for a meeting. Coach, now seventy-one years old, stood and addressed the group as we balanced plates of pizza and salad on our laps. "All of you are the best in the sport," he began. "You're here to get more out of yourselves by influencing one another." I looked around and was amazed at the caliber of athletes in the room. I saw Olympians Meb, Amy, Elva, Jen, and Nick Rogers. There was 10,000 meter standout Matt Downin and rising stars Leigh Daniel and Phil Price. Terrence Mahon, Jen's husband, was a marathoner and national champion in 20K. In that moment I realized what we were doing was big, and it elevated the marathon from a personal goal to one that included strengthening US distance running as a whole.

Coach discussed the benefits of altitude and the importance of showing up with a good attitude. Then he previewed the fall season. We were all training for various road-racing distances, but we'd conduct our main training session together in the morning. Strength training and second runs in the afternoon were on our own. He concluded with a Vigilism: "By the time you leave here," Coach said, "you're going to be so damn tough."

We got started the next morning and headed out for an easy run in Shady Rest Park on the edge of town. We ran through the forest on single-track trails that eventually merged with wider dirt roads. Mammoth had the warm pine smell I remembered. We took turns leading, found ourselves on steep hills and at dead ends, and we laughed at not knowing our way around. Eventually we made up the miles we needed that day.

Then the serious training began.

Coach had laid out my marathon program over coffee at the Looney Bean the week prior. He scooted the first month's training across the table and I glanced at it. My eyes widened. Coach had said marathon training would be a simple uptick in mileage. I knew that meant 20-mile long runs. But the increase applied to everything. Mile repeats jumped from 4 to 8 repetitions. Tempo runs went from 6 to 10 miles. The biggest leap was scratching 400s on the track and replacing them with 5K repeats. *Wow, that's a lot of work.*

"The marathon is all about endurance," Coach said. Long interval workouts and tempo runs build stamina, but the long run was the key workout for marathon training. "You've never focused on endurance so you're going to have to have a lot of emotional control, or you'll burn yourself out in the first half of the week," he said. "Emotional control" was Coach-speak for patience, meaning let your mind dictate your pace, not your emotions.

Emotional control was on my mind as the team lined up on Benton Crossing Road, known locally as Green Church Road because of the small, light-green church on the corner. The road shot across the valley toward the Glass Mountains, undulating as it went. There was a nervous, excited buzz in the air. For most of the team, it was their first hard effort at altitude. For me, it was my first 10-mile tempo run.

Coach structured the workout as an equalizer, where you chase the person ahead, fend off the person behind, and the goal was everyone engaged in a dramatic fight for the finish. Leigh went off first. Then Amy, Jen, and Elva.

I was next. Coach's command might as well have been a starting pistol. While my tempo pace was 5:30—my target marathon pace—I barreled down that road, emotional control instantly forgotten in the competitive play of the equalizer.

After sending off the men, Coach blew past me in the van, parking at the first mile. I flew by, hitting the mile in 5:10.

"Oh Lordy," Coach said.

I smiled, taking the comment as approval.

The road dipped slightly in the second mile, then climbed a bit and I charged up the incline, running the second mile in 5:10.

"Emotional control, Deena! Emotional control!" Coach shouted from the van, chuckling.

I surged down the road with Leigh in my sights, gaining momentum on the steep downhill of the fourth mile and using it to catch her on the hill. "Oh my word," she said in her delightful Texan accent as I passed.

At mile 5, the pace began to hurt. I tasted blood in the back of my throat and realized I was only halfway through.

I could have slowed but the chase was fun. The girls' workout was shorter and I had to catch them before they finished. Elva was next. She slowly came back to me on the downhill and I pulled up alongside her. "Good job," I said. Amy and Jen ran together, a tall figure and a swinging ponytail looming ahead. I reeled them in and noticed altitude had turned their usual steady breathing into labored wheezing. "Let's go," I offered, encouraging them to come with me for the downhill.

I ran on, now intent on fending off the men. Phil, Nick, and Matt were far enough back that they'd finish their workout before reaching me. Meb and Terrence, though, were threats and I looked toward the bulging mounds of the Glass Mountains for inspiration.

C'mon, win the Battle of Green Church Road.

Meb wanted it, too. When I looked back, I couldn't tell if he was straining or smiling. It didn't take long for his even foot strikes and steady breathing to grow louder behind me. "No," I said, raising my arms out to the side to prevent him from passing. But Meb just stepped out. "Keep it going," he said as he smoothly passed. He arrived at the 10-mile mark to Coach and the team cheering. I crossed a few strides later, and Meb turned back for a high-five. But I'd already cut off to the side, too busy dry-heaving to participate.

Coach didn't want to stifle my feistiness. So he educated me about the long run. "The marathon is an energy game," he said. *A game?* He had my attention. "Going out too hard and surging wastes energy. You want to be smooth and economical." In the long run, Coach said, we're training the body's energy system to more readily burn fat over carbohydrates. You see this kind of efficiency in animals that migrate long distances, he said, whales and birds notably, who glide with minimal movement, slowly releasing their energy.

This efficient use of energy translated to pacing. The game of emotional control, then, was to bottle up the excitement of competition and slowly release it over the miles.

Coach didn't set a pace for my long runs. Instead, I'd start easy and pick up the pace 10 to 20 seconds every 5K. Breaking the 20 miles down into 5K segments had the added benefit of making the distance less intimidating.

Coach created an out-and-back long-run course that started from a park in town, traveled downhill on a wide dirt road that paralleled the Sherwin Range and continued down Green Church Road before turning around and climbing back into town. The long and gradual uphill return "breeds toughness," Coach said.

The team started long runs together, running easy for the first 5K, before finding our own rhythm. At the 5K, Coach handed us our water bottles, and I picked up the pace. I was using perceived exertion to gauge my effort rather than time: running "easy" from the start and looking at my watch to make sure my increases were within the 10- to 20-second window.

Pacing, I realized, actually gave me something to do on long runs. Previously, I'd just run and the time passed slowly. But monitoring my pace and effort kept me engaged in the work in a similar way that trying to push my pace did. I looked at my watch, felt the level of my breathing, listened to my footfalls, then looked at my watch again. In between, there was time to cycle through thoughts and wander into the scenery. I admired the pines that shaded Sherwin Creek Road and wondered what to make for dinner. As I moved across the highway toward the fish hatchery and the sun-exposed Hot Creek Road, I wondered how lush the land might have been in the years before Los Angeles gained the water rights to the river. I thought about the miners who came to the area during the Gold Rush, and wondered if veins of gold were still in the river and rock. Then I'd be at the next 5K and it was time to pick up the pace again and drink more.

Fueling at each 5K was another task that kept me engaged, but it was also strategic. Science suggested that the body can absorb about four ounces of fluid every fifteen to twenty minutes, about the time elite marathoners ran 5K, so fluid stations on the course were every 5K. I had sipped water here and there during workouts, but had not needed to take in calories, so I experimented with different sports drinks to find what worked for me. I tried lemon-lime Gatorade, which reminded me of recovering from the flu as a child. Powerade's electric colors stained my mouth, as well as my clothes when it splashed out of the bottle mid-run. There was a new product on the market, a powder with protein in it. Researchers thought it would help the body store glycogen. It made me puke.

Then I tried Cytomax. Its Peachy Keen flavor actually tasted like peach tea. When I drank it, I could feel it move down my throat and into my system, refreshing my body. The crisp flavor was so satisfying that for a moment, I was no longer running on a dirt road in the heat, but sitting on the front porch, rocking gently in the breeze.

You race infrequently during a marathon buildup. Wanting to keep the competitive side of me sharp, I ran a half marathon in Virginia Beach. Ludmila Petrova of Russia was on the start, along with Kenya's Margaret Okayo. Both were running New York in the fall and were likely there to sharpen their fitness, too. The three of us took off together. The course looped through the city before finishing on the oceanfront boardwalk. My goal was to post a fast time. But it was also my first half-marathon attempt and I just wanted to see what it felt like.

The three of us stayed together through the half. The pace was aggressive, around 5:25. It started feeling challenging, but counterintuitively, I put in a surge to try to shake them in the final 4 miles. The girls went with me. I felt strained, like this was a hard tempo run, one I wanted to win. With 2 miles to go, I surged again, this time dropping Ludmila and Margaret, and tried holding the faster pace to distance myself farther. I made the turn onto the boardwalk, and seeing the finish, kicked. The finish, though, was farther out than it appeared. The struggle intensified, but I didn't want the women to see me fading and try to take advantage of it, so I held on, winning in 1:10:07. Ludmila took second in 1:10:35, and Margaret was third in 1:10:42.

Across the line, my first thought was: *How am I supposed to turn around and do that again?*

Each week I stepped into new territory. Five 1-mile repeats became seven. A tempo run jumped to 12 miles. A long run got longer, or the effort necessary to pick up the pace at mile 12, then 15, and again at 18, grew harder. I went into each longer workout thinking, *This is more than I've done before, how can I do this?* Then I'd arrive at practice and Meb and the team were ready for another battle down Green Church Road. Just knowing Terrence was also running 22 miles was comforting. It's just two miles more than last week, I told myself. I also noted that while the end was hard, most of the long run was done at a comfortable pace.

This was where the marathon was unique. In the shorter distances, the pace was hard from the first mile to the finish and I had to use mental strategies to encourage myself the entire way. Long runs taught me the marathon mind followed a different rhythm. It moved from easy to hard to very hard. So to run it effectively, my mind had to respond to the distance's ever-increasing challenge. In the early miles, the marathon mind needed to be calm to keep the pace controlled and I consciously enjoyed the time, taking in the views, while also keeping an eye on pace and fluids. Around the half-way point when the pace required more effort, the internal cheerleader stepped in—the encouraging voice that pushed me in every race. *Good job, work this hill. Just focus on the mile you're in. Drive your arms. Drive. Drive!*

The cheerleader usually shared space with the calm mind during this second phase. I'd watch a rabbit hop across the road and think about the race between the tortoise and the hare. I'd check my form, look at my watch. *You need to push a little more here.* Sometimes I'd watch Terrence ahead of me pushing through his own miles for inspiration. Or I'd think of Andrew, who was also running New York as his first marathon. He was doing long runs by himself from my parents' house. I smiled picturing him on the trails and roads I ran as a kid.

The final miles of the long run required a whole new mental level: the insistent mind. By this point, I'd be climbing Sherwin Creek Road working to pull myself out of the valley. I thought this would be the place I'd release my bottled-up excitement. But that had been beginner's optimism. I had nothing to uncork. My body felt a deep fatigue, nothing like the burn at the end of repeats. Just an unwavering desire to stop.

I can't do this.

Listen, your only option of getting to the park is to run there. You've got to do it.

I'd slap my quads to wake them mid-stride, and think, *Hi-yah!* like a cowboy prodding a horse.

Get to the next water bottle and you'll have the energy to finish this thing. But you've got to finish it.

Once Terrence was running alongside me and I told him I was in a big struggle right then. "Don't let the fatigue deceive you," he said. "There's good and bad patches in a race and it's your job to get out of the bad patches as quickly as possible and hang on to the good ones."

I looked up at Coach Vigil parked at the crest of a hill, swung an imaginary rope up the mountain, and lassoed the van, then I pulled myself to it. On the other side, I relished the flat stretch to the finish.

It was just after 6:00 a.m. in California when the second plane hit the World Trade Center. I was in my condo eating breakfast and watching the news with no volume because my roommate Leigh was still sleeping. An image of the first tower burning came on screen. I turned the volume up. When the second plane came into view, my hands went to my face. Then it hit the south tower and I knew something was terribly wrong. I woke Leigh. "Something's happening in New York City you should see."

We sat on the couch listening to news anchors try to make sense out of chaos. The word *terrorism* erased any notion of these strikes being accidents. I felt such fear for everyone on those planes, then for the workers in the buildings, and everyone's families. Leigh and I thought Coach might call off practice, but without a phone call, we arrived at the Looney Bean and Coach and the others were there. Coach gathered us around. "We have work to do," he said. "We're fortunate to be safe, and running and being with your teammates is good for trying to make sense of the news this morning."

Quietly, we headed out to Shady Rest Park for mile repeats. All of us, I imagined, were glad for the hard effort. As I ran, I felt sick to my stomach, horrified by the images of fear and destruction. I wondered what would cause someone to do that. I tried considering whether an act of terrorism done in the name of God could ever be interpreted as an act of love, but decided you can't show love by hurting others. That defies its true nature. Love was the firefighters rushing into the buildings, the EMTs from across the boroughs making their way to Lower Manhattan. I thought of all the people running away from the site and the others running to it and wondered briefly why our run mattered today. It seemed so unimportant and yet so essential. Moving through the trees and the park, the beauty of nature, friendships, and love reminded me running offers us the physical strength and mental clarity for human compassion. It allows us to improve ourselves and in doing so, bring more love to those around us. I carried that thought with me the rest of the day, sending it out into the world, and hoping it was felt.

We wondered if the New York City Marathon would still happen in the wake of 9/11. But Coach, Terrence, and I decided to train like it would. The week the Twin Towers fell I ran my first 120-mile week. Coach bumped my tempo run to 13 miles and my mile repeats to 8. That week, my mileage hit a peak of 137. Long runs he extended by time: another 15 minutes, then another.

I'd start the week intimidated by the workload, then the miles would get done and I'd come out thinking, *Wow, I can handle it.* When Coach first told me the story about Juma Ikangaa's 35-mile training run in Alamosa during his buildup to the Boston Marathon, I thought he'd exaggerated the distance for effect. Now I knew he hadn't. If you push the body, then let it rest, it adapts.

Andrew arrived in October with Aspen and a U-Haul full of our belongings. We bought a fixer-upper in the pines next to the ski lift, and the house became the central meeting spot for the team on Sunday mornings. After long runs, everyone gathered around the table and Andrew served French toast made with Southern Comfort and vanilla and offered fresh berries, peanut butter, and Nutella as toppings. Bacon and eggs were cooked to order. He started his personal training and massage business and immersed himself in supporting the team and my training. He was a constant companion, riding the bike alongside me on long runs, drawing ice baths for me post-workout, and following the sport closely. The days were easier and more joyful with him around, and he made the challenge of the marathon more fun.

In the final weeks before the taper, I made a few small adjustments. Distance had amplified the need for details, so in an effort to make the end of long runs not feel so hard, I ate more. Instead of two pieces of toast before practice, I had a bagel, which was heartier, and I added eggs or nut butter for protein. Protein helped repair damaged muscle and was considered "brain food." Whether it actually aided my broken muscles and fatigued mind a few hours later as I ran, I have no idea. I just wanted the mental security that the nutrients would be there.

In my peak long run, 23 miles, the team moved out together. We traveled down Sherwin Creek Road into the Owens Valley, passed Hot Creek to Green Church, where I made the turn and began the climb back. My body had adapted well to the miles. I felt strong and fit.

Yet, as I climbed the long hill, my legs and arms began to feel heavy with fatigue. When I reached the van, I looked at Coach. "How am I supposed to run twenty-six point two miles when twenty-three miles at a slower pace is so hard?"

"Tapering," Coach said. "You technically only need a twenty-mile run to prep you for the marathon. It's not any one run, but the accumulation of weeks that prepare you. When you've tapered and rested, the body can go the extra distance."

I didn't understand marathon training. But the mileage was there, on my body, and I decided to trust it.

A pair of custom-made running shoes arrived in time for my final mile-repeat workout before the taper. The shoes were handmade by ASICS master shoemaker Hitoshi Mimura. After falling in love with ASICS shoes the previous winter, I asked Ray to reach out to them. While he discussed possible sponsorship, I researched the brand and learned the name was an acronym for *Anima Sana in Corpore Sano*, "Sound Mind in a Sound Body." The motto spoke to the mind-body connection I was experiencing and made me more eager to represent the company. Fortunately, they agreed to take me on.

I took the shoes out of the box. They felt as light as slippers. They were white, with the company's distinctive crossed-striped logo in royal blue. *Deena* was embroidered in blue thread at the heel of the left shoe, *Drossin* on the right. I was struck by the quality of the craftsmanship and I thought of the session I'd had with Mr. Mimura that summer. A Japanese man in his fifties, he was formal, in a buttoned-up blazer. He bowed and I bowed deeper, to show respect. With a well-worn cloth measuring tape, he measured each foot, starting with the length of each toe. He then measured the circumference and height of each toe, carefully writing the Japanese number on a notepad. He measured the length of my arch, how far my anklebone was from the ground, the distance from my big toe to the top of my ankle. Then he measured them all again.

I slipped the shoes on. They hugged my heel perfectly. The toe box framed the outline of my forefoot exactly.

In Shady Rest Park for mile repeats, the team got off the line together. The first half of the mile descended slightly and I let my turnover go crazy. We made a U-turn at the end of the parking lot and I pushed, working to maintain the same quick cadence from the downhill on the way back up to the top. My new kicks seemed part of the running motion, not separate from it. Afterward, I pulled off the shoes and kissed them before putting them back in their bag. *See you on the start line.*

Coach, Andrew, and I landed in New York four days before the race. Terrence and Jen arrived early, too. My family was there, off visiting relatives who lived in the city. Coach spent hours in the Hilton Midtown lobby catching up with runners, coaches, and agents from around the world. Andrew and I lay low. We watched the Weather Channel in our room, noting when the temperature fluctuated a degree or the wind kicked up five miles per hour.

The New York Road Runners invited me to the pre-race press conference and one of the questions posed to all athletes was, "What does this race mean to you, to run in the wake of the September eleventh attack?" Athletes' answers varied from running in honor of the families who lost loved ones to being amazed the race was going on at all. My feelings were the same. I said I would run with a red-white-and-blue ribbon pinned to my uniform for the families and that it was also a gesture to all New Yorkers for welcoming the world so soon after the tragedy.

The reporters all nodded. It amazed me that the cameras were clicking and journalists were scribbling and that they thought elite runners' stories mattered. I saw, though, that they connected us with the 30,000 other runners in the race, the spectators, the volunteers, and the public safety officers. Running on the track can feel like a performance for the fans. The marathon, though, had a strong sense of community that touched me. We weren't running for them. We were running with them.

The day before the race, the Big Apple was bustling outside. New York, I thought, was alive with resilience. Race director Allan Steinfeld told a reporter that the marathon would be a celebration of life and that he expected the number of spectators to swell to 2 million. Andrew, Terrence, Jen, Ray, and I ran in Central Park that morning, past the finish line, where tourists and runners were indulging in photo ops. We paused at the statue of race founder Fred Lebow and said thank you. As we ran on, I thought that Fred would be pleased to know just how big a role the race was playing in the city's comeback.

Boarding the bus on race morning with Andrew and Terrence, I felt uneasy. The race was going to be harder than anything I'd experienced in practice. I'd be trying to run 26.2 miles at a pace I'd only ever held for 13. *You'll find a way*, I told myself as the bus pulled away from the curb. We drove through the city, watching as streams of runners filed into buses outside other hotels. The sun was just coming up as we made our way down FDR Drive and through the Brooklyn-Battery Tunnel. We joined a long line of buses on the Brooklyn-Queens Expressway, and I watched as we passed old brick buildings and smokestacks, went by Greenwood Heights, Sunset Park, and other Brooklyn neighborhoods, and finally merged onto the Verrazano-Narrows Bridge to Staten Island for the start. I turned to Andrew. "Are we really going to run all that way?" He nodded. "It's the only way back."

The bus dropped us near the Carriage House, a bar/restaurant used then by military personnel, where we waited for the start. Inside were uncovered banquet tables with bagels and Dunkin' Donuts coffee. The food was intended for the volunteers, since the elites had already eaten and moved on to obsessing about pooping before the gun.

From this point on, I was task oriented. My goal was to get the pre-race details right and stay calm and relaxed. I lay down on a towel and propped my feet up on a chair to let my legs rest. My mind wandered to Coach, thinking he could very well still be having coffee with others in the breakfast room. My parents and sister were likely layering on clothes at the hotel. I pictured Ray running in Central Park with other agents, all making predictions about the race.

After a while, I got up and put on my new shoes. I smoothed out the laces so a twist wouldn't put weird pressure on the top of my foot. I tied and then double-knotted the laces, tucking the loose ends into the crossed laces so they wouldn't come undone.

Andrew, Terrence, and I jogged for about 5 minutes, incorporating a few light drills like sidesteps and skips. I was surprised at how many people were doing 20-minute warm-ups; I didn't want to have the extra miles on my legs. I did a couple of leg swings and butt kicks to wake my legs up, and Joan Benoit Samuelson walked by.

Joan was a national hero. She won the first women's Olympic marathon in 1984, the year I started running. The Games were down the street in Los Angeles. I watched the race with my parents in our living room. Joan ran ahead of the pack, out front from mile 3. Most people expected the race to be a duel between Joan, the world-record holder in the distance, and marathoning legend Grete Waitz of Norway, then a five-time winner of the New York City Marathon. But when Joan took off, Grete didn't follow. Joan ran away from the pack, leading throughout the race, and was the first to emerge from the dark tunnel and into the bright sun of the L.A. Coliseum. In that moment, I moved closer to the television. I don't know if the image of her waving her white painter's cap was seared in my mind because I saw it, or because it became one of the most iconic images of the Olympic Games, but I'd never been more rapt watching a sporting event as a kid.

Joan was now forty-four, and still held the American record in the marathon. She was running to lend support to the race.

"These people are going to regret these warm-up miles once they get into Central Park," she quipped to no one in particular.

I smiled, pleased I was just doing drills and not making a rookie mistake.

Elite athlete coordinator David Monti called us all to the start and we lined up on the Verrazano-Narrows Bridge in a sectioned-off area for about fifty elite runners. Ray had secured a spot at the start for Andrew behind the elite women. "See you at the finish," we said. Helicopters flew overhead and boats in the harbor sprayed water. A large American flag hung above from the bridge. It was hard not to notice the void in the Manhattan skyline.

I removed my hat at the beginning of the national anthem, and began mouthing the words when I noticed Susan Chepkemei, the Kenyan standing next to me, singing along. Maybe she sang the national anthem of other countries' races all the time, or just ours. It didn't matter. She was singing it now, in New York City. My eyes stung with tears. When the song was over, I hugged her and wished her well.

The gun fired and we were off. I ran in the lead pack of about eight women that included Susan, Ludmila, and Margaret, but didn't key off them. I approached the race like a long run; the only difference was that now I had to find a way to stay on a 5:30 pace the entire distance. The pack made it easy at the start. They were patient as we climbed over the bridge into a steady headwind and descended into Brooklyn. Out on the course were eight water bottles marking each 5K segment. The New York Marathon course ran through all five boroughs. *Maybe I should view it as a five-borough tour. Staten Island, Brooklyn, Queens, the Bronx, Manhattan. We are already in Brooklyn. One down. That was fast.*

Crowds were thick through Brooklyn. People waved American flags and kids leaned into the street blowing noisemakers. Signs were everywhere: CALL IT A COMEBACK, NEW YORK, I ❤ NYC, and RACE TO REMEMBER. *How beautiful.*

As we moved through Brooklyn, the miles felt easy. The women were hovering at a 5:30 pace and I stayed in the back of the pack, enjoying the vibrant scene. I felt a hot spot under my right big toe. *Oh no, a blister. So early?* It was mile 8. I ran on, ignoring it, but by mile 10 it hurt with each step. *Is my sock bunched? It can't be the new shoes; they feel too good. A pebble, maybe?*

And so the cheerleading began. Coach's words came first: *Good thing it's four feet from your heart.*

I focused on ways to make the next mile feel easier without compromising my pace: Sipping fluids, tucking in behind leaders for the draft. The blister announced itself regularly. *It's just skin.*

The Queensboro Bridge, which took us into Manhattan at mile 16, was so quiet from the lack of cars and spectators that I could immerse myself in the hum of the police motorcycles in front of us, the harmonized breathing of the pack, and the ever-so-light tapping of women's feet across the asphalt. We exited onto Fifty-Ninth Street, took the hairpin turn on First Avenue, and all I saw and heard were people. Spectators lined the entire street four to five deep, and they screamed. It was as if we'd turned a corner and run into a U2 concert.

Margaret threw in a surge. *She feels the crowd.*

Susan, Ludmila, and the rest of the pack followed, pulling away from me. Had we been into the twentieth mile, a competitive urge might have taken over. Sixteen was too early. I was scared of what was to come.

I watched the women through miles 18 and 19. Margaret held the lead, but Ludmila wanted it, too. Their pace seemed hasty and anxious. *Their fight is on.* Joyce Chepchumba and Esther Kiplagat, both from Kenya, were in the pack, along with Svetlana Zakharova from Russia, all seasoned marathoners demonstrating an aggressive style. *I'd like to be up there someday.*

I turned left onto East 135th Street in the Bronx. The spectators dissolved, the city quieted, and I passed the 20-mile mark. Mile 20 was as remarkable—or as infamous—as the marathon itself. *The marathon starts here*, the saying goes. Reflexively, the moment grew big in my mind and in the relative quiet of the Bronx, I heard my body screaming. My hips jarred with each stride, my quads were tender, then there was the blister. A painful rhythm took over. Foot landed, the blister shouted, quads shrieked, hips jerked.

This is too much.

A few steps later, I remembered something Coach had said. "The 10K is your expertise. The last 10K of the marathon is nothing compared with all the work you've put in."

Exiting the Bronx, I felt cracked open, exposed, and barely able to run. As I moved down Fifth Avenue, I called upon my insistent mind. I searched for everything that could keep me going: lining myself up to run the tangents, getting on the right side of the road for fluid stations, avoiding potholes and manholes, taking mile splits.

I passed mile 23 and entered Central Park. I'd fantasized about charging the park's hills. Now I just wanted the pain to stop.

I'm finishing my first marathon.

God, this hurts.

I'm going to finish.

I'm never doing this again.

The crowds are unbelievably loud.

This is so amazing.

I want to be done.

I ran down Central Park South along the edge of the park, and seeing the Columbus Circle Monument, lassoed it and reeled it in. The voices of the crowds along the park were so powerful, I imagined their shouts as a breeze pushing me forward. I ran closer to the curb so the enthusiasm of their cheers leapt into my muscles. So grateful was I for them, and so desperate to be done, I practically wept as I made a right onto West Drive and passed the 26-mile mark. The finish line came into view. *Oh thank God, finally.*

I ran the last 200 meters and passed over the finish. *It feels so good to stop.*

Margaret won in 2:24:21. Susan followed in second, and Ludmila finished sixth. I followed her, placing seventh in 2:26:58, having run the fastest debut by an American woman. It was the hardest race I'd ever run.

Ray took my arm as I processed the barriers I'd just pushed through. *Wow, I've done it.* We walked toward the exit, and spotted my family. I gave my mom, dad, and sister big hugs.

"How'd Terrence do?" I asked.

"He ran 2:21, not sure what place," my dad said.

"We're going to go to Ground Zero," my sister said.

"I'll do anything as long as it involves a taxi," I said, blowing them a kiss.

As I went through drug testing at a nearby hotel, Andrew rounded the corner onto West Drive and ran toward the finish line, crossing in 3:22. A volunteer draped a medal around his neck and a silver Mylar blanket around his shoulders.

Back at the hotel, I was wrecked. I lay on the bed not wanting to move. Andrew sat in the chair, head back, feet up. My family came and coaxed us out. We taxied to Ground Zero and walked around the large city block. The streets were crowded with people, many draped in marathon medals. Everyone was quiet. We looked at the chain-link fence covered in cards and flowers. Candles and stuffed animals lined sections of the sidewalk.

I reflected on how the marathon had brought the city together, how it had brought the world to New York at this moment. A sporting event in which thousands of people from different states and countries, all with their own motivation and dreams, had traversed 26.2 miles of the city in a demonstration of resiliency and love. There was a bigness to the marathon, a power to it, that was palpable. I could barely walk around the block, but I already felt it in myself. The marathon had opened a door into a new and big way to grow. The distance itself seemed like a whole new sport, a gateway to the progress that motivated me. The pain of the final miles began slipping away and turning into curiosity. What if I got in one more long run, or a longer long run, or maybe more fluids, could I run it faster? How would the distance affect cross-country and track? I didn't know. But after a good long rest, I looked forward to finding out.

14

HOW TO CHASE THE WORLD

Mammoth Lakes, California, 2002, 2003

Victory is not the defeat of competitors, but the conquest
of heights, the transport of discovery, the affirmation of
love and technique.

—ANDREA MEAD LAWRENCE

I didn't run for a month. Andrew and I took relaxing walks with
Aspen, and I read a lot. It was hard to imagine how my sore quads
and swollen calves would transform into new speed and power. The
marathon, it seemed, had torn my muscles apart and I was exhausted
just climbing stairs. Soon though, the soreness subsided and the
swelling disappeared. My legs took the stairs as if they required no
effort at all. I started hiking, exploring trails on Mammoth Mountain and climbing up to Valentine Lake in the Sherwin Range. My
body was rebuilding itself. I imagined thousands of tiny cells flood-
ing into my muscles, stitching together each muscle fiber, adding a
reinforcement beam so it was stronger. Adaptation, a process that
never ceased to amaze me.

Returning to running was gradual. Twenty minutes was challenging at first. Eventually, I was putting in an hour around Shady
Rest Park and I noticed my legs seemed more stable on the trails.
One morning I added strides at the end and was astounded by their
lightness and ease. By the time we started cross-country training in

January, I felt like a gazelle on the open plain—swift, light, and graceful. Due to snow in Mammoth, we were in the small town of Bishop, forty miles south, where the roads and fields were clear. During lappers at Millpond Park, my legs practically bounced off the grass. I didn't stumble or fade, didn't tire as easily. My concentration was also sharper. As I ran, I saw every pothole and rut of grass. It was as if my mind downshifted the repeat into slow motion, allowing me to maneuver across the rutted grass with great accuracy and speed.

I had believed the marathon would make me stronger, but feeling the effect was astounding. The physical power parlayed into a new fearlessness in training and racing in the shorter distances. What was a 4-mile tempo run or an 8K race after the suffer-fest of 26.2? I pushed the boundaries of my speed in training and competed at cross-country nationals in February that year with a greater willingness to suffer.

When racing, it was my nature to work to extend a lead. But after the marathon, my purpose changed. Competing became less about beating competitors and more about challenging my boundaries. I wanted to get myself to a place I hadn't gone before. I had never thought of myself as someone who was afraid of the pain of racing, but now as I charged down the field during a race, I was aware of the absence of any hesitation. The marathon had so altered my perception of suffering that there was no hurt holding me back in the shorter distances.

If the marathon taught me that I could endure, it also showed me how much more there was to learn. I could push. But how could I push more? How could I get more out of my body? I found the answer in our local paper, the *Mammoth Times*.

The *Times* wrote frequently about a resident named Andrea Mead Lawrence, a dedicated environmentalist who advocated for legislation to protect the area's natural habitat. Now seventy, her love for nature was born from skiing in Vermont, where she grew up. Andrea was a natural athlete and competed in the 1948 Winter Olympics in St. Moritz, Switzerland, at age fifteen. Four years later at the Games in Norway, at only nineteen years old, she won two gold medals in the slalom and giant slalom, becoming the first alpine skier to become a double gold medalist. How did a nineteen-year-old win Olympic gold in a sport that demanded mature athleticism? What governed her pursuits, and could it apply to my own striving? Intrigued, I picked up her book, *A Practice of Mountains*.

Andrea's writing was poetic and profound. What caught my attention was that she viewed skiing as a form of creative art. Like a painter, every brushstroke mattered. She didn't just point her skis downhill and go. She was analytical, thoughtful, and experimental, and it spoke to what I'd learned about running. Running's simplicity was beautiful yet deceptive. If you viewed it as simply putting one foot in front of the other, you missed the nuance and synergy of the movement that leads to greater power and speed.

In one passage, Andrea talked about the "creation" of speed. She used a skydiver as an example. He reached fast speeds by making his body position as aerodynamic as possible, and wore clothes that further streamlined his movement. His thrust through the air was not accidental, or "falling or gliding, but a conscious effort in which all the factors governing speed must work together."

She learned this herself. During a race in Switzerland in 1948, she pumped and leapt down the mountain, trying, as she wrote, "to soar." A friend told her that her spirit was right but her approach was wrong. In skiing, he said, friction creates speed. Thrust and engagement with the ground make it possible to achieve maximum speed, she wrote. She tried it. Pushing her skis into the mountain, she felt the mountain press back through her feet, and she was unexpectedly "infused with a strange ease." Her body weight combined with her balance and gravity's pull, which had until then felt like separate parts, now blended together to propel her into what she described as "harmonious motion."

I took this idea into running. Coach had corrected various aspects of my stride years ago and I became mindful again of each part of the running motion as I ran: pushing into the ground, knee driving through the air, arm motion creating a pendulum. I pushed into the ground creating a force that would launch me forward, much like a springboard. I gripped the earth with my foot to pull it through, which activated my hamstrings and glutes for more power. This worked particularly well in lappers, where I could feel my spikes engage the grass, and in return, feel the land push me up. The power it generated traveled through my legs, helping to drive my knees forward, which I also consciously did, but now with less effort. That action helped propel my arms, which I pumped harder to more greatly propel my legs. With just the right forward lean, my whole body acted as the force for the next step. With practice, each individual movement merged into one motion, creating a cycle of momentum.

I loved that Andrea enjoyed the small nuances of mastery. She was detailed and focused, yet joyful in her pursuit. She was having fun, even being creative, in her attempts at improvement, and her playfulness spoke to my own desire to enjoy the process. I slowed down my reading, studying each line to see if there was an idea I could use. I found it in her thoughts on "daring."

At the beginning of a chapter called "Danger and Daring," she asked herself what it took to confront the limits we place on our own courage. She went on to explore her own understanding of fear. As a young skier, she viewed fear for what it was—a recognition of danger—and countered it by relying on her skill and strength. Over time, her interpretation of the emotion changed: "I began to understand fear as a process through which I could extend the practice of my own daring. It was an opening . . . of possibility, desire, reward, and strength."

This is splendid. If you meet fear with courage, you blow past it and enter into the possibility that lay beyond. It occurred to me that in skiing there was actual danger in pushing limits. Barreling down a mountain at fifty miles per hour could kill you if you fell or hit a tree. But in running, daring myself into greater speed was risky only in the sense that the pace I launched might not be sustainable, or worse, that someone might catch up with me. There was no real danger. To reach greater speed, I needed to take greater risks, and the marathon had given me the fearlessness to do it.

The year before, at the Gate River Run 15K (9.32 miles) in Jacksonville, Florida, I'd won the race in 49:09. My training suggested I was ready to run faster, so this year I decided to go out at a pace that was beyond what my training suggested. I risked being caught if I was too bold. *Well,* I told myself, *don't let them catch you.*

The Gate River Run started downtown and made a wide city loop that crossed the St. Johns River twice. The gun fired and about a hundred elite men and women surged across the line. I was at the front of the women's race. I moved forward, conscious of linking together the parts of my stride—using the ground, driving my knees and arms—but not overthinking them. I tuned into the rhythm of the faster pace, and seeing if, with a conscious effort on the parts, I could thrust myself forward into greater speed and effort.

I chose not to wear a watch, so that the only thing governing my speed was the desire to push my limits. My breathing was heavy, but there was a rhythm to it that my stride matched and I focused on stepping into a faster rhythm as I pushed. The strain increased as the miles passed. I pictured the competition hunting me from behind, and let the fear of being caught motivate me to continue. I felt a tingle and fatigue in my legs, and my shoulders hunched a little. But I kept my mind on the effort, extending my stride and the reach of my arms forward and back as I ran to try to gain an inch of road.

When I got to the base of the final bridge, the route's only climb, I smiled at it and worked the gradual rise, trying to maintain the same fast footwork all the way to the crest. The bridge overlooked the Jacksonville skyline, and then dropped you back into town, and I used the descent to quicken my turnover. Managing the many turns toward the finish, I crossed the finish line, winning in 48:12. I'd shaved 57 seconds off my time and set a new American record in the 15K.

I was ecstatic. Daring to go beyond my training and putting all my attention into moving forward as fast as possible was a simple concept, yet the execution was powerful. It felt divine to be the creator of great momentum.

From Florida, I traveled to the Olympic Training Center in Chula Vista for a ten-day stretch of training, and then flew on to Dublin for the world cross-country championships. Worlds had always been an important race for me, a place to measure my progress against the best. This year, I was ready to finish in the top five. The goal had eluded me two years earlier. The year after, in the mud and mire of Ostend, Belgium, I started with the leaders—Paula, Gete, and the Kenyans—but was overrun by their strength and finished twelfth. Now I had another year of training that included the strength of the marathon and was confident I could do it.

The US team, Coach, and Ray arrived in Dublin to a light drizzle. The championships would be run on the grounds of Dublin's historic horse track, the Leopardstown Racecourse, and we went for a shakeout run the next day expecting the conditions to be marked by gnarly mud. The fields, though, were dry. Running the route, we noted that the grass had been freshly mowed, which made for better footing, and that the course was mostly flat. *This won't be a cross-country race. It's going to be a horse race.* So I pictured myself a Thoroughbred—a powerful, muscular figure charging around the circuit, mane blowing in the wind.

Race day, the team and I warmed up together, and got into the starting corral.

"On your marks."

The gun fired. About eighty women took off down the grass. I led a strong field of Kenyans and Ethiopians, and was surprised when the only competitor to get on my shoulder was Paula Radcliffe. I'd watched Paula from behind five years earlier at my first world cross-country championships as a professional. She was a tall runner, with a long torso and long legs. She had one of the jerkiest strides I'd ever seen. Her head bobbed and her arms swung. Watching her from behind back then, I thought she was surely in over her head. But she went on to win a silver medal that year and I was the one who faded to twenty-ninth. Running shoulder to shoulder next to her now, I recalled the strength I'd seen in the leaders of previous worlds. This time, I felt that power emanating from me.

The course was marked on both sides by multicolored pennant flags, making a closed-off circuit, and I charged through it, gripping my spikes into the grass and catapulting my body forward. I finished the first loop with a slight lead over Paula. As we moved through the second loop, Paula rejoined me at the front. I pressed into the turns, grabbed the next tangent, and could see while making each turn that Paula and I were pulling farther away from the others. There was a moment in past worlds when I felt myself slipping off the leaders. Here I felt only my own strength. By the time Paula and I moved through the third loop, I knew the route and took the tangents more fluidly. We moved into the final lap and I pressed. Paula and I ran stride for stride for much of the final lap, but as we closed in on the finish line, she launched a kick and pulled away, crossing first. I followed in second, elated. I'd wanted a top five and now I was the silver medalist.

Then I looked over at Paula. She was bent over, hands on her knees. *Wow, she's beat. I feel fantastic.*

As Ray and I walked across the grass to the grandstand buildings for drug testing, something gnawed at me: Why hadn't I reacted to Paula's kick? Why, if I felt fantastic, had I not responded?

The answer came on the plane ride home. I had gone to the starting line knowing I could run *with* the best in the world but not believing I could *beat* them. I had limited myself by setting a goal based on my competitors. It was a natural thing to do. A competitor's goal is to beat the competition. But I'd settled for achieving my goal instead of pushing toward my limit. It occurred to me that while we need a plan B to turn to when races aren't going well, we should also have a plan when our strength exceeds our expectations.

Back at the Olympic Training Center, I had two weeks to prepare for my next race, the Carlsbad 5,000, and I used the time to think about how I'd approach the race. I wanted the strength of my mind to match the power of my body. How could I do that? Andrea had dared me to greater speed, so I continued slowly digesting her book in between runs. One afternoon, I came across a passage in "Danger and Daring" about a training run she'd done in Sun Valley, Idaho, before the 1947 Olympic trials. Skiing alone, she barreled down the vast white slope of Mount Baldy unaware of her speed until she reached timberline. "There," she wrote:

> Trees sounded an alarm and I knew I was going faster than
> I had ever gone before. . . . It affected me profoundly to dis-
> cover that my peripheral vision informed my rate of speed.
> Like the course diagrams of the tryout races, this measure-
> ment acted as a restriction.

So she blocked out the trees. She focused her gaze on an "ever-receding line of sight" and extended herself to get there.

The pure focus of her pursuit struck me. Could narrowing my own line of sight bring me to faster speeds? *That's how I'll race Carlsbad*, I thought. No competitors, no watch, no limits. I'll extend myself into victory.

Andrew drove down from Mammoth the night before the race. In the morning, I did a slow 20-minute shakeout run from the hotel. When I got back, Andrew had the massage table ready. I hopped up and put my face in the cradle. He began kneading my hamstrings, but quickly lifted his hands. "Your legs are humming with energy," he said. "You're ready. There's nothing I need to do here."

I warmed up along Grand Avenue with the rest of the international field, but I was already blocking them out. Once on the line, I did a practice stride out and back and took my place. *Narrow your line of sight. Extend.*

I got out fast. Later, I heard that Lornah Kiplagat from Kenya was in front of me for the first 400 meters. I don't remember her at all. In fact, I don't remember any of the competitors. I looked up Grand Avenue to the first turn, a left, in the distance, and ran to it. I took the turn, then looked for the next target. A lamppost. I chased it, working to extend myself with each step out of the speed I was in and into a faster one.

The crowd along the oceanfront road was thick and rowdy, but the sound didn't register. I'd caught the lamppost and was now focused on reeling in the timing clock stationed at the first mile. It showed 4:45 for the mile as I passed. I was aware of the split but didn't absorb it. Pace for a runner can be like Andrea's trees, a limiter, so I paid no attention. Ahead was a U-turn around a median. I put my eye on the turn, surged into it, pressed out of it, and looked up for the next landmark.

I extended myself from point to point along the course, feeling the fluidity of my stride and motion. It seemed as if nothing could stop me, because nothing was stopping me. Not a questioning thought, a tight muscle, or a hesitant stride held me back. When you're well conditioned, when your breath and your legs are in sync, and when your mind is immersed only in the task at hand, there is nothing blocking your momentum.

Psychologists would say I was "in the zone" or in a state of "flow," a term coined by Mihaly Csikszentmihalyi to describe the hyperfocus that occurs when we're engaged in something difficult and purposeful. Many people describe flow as effortless. But a race was always an effort. Flow, to me, was the absence of resistance, when you push into a pace and find nothing in the way of your pursuit. It's movement in its most freeing form.

My second mile split was again 4:45. I took the second U-turn, found the next lamppost, and ran the final mile back toward the crowds. The spectators ahead, which were six to seven people deep, were visual bait. I let their cheers penetrate my concentration and egg me on. After the final turn, I locked my eyes on the finish line and kicked with all the turnover I could muster. By the end, I was running so fast, I actually stumbled a bit.

I won, crossing the finish line with my arms raised. My time was 14:54. I'd broken the world record held by Paula, a competitor whom, two weeks earlier, I hadn't considered beating.

Andrew and my family rushed over. Coach beamed. I caught my breath, then a television camera was on me. Ray called, excited, and congratulatory texts from Meb and Jen came in. Sharing the record with family and friends made it more special. My mind, though, was on the thrill of having pushed myself to a new level and could immediately see beyond it to the next. This was a positive mind at work, a mind that after six years of being steeped in belief knew that even a world record did not cap my potential, and amidst the celebration, I was already thinking about the next chase.

The combination of marathon strength and Andrea's ideas on daring was catapulting my physical and mental growth in the shorter distances into a new realm. Now I wanted to see how that growth could improve in the marathon. I got a taste of it in Chicago when I shaved five seconds off my time from New York. But I knew I could run faster. With cross-country in winter, track in summer, and the marathon in the spring or fall, the distances worked in concert over the course of the year to elevate me—just as speed, tempo, and long runs merged into greater fitness during the week. It was this interplay, this building that excited me.

The marathon goal that felt daring, the one that would motivate me to focus, was the American record held by Joan Benoit Samuelson. At the Chicago Marathon, Joan and I had been at a press conference together and at one point she had gestured to me and said, to my surprise and secret delight, that "if there is anyone capable of breaking my record, it's the girl right there."

To run under her record of 2:21:21, I'd need a fast course and good weather. Coach, Andrew, and I discussed my options and settled on the London Marathon, which offered a flat, fast course and the chance of cool temperatures. The goal excited me, so we chose not to wait and committed to London.

I now knew just how hard the marathon got at the end. So during long runs as I climbed the hills in Mammoth, I pushed harder in the final miles. My goal was to get to the fatigue, to experience it each time, so that I'd be stronger in the race itself, both physically and mentally. If I trained harder, the race would be easier. But only to a degree. If you're pushing, the race is always hard. The strength I developed came from not being afraid of the fatigue. Every cell in my body still shouted *I'm exhausted!* by the end of each long run. But my mind was quick to respond. *Yes, but you can still move forward.*

For London, with the goal of shaving more than 5 minutes off my time, I broadened my attention beyond the long run to the entire week, giving each aspect of my preparation the same attention. We fine-tuned everything. My body had responded well to 120-mile weeks, so I ran them consistently. The program also included more long runs of 20 to 22 miles. For New York, I'd run four quality workouts—long repeats, mile repeats, tempo runs, and long runs. Now we had dropped one for alternating between long intervals and mile repeats each week. The added recovery day enabled me to run the fast days faster and the longer days stronger.

I spent afternoons in the weight room at Snowcreek Athletic Club doing a strength program designed by Zach Weatherford, the strength and conditioning coach at the Olympic Training Center.

Zach was known for turning already strong athletes into power-houses of speed, strength, and agility. Soccer players became more agile under him, rowers more powerful, and sprinters more explosive. For my program, he'd mixed together free-weight exercises and plyo-metric drills in what he called super-sets, where I did one exercise right after the other. Over the last few months these had helped me develop more explosive strength and power. My particular focus for London was on the speed drills over a rope ladder. If I could lessen the amount of time my foot was on the ground with each foot strike, that would add up to significant savings over 26.2 miles.

What struck me at the end of my buildup was the same thing that amazed me when I first started training as a professional six years earlier. Conscious and thoughtful work balanced with equal attention to rest *worked*. I felt I had the fitness and the experience to run exponentially better.

During marathon training, I began rereading Andrea Mead Lawrence's book. It had inspired my mental approach to the 15K and 5K records and I was looking for another layer, a new interpretation that would help me run even faster. I was looking to build on the flow I'd produced in Carlsbad, where I'd repeatedly taken in visuals to draw out my speed. I took time to reflect on her passage about the "ever-receding line of sight." The idea made me think of a place that could never be reached, like a constant and continuous drive forward. In Carlsbad, my line of sight was broken, from lamppost to curb to tangent. I was returning to the Gate River Run 15K as part of my marathon training and wanted to narrow my focus to one vision to allow a more constant push. So I decided I would project an image of myself ahead of me in the race and chase her.

The next morning, I was out at the front of the women's field by the first mile, chasing a woman with blond hair that flew in the wind. She had a misty, ghostlike glow to her. Her stride was aggressive, smooth, and strong. There was no hesitation in her approach, just a constant push toward an unmarked line. As in Carlsbad, the world faded into the background. I wasn't aware of the neighborhoods or the fans on the course. I kept my gaze on the faster runner about ten strides ahead. She was taking the course with speed and fluidity. I tried matching her speed, extending myself in a constant effort toward her.

It was a primitive and wild feeling to be so internal in a public space. I knew I was reaching the limit of my physical capability, but it didn't feel like a limit. It was to me an expression of my physical, mental, and emotional self in the moment.

News reports would say I was on world-record pace at the 5-mile mark. I didn't see the pace clocks. My avatar and I were battling wind on the approach to the Hart Bridge over the St. Johns River. The wind gusts didn't seem to faze the figure ahead of me, so I matched her grace. I followed her lead, willing myself close enough to draft as we descended back into the city. After a few turns through parking lots and streets, the finish line lay ahead and we kicked in to break the tape.

My time of 47:15 was 57 seconds faster than my own American record.

I capped off London training with a 126-mile week. It had been a flawless buildup of speed and endurance and I felt strong and ready.

Three days before we were set to leave for Europe, I rose out of bed and could barely walk. "Andrew, my leg is jacked," I said, cupping my calf, already worried about what this meant for the marathon.

"What's going on?"

"I don't know. It's sensitive and nervy, the whole calf."

"What'd you do?"

"Nothing, it was fine yesterday."

"Let me look." He gently massaged and stretched my calf, feeling for the tightness. "It just feels locked up. Run super easy today and see if it loosens," he suggested.

But at practice, I had to stop after a few miles. "Coach, I can't run. I can barely walk. If this doesn't get better, I won't be able to race," I said.

"Don't panic," he said. "Take the rest of the day off." But I was panicked. The marathon, my God, was hard enough when you're 100 percent healthy. Coach must've seen my stricken face because he assured me it just needed a little rest.

Andrew and I went home and he massaged and stretched my hips, quads, and hamstrings to alleviate any potential tension coming from other areas.

Later that day, with a pack of frozen peas resting on my calf, I called my teammate Terrence and told him the news. "I don't think I can run," I said. He asked about the symptoms, if I'd pulled it the day before, or felt it coming on. No, nothing.

"Then it's in your head."

"Terrence," I said, slightly incredulous. "My calf really hurts. It's not an illusion."

He countered. "I believe there is pain there, but you've had a great buildup. Maybe you're scared your best won't be enough, but it is. You just need to get out of your own way."

I resisted the idea. I skipped the next day's tempo run. My calf didn't feel much better the following day, so I forwent the two-hour long run for an easy 30-minute run on the flat, smooth surface of Green Church Road. It still felt achy. Reflecting on Terrence's words, I remembered the dreams I'd had the night before the calf pain emerged. I was doing house chores, running errands, having conversations with friends, and kept falling short in each one, failing in some way.

My negotiating self stepped in. There were two choices: give in to the pain and play it safe, or look beyond the fear to the potential. So while Andrew worked aggressively on my glutes and hamstrings, I had a little talk with my calf. "You'll be fine after this massage, and you'll be able to accomplish what we need to in the next couple weeks. Then you can take some time off," I told it. "But please, pull yourself together so we can do this."

The pain was gone the next day. My mileage for that week was short: 58 instead of 70-plus. I flipped back through my training log at the other weeks of training where one solid week after the next stacked up. I put those weeks in my head, we packed our bags, and we flew to Europe.

Coach and Andrew and I rented side-by-side apartments in Teddington, twelve miles west of central London, for a couple of final workouts and my taper. We were across the street from Bushy Park, one of London's eight royal parks open to the public, where I ran each day. Some days, Andrew ran with me. Other days, he and Coach would stand together at the park's entrance or walk while I looped through the woods and fields on cinder trails and walking paths.

One morning, Andrew and I headed out for a run and were caught by the brisk air. The daffodils seemed more peeved than we were when snow flurries began falling, uncommon in London in April. It was a quiet, intimate way to taper, like a mini camp. Stripped of the needs of home—to walk the dog, tidy the house—the day was open to just run and rest. The race and my goal were always present in my mind, a companion giving the leisure days purpose. I took longer naps, we walked for coffee, dined early.

Once at the Tower Hotel a few days before the race, we met up with Ray, and I headed to the press conference and technical meeting. The press conference was more packed than usual, and there was a lot of buzz around Paula and Kenyan Catherine Ndereba. I'd seen Catherine intermittently at races since competing against her in Georgia early in my career. Since then, she'd become a dominant force in women's marathoning, winning both the Boston and

Chicago marathons. She earned the nickname "Catherine the Great" when she broke the marathon world record in 2001, two years earlier.

Paula's own marathon progress went beyond remarkable. She had run her first marathon just a year ago in London. When I'd first heard she was tackling the distance, my thought was that her stride wasn't efficient enough. Her jerky movements and toe-running style would expend too much energy over 26.2 miles. Then she tore off the line in London as if she were launching herself into an 8K cross-country race and held that aggressive style mile after mile. "She's tough," Coach said as we watched on television in amazement. She was defying everything we thought a marathoner should be. Then, just six months later, Paula broke Catherine's world record in the marathon at Chicago, running 2:17:18. Now, in her third marathon, she wanted to break her own record, and it was all reporters wanted to talk about.

Listening to her discuss how she was confident she could run faster because key workouts from training in Albuquerque, New Mexico, were her best to date, amazed me. I, too, used workouts as benchmarks for progress, but that she believed she was ready to improve on 2:17 seemed risky. The only question I remember answering at the press conference was whether I was going to go out with Paula. No.

The technical meeting also focused on her attempt. We were introduced to the pacesetters, who would take her, and anyone who wanted to run with them, through world-record pace. Another pace group had been established for athletes aiming to run under 2:20, a new benchmark for women. The first woman to break the barrier had done so only two years earlier, when Naoko Takahashi from Japan ran 2:19:46 at Berlin. Only two other women had run under 2:20, Paula and Catherine, and others were eager to try. *That's ambitious*, I thought.

It might have been tempting to run with the 2:20 group, but I had no desire. I didn't want to risk falling apart in the final stages of the race and miss the goal of the American record I'd been training all year to accomplish. My goal was a steady and even 5:22 per mile, which would dip me under Joan's time of 2:21:21. To run that, the day needed to unfold with precision, and on race morning, I approached my routine with attention to detail. At breakfast with Andrew, Coach, and Ray, I had two dry pieces of toast with a fried egg on each. As I ate, I thought of the food powering me later in the day. I drank two small cups of coffee, and as we sat there talking, I drank one more. In my room, I showered to feel fresh, and put on my uniform. Then I grabbed a black ballpoint pen and wrote the 5K splits I'd need to hit on my left arm. (A marathon is 42K.)

On the way out of the hotel, I stopped in the lobby bathroom before loading the bus. It was an unsuccessful stop. *There's still time.*

The London Marathon course was a point-to-point route that swept through the city, hugging the Thames River through much of it. It started south of the river in Greenwich Park and finished at the most famous royal park, St. James, near Buckingham Palace. When you saw Big Ben, the finish was close. At the start, I ducked into the elite athlete tent. It smelled like sweat and Tiger Balm. Constantina Diṭă from Romania was fixing her hair. Catherine was adjusting her glasses over her headband. Paula fussed with her Breathe Right strip. I jumped up and down, trying to jolt my system. With no luck, I headed out to the grass field to jog a little, which was out of my routine. Andrew followed.

"Are you nervous?"

"No. I haven't gone to the bathroom this morning."

"At all?"

"No."

"Do you want me to kick you in the stomach?"

"Funny."

A voice came over the loudspeaker. "Ten minutes to the start." We went back to the tent and elite athlete coordinator Glenn Latimer, a graying Brit with a bushy mustache, came in. "Sweats off, we're ready to go." I walked to the line wearing my jacket and pants since there was a slight chill in the air. At the last minute, I took them off, passed them over the fence to Andrew, and went to stand with my left foot on the line.

Paula launched a torrid pace from the start.

Wow, she's really going for it.

Constantina pushed to catch her. Kenyans Susan and Catherine followed.

I found my pace quickly and locked into it, while the women around me surged and settled to find their place in the large and competitive field. As the 5K fluid station approached, I aligned myself with the table, grabbed my bottle, and ran with it, sipping until it was empty, then tossed it to the side of the road.

About a mile later, I felt it. The urge to find a bathroom. I squeezed my cheeks. *Oh no.*

I ran, focusing on the feel of the pace, and the urge went away. Ahead of me were NYC Marathon champion Ludmila Petrova and two Ethiopians: Elfenesh Alemu, and the Olympic gold medalist in the 10,000, Derartu Tulu. I ran slowly but steadily to reel them in, wanting to benefit from the energy gains of the pack. We ran steady, picking off the miles in a comfortable rhythm that matched my goal pace.

The bathroom urge returned. *No, I'm in a pack with a marathon champ and gold medalist. This is too good.*

At 10K, I hit my watch and checked my split against my arm: 32:59. Twenty-five seconds ahead of schedule. *Okay, keep it steady. Enjoy the ride with these girls.*

We were closing in on Adriana Fernandez of Mexico. Feeling the drag of the women I was running with, I gradually edged away from Ludmila, Elfenesh, and Derartu and began to pull in Adriana. The record was my goal, but if my calculations were right, pulling ahead of the girls put me in fifth place, and working my way up the field offered great momentum.

The Tower Hotel was on the other side of the bridge and I amused myself by thinking I'd love to be sipping hot tea by the window with Andrew, listening to David Gray while watching the race go by.

Paula had been out of sight for a while. *Wonder if anyone who went with her is fading.*

I crossed the half in 1:10, under the record.

Stay locked into this pace.

The course followed the bend of the river, weaving into the Isle of Dogs, where we wove around the docks and the urge to go returned. *I'm going to soil my shorts.* I had the chills and looked around for a Porta John. *You have to stop!* But ahead, I could see the silhouettes of two other runners. I focused on them to stay engaged. *Close the gap. Benefit from their fading.*

At 30K (mile 18), my split was 1:40. *How did I lose so much time?* I calmed the initial panic by thinking that all the turns we'd just maneuvered slowed me a bit. The straightest section of the course was a couple of miles ahead. Pacing there would be easier to achieve. *Okay, if I can fall 20 seconds off pace, then I can get it back.*

But it was requiring more effort to maintain the pace as I made some final turns through the Docklands. Up ahead I recognized the women as Susan and Constantina. Both had faded back from Paula's lead. The petite figure of Susan was directly ahead. *Steady. You got her.*

I kept my eyes on Constantina for a while. Five foot three with a mass of blond hair pulled into a bun, she ran with a gritty stride, determined, though she took a turn gingerly rather than swiftly. *She's fatiguing.* We'd had dinner together a couple of nights earlier with Andrew and her agent. As I passed her, I said, "Let's go."

"Go, Deena," she replied.

Passing competitors was a shot of adrenaline, not to speed up, but to feel easier staying on pace. I was running alone, on a long, straight stretch. A headwind pushed against me. I pushed back, feeling I was strong enough to keep my rhythm. Organizers had painted a blue line down the road marking the straightest path to the finish. I followed it as if it were a train track, and saw myself move across it, trying to feel like I was gliding on a rail.

At mile 23, along the River Thames, I felt the fatigue. *A little more than 3 miles to go. You do tempo runs at altitude much longer than this. You can do this.*

With 2 miles to go, I had to go to the bathroom so badly. Lose the record with a pit stop, or risk pooping my shorts? *Come on, you've come this far; you're almost there.*

Big Ben came into view. The 40K split showed no room for error. *Why did I let it get this close? I have to get going.* I grabbed my final bottle knowing it just might be the energy I needed to finish stronger.

London had countdown signage for the final stretch, and with "1 mile to go" my watch read 2:16. I couldn't calculate adding another 5:22, but knew it was still too close to relax. I pushed harder, putting my head down and racing to pass the next sign.

With a half mile to go, I had no idea what to make of the numbers on my watch, so I took in the sea of cheering fans, the marble and gilded bronze statue of the Victoria Memorial, and the grand architecture of Buckingham Palace. I made a right turn down the Mall and toward the arched balloons of the finish. The finish clock was in view, and I charged toward it. It seemed to tick faster than my legs could move. Crossing the finish, I lost sight of the clock—2:21 and something.

Andrew, Coach, and Ray were near the finish area and charged toward me. "Five seconds!" Andrew shouted, his face coming close to mine.

"I missed it by five seconds?" I said.

Coach and Ray came and put their arms around me.

"No, no," they all said.

"You *got* it by five seconds."

I cupped my face to feel the sensation of my hands on my cheeks, feel the reality of the moment.

"That was perfect," Coach said. "I'm so proud of you."

"Paula set a new world record, 2:15:25," Andrew said.

Man, that's fast. "Wow."

Ray chimed in. "Catherine was second in 2:19:55. You all ran great."

I'd placed third in 2:21:16.

I was standing with the men, just before the awards ceremony, when Joan called. "I knew it would be you," she said. Thank you, Joan. Thank you for the call and giving me something so big to strive for.

Near the awards podium, I hugged and congratulated Catherine and Paula. Catherine stood with her daughter and agent. Paula was giving a BBC interview just a few steps away, so we kept quiet. I felt a strange mingling of emotions, both proud of accomplishing my goal yet inspired by both of them. My mind replayed Paula's aggressive start. She had powered through the marathon to a world record with her grind-from-the-gun tactics. I glanced at Catherine and saw in her poised posture the same steadiness with which she had run another sub-2:20. They both, in their own style, had dared to push the pace in the marathon. I felt a little thrill. I knew there was a faster marathon in me, and these women showed me I could push my own line of daring much further out.

15

RUNNING ON JOY

Training for the Olympic Marathon
Mammoth Lakes, California, 2004

Happiness is the joy we feel striving after our potential.

—SHAWN ACHOR

One night in early summer 2003, Andrew and I went for a hike around the earthquake fault, a big fissure in volcanic rock as wide as ten feet in some places. To get there, we walked through red fir and Jeffrey pine, playing hide-and-seek among the trees. I was easy to find because I couldn't keep from laughing. Andrew and Aspen were a stride behind me when I heard him unwrapping candy and I lunged back to grab a piece. He put his arms behind him, then, looking at me, slowly brought his fists forward. "Left or right?" I tapped the left hand and he opened it. Inside was a Lifesaver and a diamond ring.

I hadn't really thought about marriage, in part because I already felt his commitment, and because Andrew was four years younger than me, I didn't want him to feel pressured. But his proposal prompted me to look up from the moment we were in—not the hike, but a focus on running—to a broader future of life with the man I loved. I threw my arms around him and said, "Of course I'll marry you."

We planned a September wedding in Kerry's Meadow in town beneath the limestone and marble formation of Mammoth Rock. Andrew and I stood facing each other underneath an arch of white roses. I reached for his hand. "Can you believe all these people are here for us?" I whispered, glancing at the rows of friends, family, and teammates. Later, my dad would give a funny toast saying he was not losing a daughter but gaining . . . a massage therapist. Coach would follow with grand words of how he'd worried Andrew would distract me from running, but that he was, in fact, the medal I was chasing. Facing Andrew, I felt rooted and firm, grounded and secure as a person and among a wide, loving community.

"We've got an Olympic year coming up," Coach said one afternoon in early January 2004. "Let's make a plan." Andrew, Coach, and I sat in a booth at the Base Camp Café to discuss the year ahead. I told Coach exactly what I wanted: to run cross-country, then clock a fast 10,000 in Athens. "There's no guarantee of fast times in the Olympics," Coach said, pointing out that the Games were often tactical and Athens would be hot. "What about the marathon?"

I looked at him. I hadn't thought about the marathon. To me it was a spring and fall event, not summer. I also felt I hadn't run the 10,000 to my potential and wanted the chance to do it.

Coach leaned back in the booth. "What's the goal of running in the Olympics?" he asked.

"To medal," I said.

"Okay, to finish in the top three in the 10,000, you'd have to run a closing lap of 60 seconds, which even on a good day would be unlikely," he said. "The fastest women's Olympic marathon was run in 2:23. Your London time was two minutes faster than that."

I could feel Andrew getting excited next to me. He followed the sport, kept records of my marathon splits, and printed out lists of athletes' times and other data, comparing, looking, thinking. He shuffled through some papers and pulled out a list of the world's all-time fastest marathons. He laid it on the table. "Out of the women likely to compete," he said, pointing to names on the list, "you have the fourth-fastest time." Paula Radcliffe, 2:15; Catherine Ndereba, 2:18; Margaret Okayo of Kenya, 2:20; and me, 2:21.

There it was in black-and-white. I had a chance to medal in the Olympic Games. A buzz of excitement pulsed through me and I got fidgety in my seat. "Great," I said, breaking into a smile. "Let's run the marathon."

The Olympic marathon trials were in St. Louis, Missouri, in early April. My buildup was solid, but not aggressive. Just enough, I thought, to be fit enough to win the race and move on to training for Athens. Race morning, Blake Russell, a strong contender for the team, took the lead. I held back. My plan was to expend as little energy as possible and take over the lead before the finish. Just before the half, a rock stuck to the bottom of my shoe and it disrupted my stride. After a few attempts at shaking it loose, I finally sat on the curb and pried it out. Back in the race, I worried I'd lost too much time to catch Blake, and picked up the pace, gaining ground in mile 15 and finally passing her for the lead in mile 17. At mile 21, my legs had no spring or giveback and my pace slowed. I climbed the hill at mile 24 feeling like I was slipping backward. I felt vulnerable, knowing I didn't have it in me to respond to a challenge. Then, I heard the sounds of rapid footsteps. Colleen De Reuck, a South African now competing for the United States, flew past with the speed of a sprinter.

I ran the rest of the race scared I wouldn't make the team, but I also ran guiltily. I'd gone through the motions of training without applying the mental focus and had taken winning and making the team for granted. Race week, I'd prioritized media and sponsor events over final preparations, was on my feet too much, and hadn't paid attention to tapering, hydration, and nutrition. As a result, I'd started the race underfed and underrested.

I cringed. *Complacency had risked everything.*

I held on for the last two miles and crossed the finish line in second, feeling lucky, and immediately committed to getting it right. Nothing can slip through the cracks. Focus matters. Details add up. *That's how I'll prepare for Athens.* I congratulated Colleen on her win, then we turned to cheer for Jen Rhines as she claimed the final spot on the team.

A month later, the three of us met at the Olympic Training Center in Chula Vista along with the men's marathon team: Alan Culpepper, Meb Keflezighi, and Dan Browne. Coach, Andrew, and other coaches and spouses attended, too. In order to give the US the best chance to medal in Athens, the Olympic Training Center hosted a three-day marathon summit. The summit represented years of research on the factors that influence performance by two Ph.D. physiologists, David Martin, a researcher at Georgia State University, and Randy Wilber, a senior physiologist for the US Olympic Committee.

We sat in the conference room on the side of the track and Dr. Martin summed up the challenge on the first day. "The competition will be tough," he said, "but you'll face a harder foe in the three H's: heat, humidity, and hills." Dr. Martin was tall, with messy hair and the demeanor of a mad scientist in his element. His voice was soft and raspy and he spoke with the enthusiasm of someone fascinated by nuance.

He started by introducing Athens, a sprawling ancient city of white buildings, distant hills, and pockets of green. We'd be running on the world's most historic marathon course, the same one used by runners in the first modern Olympic Games held in Greece in 1896. The route began in the small town of Marathon and traveled west toward the city, finishing in the open, white-marble stadium in the heart of downtown.

Dr. Martin's intent was to show the area's abundant sunshine and point out that "radiant energy abounds," meaning that heat would be collected and released off buildings surrounding the course and from the pavement on which we'd be running. "It's a guarantee that Athens in August will be hot," he said.

He went on to detail the challenge of heat stress. During exercise, metabolism increases and we produce our own heat, which is why we feel warm even running in cold weather. The body releases heat through the skin as sweat, and as it evaporates, heat dissipates and our core body temperature remains low enough for optimal function. A cool environment helps keep core body temperatures low, which is why 50 degrees is considered ideal conditions for the marathon. A hot environment elevates core body temperature, forcing the body to work harder to prevent heat from building.

Temperature, though, is only one factor. Humidity acts as a shield of sorts. The moisture traps heat in the body and prevents evaporation, thus hampering the body's cooling system. Pace also comes into play. The faster we run, the more heat we produce. Heat, humidity, and pace all elevate core body temperature. The athlete's challenge, then, is to run at a pace that allows the body to release enough heat to avoid overheating.

That's what happened to Gabriela Andersen-Schiess, the runner who suffered heat exhaustion in the 1984 Olympic Marathon. Dr. Martin showed a slide of her on the track, her face drawn and her body leaning to the left. The temperature that day rose into the eighties and her pace exceeded her body's ability to release heat under those conditions. Her core body temperature rose, causing her to slow to a walk in the final lap on the track and stagger across the finish. Seeing that image of her projected on the wall, I was reminded of why I'd avoided the marathon in the first place.

Dr. Martin didn't shy away from saying that as humans we live "precariously close to our thermal death point." But the rest of his presentation evoked the grandness of the challenge, the amazing interplay of human function and environment, how we could control nothing, yet prepare for everything. "You can learn," he said with clear relish, "to beat the heat."

He began laying out the primary methods of succeeding in hot conditions: (1) Acclimatize; train the body to handle heat. (2) Increase fluid intake, since sweat evaporation is the primary means of cooling; if the body cannot sweat, it loses its ability to cool itself. (3) Get fit; the fitter you are, the more efficient the body's cooling system.

Which brought us to the third H: hills. Dr. Wilber, or Randy, as he preferred to be called, had flown to Athens to meet with the organizers and spent a day walking the entire course with a video camera, capturing each undulation, and handing us our own copies on DVDs so we could become intimate with the terrain. "Out of the town of Marathon, the first 5K is a little downhill and flat, ideal for an easy start," he said. But just before 10K, the climbing began and continued for 13 miles, though there were periods of relief. The hills were subtle at first, he said, with the hardest climbs between 20 and 25K. Another steep section led to mile 19, followed by the seven-mile descent into the city. Coach leaned over to Andrew and me and said, "If there is anything we have an abundance of in Mammoth, it's hills."

On the third day, we sat with folders stuffed with handouts, and Dr. Martin stood at the front of the room. "We've given you a lot of information," he said, smiling and with an air of anticipation for what lay ahead. "Adopt as much as you can, but if you leave with only one bit of advice, let it be this: Go home and get supremely fit."

Back in Mammoth, Coach, Andrew, and I identified precisely how to implement the advice. We started with the long run, addressing all the challenges we'd face in Athens. To prepare for the heat, I needed to train in the heat. Mammoth in the summer could get into the eighties, but the climate was dry. Randy had recommended wearing white in the race to reflect the heat. So to create a more hot and humid environment while training, I'd wear black leggings, a black long-sleeve shirt, and a black cap to draw the heat to me.

For the hills, we wanted to do more than train for the climbs; we wanted to prepare for the precise timing of the elevation changes in the race, ideally on a sun-exposed route. Coach studied our running routes and strung together roads that mimicked the timing of Athens's hills. I'd begin at a park in Mammoth with a slight downhill for 5 miles on Sherwin Creek Road. Across Highway 395, I'd roll through the middle miles on Hot Creek Road, feeling the beginning of Athens's hills. A left over the river and up Antelope Springs Road was where the real climbing began: 7 miles on an undulating stretch that eventually rose steeply out of the valley until mile 19—the same as Athens's final climb. Over the hill was a long descent, as if I were dropping into the ancient city, that allowed me to extend the run from 20 to 23 miles. I'd run the route every Sunday for ten weeks before leaving for Athens, learning to better pace the first half so I'd be strong in the hills.

Heat, humidity, and hills would require more fluids and more mid-race carbohydrates, but how much? Too little would leave me depleted. Too much could weigh me down and lead to stomach problems. Before the first long run, Coach put down a bathroom scale in the parking lot and weighed me. As I ran, I drank the usual four ounces of Cytomax every 5K. At the finish, Coach put the bathroom scale on the side of the road, and I hopped on. The goal was no weight loss, indicating enough fluids had been ingested to offset what was lost sweating. I'd lost weight. I'd also felt tired and sluggish at the end, so on the next long run, we doubled my fluids to eight ounces every 5K, and used more powder to increase the carbohydrate concentration. Eight ounces trained my stomach to handle more fluid and absorb more calories. If I sensed it was too much, I could stop drinking. Coach weighed me for two more long runs. I lost no weight and we stuck with the eight-ounce routine.

Coach and I then looked at ways to build supreme fitness. I was already hitting 120 to 130 miles a week during marathon training, so I didn't need more mileage, but we needed to maximize that mileage. We accomplished that in multiple ways. First, Coach added a second long run of 20 miles on Wednesdays. Then, we kicked up my training paces a notch to target a 2:20 marathon. I wouldn't run that fast under hot conditions, but we knew it would take that level of fitness to medal. Next, we moved repeat workouts to Lake Mary at 9,000 feet for a better altitude effect.

Finally, to ensure I would be challenged in every workout, we hired three men to pace me. My teammate Matt Downin, a University of Wisconsin grad, put the word out to recent graduates from his alma mater, and a few weeks later, Colin Steele and Joe Eckerly, along with Derek Tate from Oklahoma State—all 14-minute 5K guys—were pacing alongside me.

They were a formidable crew. Colin was twenty-two, skinny, and blushed easily. Joe, twenty-three, was stalky in appearance and reckless in practice, giving his all until he fell apart. Derek was the oldest at twenty-four. He was using the summer to build mileage before joining the Hansons-Brooks elite team in the fall.

The men trained with me daily. With Coach driving the van and detailing workouts, Andrew helped orchestrate when and where the men would tag team to push me. Colin, Joe, and Derek jumped in and out of the van like a relay team to cover the mileage, willingly submitting to the playful competition that fed my drive. I studied the men for signs of fatigue—Joe's upper lip peeled back, Colin leaned slightly forward, Derek's head tilted sideways—and tried to break them. They pushed back, trying to one-step me. We finished most workouts with our hands on our knees.

The men all had strong running résumés and I'd anticipated they'd continue to push me in workouts. What I hadn't expected was how committed and positive they'd be. Once, at the end of a 130-mile week, Joe and I were climbing Antelope Springs Road in the hot sun. I was overheated, fatigued. Coach passed in the van and double-tapped the door with his hand to encourage us. I responded by saying, "I can't do this." Joe didn't miss a beat. "Me neither," he said, taking a breath as he pushed up the hill, "but we are." Derek once put his hand on my back going up a hill, to keep my momentum going. On a brutally windy day, when I wanted to forget the whole workout on Green Church Road, Joe and Derek strode out a few steps and formed a wall in front of me, taking the full force of Mother Nature's fury.

Training had never been more engaging and the work more fun and collaborative. After long runs, Andrew cooked us French toast piled high with fresh berries. Some evenings, I cooked lasagna or grilled burgers for everyone. We sat around our dining-room table. Coach told the men his stories about the Tarahumara, Juma Ikangaa, and other runners. The men swapped tales of the struggle of the day, while Andrew cracked silly jokes. We retired early.

We were a small team working toward a common goal of earning a medal for our country. Life was simple, it felt purposeful, and I was at my happiest. I was aware on some level that joy was at the heart of the process, making it work. The more enjoyable the experience, the more effort we all put into it, and the greater the satisfaction. We were throwing more mileage and intensity at my body, and it took it. More than took it, my body thrived. I woke each morning feeling like "Let's go!" There was a lightness in my stride and a fierceness in my limbs. To train to earn an Olympic medal is to push your body to its edge. Yet I did not feel I was moving toward the edge. I felt like I was climbing toward a peak that had no limit.

Indian researchers investigating the "biochemistry of belief"—a phrase I love because it captures the mind-body connection so precisely—wrote that "each and every tiny cell in our body is perfectly and absolutely *aware* of our thoughts, feelings, and of course, our beliefs. . . . If you believe you are fragile, the biochemistry of your body unquestionably obeys and manifests it. If you believe you are tough, irrespective of your weight and bone density, your body undeniably mirrors it." The body experiences joy at the cellular level. Satisfaction, gratitude, and other positive emotions keep stress hormones at bay. Social connections and purpose are like "nutrients for the human body," another researcher wrote. I couldn't have told you that then, but I certainly felt it.

Training for Athens meant leaving no stone unturned, no detail left to chance. I wanted to stand on the starting line knowing I had done everything possible to succeed. Andrew and I continued our routine of morning stretches, post-workout ice baths, and massages. I'd also cleared my calendar of all other commitments, cut back on wine and sweets, and bumped up my fruits and vegetables to increase my electrolyte intake.

I worked to nail the time goal of each workout by using all the mental tools I'd gathered over the years. In the quiet of morning, on the massage table with Andrew prepping me, I reminded myself of the purpose of the workout ahead and set an intention of staying engaged in the workout and reveling in the process. After workouts, I identified the positive aspects of the session and was amazed at the length of my mental list.

I also found creative ways to stay focused and positive. In the middle of the workout when one of the men cried "mercy" and another hopped out of the van to join me, I emulated his fresh stride, adding a little bounce to my step and mentally resetting by telling myself I, too, was just starting. Sometimes I felt better simply by relishing the idea that it took three men to match my work. When the road ahead appeared long, I took inspiration from the mountains that stood over us.

Two-mile repeats around Lake Mary proved to be a long burn. The uptick from 7,000 to 9,000 feet, plus doubling the distance, left me aching with effort. *Just ten minutes of hard running,* I'd tell myself. *That's not too much to ask.* Sometimes, mid-repeat, I'd remind myself that the fatigue was the feeling of progress.

I knew what pushed me—the thrill of being chased—and I created those situations as much as possible. On Tuesdays, when Meb was also running repeats at Lake Mary, I would cut through a trail in the final half mile, along with whoever was pacing me, and we'd emerge just ahead of him. Back on the loop, I turned to stick my tongue out at Meb as I worked hard to fend him off, the spirit of the chase recharging both of us. Once, at the end of a long run, I was climbing a hill through the forest and heard the sound of gravel crunching behind me. It was Coach in the van. I pretended he was a competitor about to catch me and accelerated, running the final 2-mile stretch faster than the week before. At the 20-mile tree, I did a little victory jig and turned to see Coach laughing in the driver's seat.

Mostly on long runs, though, I pictured myself in Athens. Colin and Derek usually guided me through the first half of long runs, pacing me with their steady rhythm and sophomoric humor (it's hard to run fast when you're laughing). Then Joe took me through the big climb. Halfway up the hill, the road curved north and the valley appeared below. This was the point when Coach usually pulled up alongside us, thrust his arm to the air, and shouted, "This is just like Athens!" It cracked me up because despite the hills, the scene was nothing like Athens. Mammoth was at elevation, the heat was dry, and we were on dirt roads in the morning. The race would be at sea level, in humid heat, on paved city roads in the evening. Still, as soon as Coach shouted "Athens!" I saw the long avenues, big climbs, and barren strip malls. Sometimes I pictured myself entering the ancient marble-white stadium and earning a medal. Mostly, though, the scene was of me running steadily in the middle miles. I saw myself maintaining form and focus, felt the sun on my shoulders, the dryness in my mouth, and the fatigue and heaviness of the heat. Then came the actual real sensation of cooling fluids on the back of my throat when Coach handed me my water bottle.

Dr. Martin had given us a handout on the history of the marathon, and one evening I read through the story of how it all began. In 490 BCE, the Persians were on a tear. They pillaged towns on the Greek Islands and pulled up on the shore of the Bay of Marathon to prepare to attack the city-state of Athens twenty-five miles away. The Greeks were greatly outnumbered and dispatched a messenger to Sparta to request backup. Messengers ran on foot and the running soldier, Pheidippides, took off, covering the 150 miles in about thirty hours. He returned with disappointing news. The Spartans were unavailable until the conclusion of a religious festival a few weeks away. Unable to wait, the Greek general Miltiades launched a surprise attack at Marathon, a brilliant move that sent the Persian army fleeing.

Legend says the general dispatched Pheidippides again, this time to bring news of victory to the king in Athens. In full armor, in the midday heat of a Mediterranean summer, Pheidippides ran, traveling across the sunbaked coast, up and over rocky hills to the center of Athens. When he arrived, he burst through the door of the state house and shouted a single word, *"Neikhkamen!"*—We have won!—then collapsed and died.

I found the strength and will of Pheidippides to carry out his duties heroic and inspiring. A French professor named Michel Bréal was also moved. He read a poem about the runner's epic journey and loved it so much that in 1894, when the French were trying to convince the Greeks to revive the Olympic Games, Bréal suggested they honor Greek history by adding a distance race from the town of Marathon to Athens. The Greeks loved the idea and the modern Olympic Games—and the marathon—were born.

On April 10, 1896, four days into the Games, seventeen men set off from the dusty town of Marathon. Most of the men were sprinters and went out too fast. But Spyridon Louis held back. Spyridon was a twenty-three-year-old Greek water carrier and a late entrant to the race. He had spent much of his youth running back and forth from his village six miles away from Athens to help his family deliver water. In the race, Spyridon ran with patience and confidence.

He trailed the leaders at the half, but proclaimed to the crowd as he passed that he would win. Knowing the course, I could see in my mind a black-and-white image of an assured Spyridon running. He was climbing, slowly picking off runners as he moved into the twentieth mile. I laughed when I read that he refreshed himself with half an orange and a shot of cognac, courtesy of his girlfriend and future father-in-law. I would have preferred slightly chilled white wine. At mile 22, he made his move. He shot past a fading Edwin Flack of Australia to take the lead and flew down the road, trailed by cheering children. A course monitor on horseback galloped ahead and entered the Panathenaic Stadium announcing that a Greek was in the lead. As word spread, the crowd of 100,000 rose to its feet and cheered when Spyridon appeared on the track and pushed on to the finish, winning the marathon.

Understanding the history connected me more closely to the distance. It gave the marathon greater beauty and I trained with its spirit in me. The race itself would be a pilgrimage, a journey over land where the marathon and the Olympics were born. I felt grateful to Pheidippides and Spyridon, but also to the pioneers of women's marathoning, Bobbi Gibb, Kathrine Switzer, and Joan Benoit Samuelson. Bobbi jumped into the Boston Marathon in 1966, when women were barred from running. Kathrine did the same the following year when Jock Semple, the race director, famously tried to pull her off the course. Despite his efforts, she finished the race, and images of the scuffle catapulted the limits placed on women runners into the national spotlight. Eventually that situation, along with the efforts of Kathrine and other activists, led to the women's first Olympic marathon in 1984.

Sometimes as I ran, I saw Joan enter the L.A. stadium and wave her white hat, or Kathrine courageously running after being attacked. Bobbi's long ponytail came to mind, or the image of a young Greek runner entering the ancient stadium. There was a long line of history and it felt like I was running each day with their influence.

In early August, Andrew, Coach, and I flew to Crete, where the

US track and field team spent sixteen days acclimatizing to the heat and time change. The marathoners ran at 6:00 p.m., the race's starting time, in order to get our bodies used to a hard effort in the evening. Andrew rented an old rickety bike and pedaled alongside us, everyone's water bottles weighing down his backpack. Sweat dripped off his nose as he put 170 pounds of torque on the pedals, attempting to climb the hills wearing flip-flops. Each workout I pictured myself in the race running steadily toward a medal, sweat flying off my fingertips. Every evening, after a light massage, we swam in the Mediterranean before sitting down to dinner, the fresh local cuisine nurturing the work.

The night before we left for Athens, Andrew and I had dinner on the oceanfront terrace with Coach and Caroline. The evening was warm and we took in the sound of waves crashing on the beach. I was filled with a well of gratitude for all the people who had brought me to this moment. For Coach and Andrew, who had created the buzz of potential for a medal in our meeting, and the physiologists who over a few days had given us knowledge they'd gathered over a lifetime. My training partners' commitment to the goal touched me. Everyone gave so much so willingly and I would race with the same generosity.

The marathon was a couple of days away and I felt fulfilled in a way I never had before a race. The summer had led to big gains physically and mentally, but I was elevated in a permanent way. There was a feeling of strength that wasn't just part of the marathon buildup, it was part of me. It seemed fitting to be going into the games as Deena Kastor, as if my evolution from lost college runner to world-class athlete had been somehow formalized. I found it difficult to find the words to thank Coach. "This summer was incredible," I said, "Thank you." We smiled. I told Coach that I felt so transformed that while I knew earning a medal was the goal, it almost no longer mattered.

Of course, I still intended to snag it.

16

GO! GO!

Olympic Marathon, Athens, Greece, 2004

Like wine thro' clay, Joy in his blood bursting his heart,
he died—the bliss!

—ROBERT BROWNING, "PHEIDIPPIDES"

On the athlete bus to the start, we drove on the actual racecourse, Route 83, Marathon Avenue. Most of the women had their heads back, their eyes closed, dipping into the quiet space athletes go to before competition. I stared out the window and watched the heat radiating off the pavement, the cement buildings, the dirt fields, and the rooftops of the police cars escorting the bus. The tightest squiggles seemed to hover over the road's freshly laid blacktop. I joked to Julia Emmons, the US Olympic assistant coach, that I would have taken potholes over fresh, heat-emitting asphalt. She pointed to the olive trees the Greeks had planted for shade. They were three feet tall.

The highway road narrowed as we approached the town of Marathon. Marathon, for all its fame, didn't match the hype in my head.

I thought there'd be a big gold-plated sign arcing across the road that read: THE EPIC BATTLE OF MARATHON, or something, but it really was just a sleepy village. The streets were deserted. The only sign of life was a soda shop with a lit Coca-Cola sign in the window.

Out front, three Greek men sipped espresso and smoked, their bellies sticking out beneath white T-shirts. They waved as the bus went by.

The bus looped around the soda shop and onto Marathon Avenue, stopping in front of what looked like a bunker—a short, cement building. I grabbed my things and walked down the aisle. As I passed the driver's seat, I looked at the dashboard thermometer. It was flashing between 38° Celsius and 101° Fahrenheit. I gasped. *I trained for heat, but not triple digits.* Earlier that day, 10,000-meter runner Abdi Abdirahman was helping me lug an ice chest carrying our team's ice vests to the bus. He couldn't get over the heat. "People are going to die out there," he said, sweat glistening on his face. I thought he was being a bit dramatic. It was warm, but it didn't feel that hot. Now, walking from the air-conditioned bus to the outside, the rush of ovenlike air was suffocating.

I called Andrew.

"Go out slooooooowly," he said, dragging out the adverb for emphasis. That was the plan, but I modified it on the spot: I'd go slower than slowly. I tucked my phone into my bag and ran to catch up with Julia, Jen, and Colleen, as well as our FBI agents (all US marathoners had one because of the Iraqi war and the risk of being on an exposed course). We walked on the narrow path, and the glare of a white-hot sun pressed heavily against my eyes. I decided a conservative start and fluids were the only things that would save me from sharing the same fate as Pheidippides.

A set of steep stairs led us down into a small locker room, part of the municipal stadium. The air was cool. Jen, Colleen, and I found a quiet corner, put on our ice vests, and slid down to the cement floor. I hugged the vest to my body, staring outside, surprised to see the other women jogging back and forth in the sun. We sat quietly, talking a little about the beauty of Crete and the leisure feel of our camp setup there. Jen and Colleen left a little while later to do a short warm-up. I sat holding my racing flats in my hands and reflected on all the workouts I'd done in those shoes until the announcer called us to the line.

The start was staged just outside the locker room on a wide cement lot. After the huge starts of 30,000 runners in Chicago, New York, and London, lining up with just eighty-two women felt anticlimactic. We stood three deep. I remember other women yawning, taking deep breaths, clear signs of easing anxiety. I felt very calm. On the starting line of most races, there's always that little bit of anxiousness that you won't meet your goal. You wish for one more long run or magical speed session to boost your confidence, or you worry about uncontrollable things—a blister, a bathroom break. Athens was the only race when the hint of fear was absent for me. While it was hot, I could feel the temperature had already dropped, and at 6:00 p.m., I knew the worst of it was over. I trusted my plan: a slow start, then start picking off women. I also felt like I had privileged information: I knew the course intimately even though it would be my first time running it. I'd seen every turn and hill, I knew its rich history.

Music played out of a single speaker. A helicopter flew overhead. An official signaled the start was near, then the pistol sounded and we, along with a few media trucks leading the way, were off.

Run your own race.

The pack ran across the lot between cement barriers and onto Marathon Avenue. I stayed near the middle, off the leaders, to avoid being pulled into a fast start. Spectators lined the roadside, cheering and ringing cowbells. The course had few turns, but the first came a few miles in, a left that would take us around the Tomb of Marathon, the site of the battle and now a burial ground for Athenian soldiers who fell there. I put my eye on the turn and ran the tangent as closely as possible without jostling for it. My goal was to stay as relaxed as possible, to find the balance between the shortest line without wasting energy on unnecessary moves. We followed the road, running around the tomb, a mound of dirt and grass to our far right. I thought about the Athenians' surprising win, and Spyridon's unexpected victory, and felt a harmony with the course's history.

At 5K, I grabbed my bottle and sipped the fluid, knowing it was the hydration and calories I'd need later in the race. A sponge station appeared and I squeezed water on my neck and wrists. Trying to disengage from actually racing so early in the race, I remained slow and passed the time calculating the amount of fluid I'd consume over the course of the race—eight ounces times eight bottles, plus water, about seventy ounces.

By the time I grabbed my bottle at 10K, the hills began. *Here they come.*

The road ahead was long enough that I could see the leaders. *All the players are there. Paula. Catherine. Her arm carriage is so tight, distinct. The Japanese look strong. Rumor is they're well prepared.*

I felt a weight, a heaviness at my back, and glanced to see a long line of girls strung out behind me. *I don't belong back here. I belong up there.* I took a small step to the left and made a minuscule increase in pace, shaking the women and feeling immediately lighter.

A Moroccan runner pulled off the side of the road and bent over. It was only 10K, too early for puking. *I don't want to end up like that. Okay, hold back.*

Up ahead, Paula had moved to the far left, avoiding the pack, the tangents, the crowds. Catherine, Margaret, and the Japanese were all pulling farther ahead.

You need to pick it up.

But if I pick it up, I could end up like these other girls, dropping off like flies.

You're thinking too much about the heat. Forget the heat. Focus on staying cool instead. Fluids and sponges.

I ran steady, encouraging myself to drink my fluids despite their having been warmed by the sun, and squeezing water from sponges on my wrists and neck.

I crossed the half and looked up. The leaders were no longer in sight. *Shit, I better get going.* Other women's strides were already slack, a reminder of the draining effect of the heat. Overheating makes you feel flushed, hot, and heavy. But I felt none of that, I felt fantastic. *Pick it up then.* I inched up my pace, pushing gently on the hill. Adrenaline rushed in as I passed competitors and saw some of the best runners in the world coming back to me.

"You're in twelfth place!"

The information came from a tall, overdressed man in slacks and a utility vest on the sidelines, Jen's FBI agent. Unlike pro cyclists, who communicate with coaches via earbuds, and ultrarunners, who learn about competitors through their crews, marathoners are on their own during competition. Your understanding of the race is based solely on what you can see and trusting in the information coming from the spectators. Knowing my place gave me a focus and I began counting down. *Eleven.* Italy. *Ten.* China. *Nine.* Russia.

I rolled through the hills, steadily climbing, and heard Coach shouting, "Just like Athens!" mid–long run. I'd been right, the two were not alike. Mammoth was more punishing, the hills steeper, the climbs longer. I'd overprepared.

The possibility that I might not medal was there, but I never allowed it to become a thought. I just ran. I shifted between hunting women and taking in fluids. Sometimes, I listened to the tapping of my racing flats on the pavement. Barely audible over the cheering from the sidelines, the tap was light and fast, and I ran enjoying the rhythm. I crested a steep hill, ran down the gradual descent, and seeing no one ahead to catch, felt an urgency.

I'm running out of real estate.

I entered a tunnel, tossed my glasses to the side of the road and emerged, hammering the pace.

I passed Naoko Sakamoto from Japan and moved into seventh. I passed Asha Gigi from Ethiopia for sixth. I overtook a Serbian runner, then another Japanese runner, which put me in fourth. One more.

As I approached the twenty-fifth mile, lights lit the road, the crowds grew rowdier, and I spotted the outline of a small runner ahead. I watched her from behind. She stumbled a little and I knew she was suffering. More quickly than I thought possible, the red, green, and yellow uniform of Ethiopia's Elfenesh Alemu came into view. Her feet were overpronating and there was a slight caving in at her knees. *This is your move. Make it a decisive one.* I passed swiftly, with perfect form, tucking in my chin, dropping my shoulders, and holding my breath. I kept my peripheral gaze open to see if she'd go with me, but she was fatigued and had no response.

The lights of the stadium ahead were bright.

"You're in fourth!"

Fourth?!

I wondered briefly if Elfenesh was right behind me and the spectator was talking to her, but she wasn't.

Had I miscounted? Is he right?

Just keep going.

Up ahead, the motorcade and the leader turned left into the stadium. Seconds later, Catherine veered left and disappeared into the lights. I made the turn shortly thereafter and entered the stadium. A roar from the crowd let me know I was in third but I couldn't fully believe it without confirmation. The announcer spoke first in Greek, then in French. Absurdly, I thought that if I'd taken French in college I would know if I'd medaled by now. Then, in clear English, came the distinct and familiar voice of Garry Hill, editor of *Track & Field News*, booming over the speaker, "And third into the stadium, Deena Kastor of the United States."

I cried through the final lap, surprised at how intimate the moment felt. Although surrounded by tens of thousands of people, with millions more watching on television, my world was narrowed to my family, Coach, Andrew, and Ray in the stands. I threw my arms up across the finish and stepped over Catherine, who was puking in lane 1. I put my hands over my face in disbelief and turned toward my family with my jaw dropped. *Can you believe it?* They were jumping up and down.

NBC interviewed me trackside, and I noticed gold medalist Mizuki Noguchi throwing up at my feet. *Look at these girls, wow, I feel great.*

My sister climbed down the stadium steps to the edge of the track and reached out her arm. "Dee, that was amazing, I can't wait to celebrate." I grabbed her hand, telling her having everyone here was my celebration.

As I made my way toward the exit tunnel, Andrew leapt over the railing and gave me a folded piece of paper. It was the "I love you" note we passed back and forth during pivotal times. I kissed him. "Coach is sitting right there," he said. We walked over and I took both of his hands. "We did it," I said. He nodded with glassy eyes and pursed lips.

An hour later, I emerged from drug testing to a view of the ancient columns of the Parthenon lit up against the night sky. It took more than a few attempts, but Ray finally hailed a cab and we drove through the city, turned down an alleyway, and pulled up in front of a small restaurant. The front patio was draped in lights. Even at 11:00 p.m., patrons packed the tables. My mom, dad, and Lesley sat with friends and cousins who'd come to Athens, along with Coach and Andrew—about twenty people total. When I walked through the door, everyone in the restaurant stood. *"Opa!"* the Greeks exclaimed, an expression for the celebration of life. Ray and I joined our group and we passed plates of food across the table, wine flowed, stories were told.

"She called me to say it was a hundred and one degrees," Andrew said. "I remember looking at my watch, it was four o'clock."

"Well, she really executed the plan," Coach said.

"I couldn't believe they weren't giving us more updates," my mom said.

"Did you see Paula dropped out?"

"We were sweating just sitting there."

"All the people in this pub were glued to the television . . ."

"Oh, and when you came into the stadium . . ."

The medal ceremony was the following day in the modern Olympic Stadium across town, a sleek building that seemed out of place in ancient Athens. The stands were packed for the many final rounds taking place. Mizuki, Catherine, and I followed a woman dressed in traditional Greek attire holding our medals on a pillow. At the center of the infield, we stood behind our designated podiums and waited for the announcer. "Attention to the infield for the medal ceremony of the women's marathon."

I was the first to be introduced. When my name was called, I stepped up and waved to the crowd. Sebastian Coe, four-time Olympic medalist and a British lord, placed the bronze medal around my neck. Then he put a laurel wreath on top of my head. This moment stood out for me. The wreath was made from the branches of the ancient olive tree in the Acropolis known as Athena's Tree. According to myth, when the ancient city of Attica was built, two gods wanted to be patron of the beautiful new city. Poseidon, the god of the sea, laid claim. Athena, the goddess of wisdom, challenged him. To settle the matter, Zeus asked them each to present the citizens of Attica with a gift and let them choose. Poseidon struck a rock with his spear and out poured a spring of saltwater. The salt, though, meant the water had little use. Athena made an olive tree sprout from the ground of the Acropolis, a gift of food, wood, and leaves. The people chose the tree.

To honor the history of the marathon and its significance to Greece, the marathoners' wreaths were made from the leaves of the sacred tree. Branches were carefully pruned and woven together. When it was placed on my head, I felt its gentle weight connect me to the marathon's lineage, linking me all the way back across the land we had just run to Spyridon Louis and his victory in the first modern Olympic Games; to Joan and her triumph in the women's first Olympic marathon; and to the Battle of Marathon itself and the messenger Pheidippides. It felt rhythmic, beautiful.

While gold medalist Mizuki was being introduced, I took a quick moment and held my medal in my hands, angling it up to see the winged goddess of victory emerging from the center of the very stadium I'd circled the evening before. A sharply dressed official signed to the three of us to turn for the raising of the flags. As I watched the Japanese, Kenyan, and American flags rise together, I felt overwhelmed by the sight of the broad stripes and bright stars climbing the pole. The Japanese anthem played, but I couldn't help but run through the words of the American anthem. I paused on "perilous fight." It brought me back to the tunnel at mile 19. That was the moment I let go of caution, when I fully released myself from worrying about the heat and ran as if I were hammering a 10K.

Stepping into that place of risk had felt momentous. I'd felt light and free, as if I were going after something instead of holding back. My God, what if I'd gone earlier? Could I have caught Catherine? Could I have won? What if I dared myself to do it, to challenge the boundaries of my fitness in the marathon? What, I wondered, would happen then?

17

THE MEANING OF WINNING

Chicago Marathon, 2005; London Marathon, 2006

*We must think over and over the kind of thoughts
we wish to dominate our lives.*
—HENRY DAVID THOREAU

"I want to win a marathon," I told Terrence over coffee at the Looney Bean.

Terrence sat across from me sipping a quad Americano, an intense afternoon drink befitting the drive and focus of my new coach.

Before Athens, Coach had told me he had spent the last four years mostly away from Caroline and that he wanted to be home with her. "Of course!" I'd said, holding back the thought in my mind a moment before giving it voice. "Will you still work with me?"

"Yes, yes."

But Coach added he was looking to see if there was another person who could lead the Mammoth team, and he had Terrence in mind. Over the last few years, Terrence's career had shifted from running to coaching and he'd spent many afternoons picking Coach's brain about training and altitude. "Terrence has a good mind," Coach said. He admired his persistent questions and his eagerness to learn and grow. I appreciated his frank counsel. Terrence had guided me through the London calf scare as a teammate, and his opinions and advice were helpful. I believed he could get me to the next level.

"Okay," Terrence said, "but let's look at the big picture, four years out to Beijing."

I told him that a shinier medal in Beijing was a goal and that I wanted to run sub-2:20, too. "But right now, even with the American record and a medal in the marathon, I still haven't won a marathon and want to."

Terrence nodded. "Why not aim to win *and* run sub-2:20?" he said. "You're ready for that now." I agreed. We discussed London and Berlin, but in the back of my mind, I knew which race I'd run: "Let's go with Chicago," I said. "I want to win on US soil."

My training under Terrence changed in small but significant ways. He was a product of Coach's approach and kept my mileage high and the week's mix of speed, tempo, and endurance workouts the same. But when it came to the specifics of speed and tempo sessions, it was a new ball game. Terrence didn't want me comparing current workouts to past seasons. With such a strong buildup to Athens, where I was running workouts that indicated a sub-2:20 was possible, he thought if I saw slower times on my watch, it would hurt my confidence. So rather than straight 400s or mile repeats, he incorporated multiple distances: alternating miles and kilometers, for example, or descending ladders (mile, kilometer, 800, 400). On tempo runs, he wanted the pace to be steady, not faster in the beginning.

The shift proved challenging. During repeat sessions, holding back to hit a pace so I could finish faster in shorter repetitions played against my aggressive nature. Once I held back, it was as though I locked into that easier pace, making it hard to psych myself up for the final repetitions. After a few weeks, Terrence saw it was ineffective and told me to just go for it in speed workouts.

His guidance for tempo runs was subtler. Holding back in the early miles was resulting in slower overall times. But Terrence still believed I could benefit from more even pacing. He let me run them as I wanted to, but asked me to write down each mile time in my training log. The practice of recording each split made me more aware of my fast start and slower finish—pacing that was ineffective in the marathon. It encouraged me to modify my approach, and while early miles were still a little faster, the difference in pace from start to finish was less drastic.

The Mammoth team had a new mix of mostly young athletes. Meb and Jen were still there. But Terrence had seen how effective working with the men was during Athens training and he said a specific training partner would be a valuable asset in my pursuit of a win. He recommended I hire Mike McKeeman.

Mike was a steeplechaser, twenty-eight, lean and muscular, with dirty-blond hair and an all-American look. He lived in Ardmore, Pennsylvania, and moved to Mammoth to help me train. Mike was quick-witted and funny. Upon request, he could belt out a perfect rendition of Bon Jovi's "Wanted Dead or Alive" (useful on road trips). But it was his mathematical mind that was most useful. Whenever Andrew or Terrence shouted a split, I simply said "math," and a couple of strides later, Mike would state our predicted finishing time.

Mike also knew pace. In Shady Rest or out on Green Church Road, it was as if Mike opened a filing cabinet and pulled out the 5:05 or 5:18 folder. We'd get off the line and, in two strides, Mike was on pace and stayed there, unaffected by wind or moving from asphalt to rugged dirt roads.

Having Mike at my side allowed me to work on pacing without overthinking it. I could fall into his rhythm without fussing about whether I was too fast or slow. Mostly, Mike did what the three men had done for me before Athens. He kept training fun, which remained the single most important factor for me. One day when he complained about the hills and the heat, I said, "C'mon, be positive." He replied, "Okay, I'm positive this sucks." I laughed so hard I could barely hold pace. Mike just ran on.

Terrence had a strong, intuitive side and he brought a spiritual, holistic element to my quest to win. Once, we were having coffee at the Looney Bean with Jen and Andrew, and I fussed about how my time in a tempo run had in fact been slower than the year before. "No two training cycles are alike," Terrence said. "It's your job to run your best in the season you are in. There is no benefit to judging if you are better or worse than before. Find a way to be your best in this moment."

We discussed the cosmos, power versus force, and intuitive healing. One of the most fascinating conversations was on universal energy. "I'm reading this book," Terrence said, which was often how topics emerged. "It's based on the understanding that everything is alive and has a vibration. Trees and animals and everything around us, and how we're all connected by it."

The four of us talked about how we could benefit from being conscious of the exchange of energy around us. "What do we take and what do we give?" Andrew asked rhetorically.

I brought this idea to practice. The mountains had previously been a source of inspiration and distraction. Now as I ran, I imagined them filling me with their strength and beauty and I offered my gratitude back. Sometimes before workouts, I stood outside barefoot to absorb the earth's energy. I felt the dirt or the grass under my feet. I took deep breaths, feeling the oxygen move through my chest to my legs, and exhaled my positive energy back into the world. I also pushed down into the earth to feel grounded, and to plant my own energy into the environment.

Simply being aware of this exchange added a richness to my running. I sometimes looked more closely at a single object—sagebrush—and considered its soft, warm energy. Or I took a moment to appreciate the caring way in which Andrew handed me my water bottle, and the selflessness of Mike as he ran farther and harder than he ever had before. With these small acknowledgments I felt closer to the world around me.

Training was going well when, about four months out from Chicago, I rolled my foot on a pinecone while walking Aspen. I limped home. It hurt to walk, so I skipped the evening run. *Maybe it's just a little tendon strain*, I told myself. The next day during a 10-mile tempo run with Mike, the pain was so intense, I aborted the workout at mile 4.

An MRI at Mammoth Hospital showed my cuboid bone had a stress reaction, a weak spot, which is a precursor to a stress fracture. "You're going to have to take eight weeks off any weight-bearing exercise," the radiologist said.

I cupped my face in despair, *No, things were going so well.* Then I looked at Andrew. "We'll have to count backwards from the race and see how to make it work," he said.

Terrence's reaction: "Let's continue workouts in the pool."

The next day, Terrence and I went back to Mammoth Hospital and I ran on the underwater treadmill. Chest-deep, pushing against a jet stream, I listened to Terrence tell me about a conversation he'd had with a friend of ours, Peter Roth, a New York–based intuitive healer. "We talked about divine order," Terrence said, as he increased the jet pressure. "It's a matter of trusting that everything is unfolding as it's supposed to, even if we don't understand it now. It's about not resisting or fighting the situation. Who knows, maybe this setback is actually keeping you from peaking too soon." *The rigid tree snaps in the wind*, he wrote in an email. *The flexible tree sways and develops stronger roots.* I chose to be the flexible tree.

My foot didn't hurt in the water. The calculations for the water level and my height put the buoyancy lift at 75 percent of my weight, meaning in the water I weighed only twenty-five pounds. Every morning Monday through Saturday, I worked out in the pool. Without the pounding of running, my body could actually handle more intensity and we made each day a hard hour. Sometimes, I did 30- to 60-second sprints with 10 seconds of recovery. Other days, the reps consisted of a sustained 6 minutes hard, with 30 seconds off.

The workouts were among the hardest of my life. I was light, but water gushed out of the jets at the front of the pool and I had to pump my arms and legs in an exaggerated way to overcome the thrust. If my mind wandered, the heart-rate monitor gauging my intensity beeped, indicating I'd dipped below the target of 185 to 190 beats per minute. Then I'd have to refocus on driving forward.

Terrence egged me on—"Stay with it, only two more minutes"— and sent thoughtful emails on mindfulness. He quoted spiritual leaders like Maya Angelou, Deepak Chopra, and Lao-Tzu, an ancient Chinese philosopher. *Our only task*, he wrote, *is to follow our path no matter how crooked the course.*

Andrew oversaw my workouts on days Terrence was with the team. He brought a speaker and played upbeat house music. He managed the jets and would kneel at the water's edge shouting, "Pump, pump, pump!" Every 10 minutes or so he handed me a bottle of ice water to keep me hydrated in the pool's hot and humid environment. Sometimes, on long intervals, he could see my boredom and would do a little jig for entertainment.

Thanks to Terrence's calm belief and Andrew's support, I stayed in the mind-set of winning Chicago. The challenge of the workouts themselves gave me confidence that my fitness wasn't suffering, and I focused on staying off my feet in between pool workouts to give my body the chance to rest and my foot the space to heal. The lack of worry kept stress hormones low, aiding the healing process. Additionally, endorphins and oxytocin flooded my body during workouts with anti-inflammatory properties, helping to create an environment that also supported healing.

Five weeks later, an MRI showed no sign of injury and I was cleared to run. I felt antsy. I was grateful that the pool had kept me focused and maintained my fitness, but only running would allow me to win. *Let's get after it*, my body and mind were saying. Terrence, though, made sure the return was gradual. We balanced workouts in the pool with workouts on land and kept the timeline open to allow my body to transition organically. I trusted the process because I trusted Terrence, and I didn't want to take any steps backward.

After the buoyancy of the pool, I felt a little heavy running at first. But without the water holding me back, there was also a rejuvenating freedom to feel momentum in running again. I felt no residual pain or tension in my foot, and two weeks later, I was back to full-time running.

One of the unexpected benefits of the pool was that it extended my concentration. Similar to how the marathon sharpened my mental acuity years earlier, the constant attention required to keep my heart rate high gave me a greater ability to narrow and sustain my attention on the roads. My mind wandered less and I had a tighter focus on pace and effort.

Every other week, Terrence had me do a simulation run, a long run in which every mile—rather than every 5K with Coach—was slightly faster. It ended in marathon pace (5:15 to 5:19). The workouts gave me more responsibility to pace, encouraging me to mature as a competitor. They were also a mental challenge. Previously, when the goal had been effort-based, I finished each workout feeling accomplished. Now, when I didn't hit the specific pace in simulation runs, it left me worried about my ability to run the marathon that fast. So I used the slower times to motivate me to push harder in the next run. When I was able to run the pace, I gained greater confidence. In both scenarios, my goal was to interpret the numbers in a way that served my goal.

Three weeks out from Chicago, Mike and I headed to the Philadelphia Half Marathon. It was a tune-up race for the marathon, but Terrence turned my attention to the times I was hitting in workouts, and encouraged me to challenge Joan Benoit Samuelson's American record in the half marathon of 1:08:34. Mike and I set a goal of running under 1:08.

Mid-September in Philly was hot and humid. On the starting line, I joked with Mike: "The humidity feels exactly like being in the pool. It might have prepared me for this heat." It was said in jest, but everything we say and think has an effect on our perception. The humidity sat on my skin and rather than interpreting it as a hindrance, it became moisture and air supporting me.

Mike and I went out at a 5:05 pace. We only needed 5:10 to earn the record, but I was excited and locked into it. Two miles later, I said, "It's too much." We dialed it back to 5:10. The course made a sweep through historic downtown before extending for 8 miles out and back along the Schuylkill River. Mike and I had taken the lead in the women's race and were pacing alongside Steve Spence, the 1991 world championships bronze medalist in the marathon, along with other men. Some faded as we moved along the river, others joined us from behind.

For miles I enjoyed the ever-changing dynamic of the pack. It gave me something to focus on. I saw Mike and me as this nucleus and everything else as happening around us.

I began to suffer on the return. "Come on," Mike said, feeling my drag. "We only have 5K to go!" *Oh no, we still have 5K to go.* The difference in our reactions caught my attention. I thought about how I alone had those opposing reactions depending on my fatigue level. In Carlsbad, when I felt strong, my thought had been, *Sweet, only a mile to go.* In New York, when the pain was great, the final miles seemed long. Recalling New York assured me I could finish despite the fatigue.

Immersed in these thoughts, the miles went by and we approached the finish. Mike surged ahead, running an amazing 1:07:46 in his first half marathon. I broke the tape in 1:07:53, winning with a new American record. I gave a nod to the universe. I couldn't help but think that the injury had been perfectly placed far enough back in the year that it actually helped me peak at the right time. If I was capable of breaking the American record in the half, I was confident I could win Chicago.

On the day of the race, Andrew and I walked out of the Chicago Hilton with Terrence, Mike, and Ray into a gorgeous morning. The sun was just peeking over Lake Michigan as we made our way across Michigan Avenue and into Grant Park. The streets were blocked to traffic, but up and down the avenue runners emerged from each intersection, all of us funneling toward the start.

As we walked, I anticipated a philosophical pep talk from my coach. Terrence, though, simply put his arm around me and said, "Define yourself." I waited for him to say more, but he was quiet. Ray and Andrew were talking and the conversation moved on. At the elite-athlete tent, we all slipped under the flap and found a couple of vacant chairs in the corner. Mike sat and put on his racing flats. He'd done all the marathon training but was opting to run the first 20 miles with me before pulling off. Terrence, Ray, and Andrew stood above us talking as I slipped on my shoes and tied them, thinking about Terrence's words. *Define yourself.* Their simplicity told me he believed I was ready to win. I grabbed that confidence and headed out to do it.

Mike and I tucked into the roped-off section for the start. We were surrounded by about fifty elite women and men, and in front of the masses, an aspect of Chicago I loved. Other marathons separated the professional women from the remainder of the field for broadcasting reasons. Chicago built the excitement of the whole race with a mass start, streaming forty thousand runners right behind us. I felt the anticipation of everyone there and was anxious for the gun to fire.

"Ten seconds to the start." Mike Nishi, head of operations for the Chicago Marathon, stood on the side of the starting corral, earpiece pressed to his head, multiple walkie-talkies strapped to his vest. He held up his hand. Five seconds.

The gun fired and I launched into a hot pace. I was surrounded by elite men, mostly Africans in blue shorts. Mike was somewhere behind, probably shaking his head at me. *What? I'm excited.*

A group of us began to find our stride and we emerged out of the mass into a pack of about twelve. That's when I noticed Constantina Diţă of Romania on my right shoulder. *No, wait, you shouldn't be here.* Constantina had won the world half-marathon championships the previous weekend. She threatened my win. Instead of trusting the race to unfold, my ego took over and I tried to force the win with each step. If I were a peacock, you would have seen my feathers fan up as I pushed into the pace.

I needed to hold a sub-5:20 pace to run under 2:20. Terrence's instructions were to go out at 5:20 pace, then drop to 5:15 in the later stages. I hit the first mile in 5:08. Mike was a few strides behind and he said in a cool voice, "A little fast." I was quick to respond, "That mile must be short."

Constantina came closer, pulling up on my shoulder to take advantage of my draft. *Shake her.*

I put in a surge. She responded right away. I tried again. She stuck with me. *Try again.*

We danced through the first couple of miles this way. I focused on her, wanting to make sure I was in the lead. If she had the slightest advantage, I kicked it up a little, surging, I noticed, right past the 5K fluids table.

Oh, you gotta focus.

I ran on, dropping Constantina. I knew the pace was fast, but only later would I learn I was on world-record pace at the 6-mile mark.

At the half, Constantina pulled up on my shoulder again. Her presence was irritating me. *Make a move she can't cover.* I peeled off my gloves and threw them on the side of the road as a signal that the race was on. She fell back.

I powered down the middle of the street surrounded by Mike and other male competitors. When needing to navigate an upcoming tangent, I elbowed the guy next to me to move over.

At mile 15, the men and I were on a sub-2:18 pace. Constantina pulled up on my shoulder again. *Damn, she's tough. How many surges is this going to take?*

Mike and Clint, a US marathoner with a chiseled face and broad shoulders, pulled in front of me to take the headwind through the city. But with Constantina there, I needed to be out front, and I elbowed my way between them, taking the lead.

I kicked it up at mile 20. She didn't respond, but I couldn't settle. She'd rallied every other surge, so I needed to keep pushing. Crossing the Chicago River into Chinatown, I passed the 21-mile mark. Suddenly, my body sputtered, like a carburetor jolting from lack of gas. It was an immediate energy drain.

Okay, one mile at a time.

But the mile felt impossible. Unlike New York, when my hips and legs were sore and tired from the repetitive pounding, here, the abrupt lack of energy left my whole body limp. I settled on one step at a time. *You can still win with each step.*

Along Michigan Avenue, the crowds cheering let me know Constantina was chasing. I fought the urge to look back and made the right onto Roosevelt Road, the race's only hill. The day before, the ten feet of vertical climbing up and over the bridge had appeared insignificant, puny even. In that moment, it was a mountain. I'd never been so deep in the fight, so consumed by the simultaneous pull of fatigue and drive. *One step at a time.*

I crossed the twenty-sixth mile and used the left onto Columbus Drive to glance over my shoulder. Constantina was right there. I tried disassociating from the pain by starting to count to 100, but the crowds cheering rose to a roar, telling me she was closing in. I reverted to begging. *Please, let these steps be enough.* A few more strides and I was over the finish in 2:21:25, my arms raised just high enough to clear the tape. My hands went right to my knees.

Wow, I thought winning would feel better than this.

A few seconds later, Constantina patted my back. "Congratulations," she said. I had no energy to respond.

The immediate aftermath of Chicago was a blur. My body was so depleted, race director Carey Pinkowski gripped my arm to keep me standing. Terrence, Ray, and Andrew were there, and my parents and sister came rushing out of the VIP tent. I heard my mom before I saw any of them. "Oh my God," she said, seeing my pale face, "someone get her a chair."

After a long shower at the hotel, I sat on the floor with my legs elevated against the wall. My parents and sister arrived. Lesley kept bringing me sports drinks and sodas. "I can't believe people are still finishing," she said, looking out the window.

Back in Mammoth, I took a month off. As my body recovered, my mind did its usual turn toward the next race. What did I want to accomplish?

I knew right away. I wanted to win a marathon feeling better. The exhaustion I felt after Chicago showed me I had run the race incorrectly. I had allowed the need to win, and the fear of losing, to hijack reason. I'd made reckless moves and missed water bottles. I had run to exhaustion, but I had not run to my potential.

What did a winning performance look like?

I pictured Joan Benoit Samuelson emerging from the dark tunnel on the track of the L.A. Coliseum. She was in the lead of the first Women's Olympic marathon. It was hot and her dark hair was matted with sweat. As I watched her make her way around the track and wave her white painter's cap to the crowd, I was struck by her grace. Her acknowledgment of the crowd was subtle yet heartfelt, a display of gratitude and humility. Her focus was internal yet outward, her performance for the advancement of women's running, yet also deeply personal.

Twenty minutes after Joan won gold, Gabriela Andersen-Schiess of Switzerland entered the stadium severely dehydrated. Her body leaned far to the left, as if her limp dangling arm were weighing her down. This image had initially deterred me from the marathon, then it had shown me the danger of heat before Athens. Now it inspired me. She shooed away medics, knowing that if they helped her, she would have been disqualified. Gabriela limped around the track to applause, completing the final lap in 5 minutes and 44 seconds and finishing thirty-seventh. In Gabriela, I saw perseverance, determination, and fearlessness. She had to have known she was practically running sideways, that her world was tilted. Yet she ran on.

In running, you learn that the way you run matters more than place or time. These women knew this. They ran to their physical, mental, and emotional capacity that day, displaying the strongest version of themselves. I wanted to define a win not by fear and ego but by knowledge and wisdom. I decided I had it in me to draw out the better sides of myself to make it happen. I would race to express everything I'd learned and all that I had become.

Terrence sent me a quote at the beginning of 2006. It was from legendary track and field coach Bill Bowerman: "Everything you need is already inside." What I needed, I had. What I was seeking, I was. The accumulation of miles and wisdom were present, waiting to be written in the race.

Terrence sat with Andrew and me at our dining-room table. I laid out a wall calendar, flipped to April, and put my finger on Monday, April 17, Patriots' Day. Every elite marathoner dreams of winning Boston, but because I was born there and my mom was raised in the small town of Hull nearby, the race had a personal draw. Then I tapped Sunday, April 23, the London Marathon. The flat, fast course offered the chance of a fast time, and a sub-2:20 still tugged at me.

I couldn't make a decision. Terrence and Andrew had no opinion. I called Coach. "The choice has to come from you," he said. "The commitment to the training is driven by whatever your desire is for the race."

For the good part of a week, I played with the choices in my mind. A win at the prestigious Boston Marathon would be a new level of progress, as would putting the American record further out by going sub-2:20. One day I'd decide on London and feel the tug of Boston. The next day, I'd try on Boston and London would call.

So I let Aspen decide. I grabbed her stuffed bear and moose and put them in the driveway, designating the bear as Boston and the moose as London. Back inside, I stood at the front door, opened it abruptly, and told her, "Go get your baby, go get your baby." Aspen sprinted outside and fetched the moose. I started preparing for London.

I trained with a freedom I hadn't felt in years. I ran with trust and with the intention of cultivating all that I already knew. There was a lack of self-consciousness in my preparation. I became less attached to the pain of training as I matched the challenge of Mike's fast pace. The fatigue was there but I didn't claim it, or maybe I became desensitized to it. Discomfort existed alongside strength, and fatigue was a part of endurance. It took less self-talk, less cheerleading to execute workouts. My mind stayed with my body and my body supported my mind. I felt light, as if my upbeat spirit had sprouted some wings.

When Terrence sent me an email with my London workouts, he sent a series of beliefs and existential questions. He wanted to know if I had it in me to dig deeper, if I had the strength to keep fighting, the desire to meet my human capacity. He encouraged me to meditate, pray, reflect, and free my mind from mental roadblocks. He told me to not be limited by time, age, experience, or talent. He said other athletes came before me, others would follow, but London was my moment.

About a month out from the race, Terrence sent me an email that read:

You will win the 2006 Flora London Marathon!

Yes, you will do it!

Winning London will be difficult. It may be the hardest thing you have ever done. But remember that it will happen.

Every day that you get up from now until London, I want you to ask yourself these questions:

Who am I today?

Am I going to be the person that I know myself to be?

Am I going to be the person that my family, husband, coach, and training partners know me to be?

By asking yourself these questions, you will set the tone for the day. You will give the day a sense of purpose. You will put your mind and body in order before embarking on this journey.

I finished reading the email, pulled out a piece of paper, and wrote:

WIN

2:19

London: Swing at it!!!

Three weeks before the race, Andrew, Mike, and I settled into a second-story apartment overlooking Bushy Park, not far from where we stayed the last time I ran London.

As we trained and rested, I felt confident in my fitness. Mike and I had run a tune-up race at the Berlin Half Marathon, and with a little kick from him in the middle miles—"This course must be short, because we're on American-record pace"—we went for it. I set four American records that morning in the 12K, 10 mile, 20K, and the half marathon (1:07:34). I held on to that success as a sign of my fitness for London and wrote "2:19" in red lipstick on the bathroom mirror.

We passed our leisure time in Teddington solving sudoku puzzles and playing cards. Andrew and Mike kept letting me win at gin. Andrew turned his cards so I could see them, or he passed me a card I needed even if I hadn't asked. Mike would have a hand full of melds, but would throw them down, saying, "I'm out. Deena won again!"

"Please," I said. "I can lose at a game of cards without losing my confidence in the race."

Terrence arrived for the final week. He ran with Mike and me during our last tempo workout. I pushed and strained to run the 6 miles at race pace (5:15 to 5:20). Afterward, the two men stood loose and jovial with Andrew, talking in their best British accents. I experienced an intense moment of pre-race panic. "How am I supposed to keep that pace for twenty more miles when six was difficult?" I said. I was actually fighting tears. The men looked at me in shock. Andrew put his arm around me.

Then Terrence said, "The problem isn't the pace or your fitness. The problem is your perception of the pace. You think it should feel easy when the pace is actually very hard." He went on to loosely quote a character from the movie *The Matrix*: "It's not the spoon that bends, but your mind that bends the spoon." The guys laughed.

Is confidence that fragile? Can trust turn on one workout?

We have to repeatedly return to the thoughts that support our desires. We have to manage our emotions in order to keep belief, trust, and confidence as our energy and driver. Chicago had reminded me of that.

Of course you're ready, I thought. *It's a single workout. You just ran a personal best. You had three months of solid training.* The pace was going to be hard and I accepted the challenge.

Race morning was cold and drizzly, and on the starting line I closed my eyes and turned my face to the sky, letting the rain pour down while the earth's energy came up through my legs. Crouched on the starting line, eyes straight ahead, I breathed in and exhaled one calm thought: *Trust.* At the gun, Kenyans Salina Kosgei and Susan Chepkemei jumped to the lead. I tucked in behind them, feeling the ease of the early miles. I knew from the pre-race technical meeting both women were also aiming for sub-2:20. I felt composed, knowing we could work together to push past that time barrier.

The race was down to the three of us after the first mile, along with official pacers Mike and Henry Tarus, a tall Kenyan with a long back-kick. The women and I spent the first couple of miles trying to find the magical line between sustainable and too fast. We took advantage of the slight downhill third mile and ran a 5:00 flat, then settled in behind Henry and Mike.

The women were on my shoulder, but I felt no need to drop them. I was confident I'd be the one to sustain this aggressive pace, and so their presence didn't shake me. I ran the tangents, drank my fluids, and enjoyed the relative ease of the effort, knowing it would get harder later.

Salina began fading at mile 12. We ran on. Mike, Susan, Henry, and I crossed the half in a perfect 1:09:48. Mike was a half stride ahead and to my left, and I wished I could catch his eye to see if he had a reaction to the precision of the pace. Instead, I offered a "Nice" under my breath.

I smiled, remembering his fear-stricken face at the pre-race meeting. Race director Dave Bedford had told the men they needed to stay precisely on a 2:20 pace, a challenge for any runner, let alone a newcomer like Mike, who was running his first full marathon. Dave had looked straight at Mike, and said, "Two-nineteen, pigs. Two-twenty-one, pigs," indicating if the pace wasn't perfect or he gave preferential pacing to me, he'd be fed to the pigs. Mike had left the room pale.

Rain came down. I tilted my head up so my face could catch a few drops under the bill of my cap.

Susan stayed with me longer than I expected. *Trust you'll be the one to carry this pace.*

Maybe, I thought, *she'll last another mile*. When the mile came and went and she was still with me, I waited for the next mile, watching for signs of fatigue. They started on a winding stretch in the Isle of Dogs. Susan took the corners with a stutter in her step. At mile 20, the slap of her feet on wet pavement grew louder.

I feel good. Should I make a move?

No, don't blow it. Be patient.

I'm not sure if I picked up the pace or if Susan faded, but either way I found myself in the lead.

She rallied, but it didn't worry me. I stayed steady and she faded for good that time. Mike fell back at mile 21. Henry dropped out at 24.

I ran alone in the London drizzle as people poured out of pubs, pint glasses in hand. A few raised their glasses toward me. I tipped my hat. *Thank you.* I felt sharp, focused, and internal, but could see and hear everything. My breathing and foot strikes blended with the movement and cheers from the crowd.

I locked my eyes on Big Ben, and after making a brief tribute to Chevy Chase's European vacation movies (the things that come to mind!), I reeled in that massive, beautiful clock like it was my biggest rival.

My 40K (1.24 miles to go) split showed sub-2:20 would be close.

Get uncomfortable.

Breathe in the crowd's energy, put it in your legs.

My breathing and foot strikes began feeling out of sync, so I projected an image of a smoother me running ahead and, after matching her fluid stride, lunged forward to catch her. I pushed hard, feeling the miles in my legs yet trusting I had what it would take to continue.

With a half mile to go, a heavy armor of fatigue settled on my body, making every movement feel forced. *Be a knight!* I suggested to myself and imagined charging toward Buckingham Palace, moving with a warrior's will past the gold-winged statue of the Victoria Memorial, and turned onto the Mall.

It wasn't the most elegant of finishes. I squinted in the rain, trying to read the number on the finish-line clock. Sprinting the last stretch, I broke the tape and won in 2:19:36, becoming the first American woman to run under 2:20.

Someone draped an American flag over my shoulders. Its weight felt like being draped in the accumulation of years of learning and all the people who had taught me. There was Bill, sending the team to play in the mountains. Lance keeping faith in my ability even when I'd lost my own. There was Coach, reminding me to bring a good attitude, to get tough, to focus on building the person. I felt Terrence's calm wisdom. Andrew's love and devotion. My dad's bottomless support, my mom's constant attention, and my sister's pride. Every teammate and competitor who had pushed me, and every fan who'd cheered. Each mountain, road, and blade of grass that had inspired me. I was the sum of everyone and everything that had built me.

I grabbed the corners of the flag and lifted my arms toward the cameras above the finish line. I'd turned in time to see Mike running down the final stretch. His stride still looked strong, though his face wore a marathoner's fatigue. I clapped as he took his final steps over the finish line, stopping right in front of me. "Why did I let you talk me into this?" he said. I smiled. He ran 2:20:27, qualifying for the Olympic marathon trials. "Why," he asked, "why would I do that again?"

Terrence, Andrew, and Ray were there in the finish-line area to congratulate us. A reporter started asking questions. "Deena, did you know you ran perfect splits? The first half of your race was exactly the same as the second: 1:09:48."

"No," I said, a curious smile forming. "I didn't know." I took the symmetry, though, as a sign that I had done it, I had defined myself with a race that was the most authentic expression of who I was. A balance of caution and daring, desire and will, joy and gratitude, athlete and person. That harmony was right there on the clock.

PART IV

Play

18

A SANDWICH ON THE DECK

Olympic Marathon, Beijing, 2008

Sport is a personal journey.
—RAY FLYNN

No doubt they were going to hate the Americans. It was a weekend, and the government security forces had shut down the main road to the beach in the coastal city of Dalian, China, so a few US distance runners could get in a good workout. As the six of us warmed up—me and the other US marathoners competing in the 2008 Games—I thought I should've swapped my USA shirt for one with a Canadian maple leaf. Cars extended for miles at each end of the 9-mile stretch of road reserved for our long run. The sun was bright. The ocean was a few feet away. But no one could get to the beach until our workout was done. I waited for horns to start honking, for people to give us the bird. Instead, families stepped out of their cars and started clapping and taking photos.

The plan was to run the out-and-back route for an 18-mile simulation run, in which I'd begin at a 6:20 pace and gradually build to marathon pace by the half. Terrence ran alongside me and Andrew shadowed us on the bike to give fluids. The miles came easily and I dropped to 5:30 for the second half. The final miles were faster than race pace, indicating I was strong and fit.

After the workout, Andrew and I ate lunch with Terrence and Jen, who was running the 5,000 meters at the Games, at the hotel restaurant. We talked race strategy. "Go out with the pack but controlled," Terrence said. "Then at 10K, run to win."

Afterward, Andrew and I wandered along the beach collecting sea glass. "The plan feels exactly right," he said. "I know you can do this. I know you are ready." He was offering me support for the hard task ahead, but I was acutely aware of and grateful for the constancy of his support, his steadfastness, and how important he was to me. We were holding hands and I gave his a little squeeze.

Beijing's marathon course started on the East Road of Tiananmen Square at seven thirty in the morning. After doing some of our workouts in ninety-degree heat, it was blessedly overcast, in the low seventies, though humidity was nearly 90 percent. I lined up with calmness, knowing my strategy was not to hype myself up until I was farther into the race. When the gun fired, the entire field ran so slowly we moved as one pack, tripping and jostling for space and rhythm.

The lead truck took us around Tiananmen Square. I kept my eyes on the truck to gain a sense of the upcoming turns. We passed through the north gate of the Temple of Heaven, a stunning blue-tiled structure set in a vast garden. As I ran down the tree-lined avenue in the middle of the pack, nearing 5K, I felt a little tension on the top of my right foot. A few strides later, I heard what sounded like a Popsicle stick snapping in half. I went down. Women stumbled and moved around me. Stunned, I tried standing up. My foot couldn't hold my weight and I fell again, realizing that the snap had been my foot breaking. I immediately felt nauseous from the sound, the idea of it breaking, and the reality of having my plan for gold gone so quickly. Usually in a race, you have a few miles to understand or accept defeat. This was sudden.

I sat on the roadside and the pain kicked in, a burn and throb that pulsed up my leg and seized the rest of me. I held my foot tightly, trying to make the pain stop. The final three competitors went by, followed by a white van. When it pulled over, two Chinese women in slacks and polo shirts jumped out. They each took an arm and hoisted me up. "Thank you," I said. I hopped with their help to the van and climbed into the seat behind two other Chinese volunteers, a man and a woman. I was the first athlete they'd picked up. One of the women handed me a white towel and I sobbed into the rough fabric. The pain was intense.

My foot was swelling inside my shoe, so I took it off and watched it blow up to the size of a football. It swelled so much I thought the skin might rupture. We passed a medical tent and I had the option to get out but didn't want to sit on a cot on the roadside. One of the women jumped out and grabbed two small sandwich bags of ice. I placed one under my foot and rested the other on top.

I felt angry at my body, and instantly blamed it for being weak and making me feel incapable. Why couldn't this have happened last week, or better yet next week, or better still not at all?

The towel woman, whose name I wished I'd gotten, gently rubbed my shoulder. She pointed toward a temple, and began telling me its history. Thank you, I told her, but I'm not up for a tour right now.

I stared out the window in disbelief that I was completing the marathon course in a van behind the last competitor. I got dramatic thinking my slowest marathon to date would be in a vehicle during the Olympic Games I'd hoped to win. I looked around at the empty seats. *Why me? Why was I the one?*

I caught my tone. *Well, no, wait a second, I'm not a victim here. This is a big deal, but maybe a big deal has a big lesson to teach.*

I shifted. *Why? Why did this happen?* It was the better question than "Why me?"

I started thinking through the process. It seemed too simple to accept the break as part of the consequence of pushing limits, because our bodies are strong and adaptable. They can withstand the impact, so what had I missed? Asking the questions allowed me to look forward to better understanding. I didn't win gold and didn't yet have answers, but here positivity was doing its best work. After a crushing blow, the consistent practice allowed me to arrive at a place of acceptance and relative peace in record time.

We picked up a number of runners. Women from Russia, Japan, and Portugal climbed in. Gete Wami from Ethiopia joined us toward the end. My US teammate Magdalena Lewy-Boulet appeared at the door. "I'm sorry," I said. She nodded as she made her way to the back.

Ray and Andrew were standing outside the Bird's Nest Stadium when the van pulled up. "I'm fine," I said when I saw the look of worry on their faces. Ray looked at my foot. "I'm so sorry, Deena." "I'm pretty sure it's broken," I said. Andrew picked me up. "Constantina won gold," he said, knowing I'd want to know. I smiled. It told me I could have been up there. At the same time, having a friend on the competitive circuit, a feisty runner with the aggressive style I admired, earn the medal, felt good. I was happy for her.

A couple of USATF staff helped me into their car and drove all of us to the Olympic Village. Andrew carried me into the village hospital. X-rays showed a complete fracture of my third metatarsal. We called Mike Karch, an orthopedist in Mammoth, who viewed the images from his office. "It's actually good you went without medical attention," he said. "The pressure from the swelling reset the bone perfectly."

Looking at images, I was amazed how all those jagged pieces squeezed back into place. Just a few hours earlier my bone had cracked, but my body was already hard at work healing itself. I apologized for my anger. *I was upset,* I whispered to my foot, *I'm sorry.* I closed my eyes and took a moment to be grateful for all my body had given me over the years.

Before hanging up, Dr. Karch was emphatic that I let nothing, not even a bedsheet, touch my toes. To displace the bones and disrupt the healing already taking place would mean surgery.

That night, I stayed in the room at the Olympic Village with

Jen, who was competing the next day. We lay on opposite sides of the room in the dark, my casted leg elevated, and talked about the highs and lows of the Olympics. It was the medals that were celebrated, but we wondered if most athletes went home disappointed. "Maybe some are really happy to just represent their country," Jen said. "Yeah, or to run a personal best," I said.

Jen's and my ratios would be similar: two disappointing, one good. Jen failed to advance to the finals in the 10,000 in Sydney and missed her top-10 goal in the marathon in Athens. In Beijing, though, she had her Olympic moment: in a packed stadium under the lights, she'd qualified for the final in the 5,000. I had unmet hopes in Sydney and Beijing, but a bronze from Athens.

Reflecting on the spectrum of what the Olympics offered athletes helped me further cope with the turn of events in Beijing. I took it less personally and saw the disappointment more generally. I was running the gamut of the Olympic experience.

Andrew and I flew to Southern California the next day and spent two weeks at our beach house in Oxnard. With the Olympics over, there was no need to maintain fitness or look ahead at other competitions. We agreed there was nothing more important than my health, and we opened the space ahead to focus on healing.

I avoided caffeine and alcohol in order to give my body the purest space in which to absorb the abundance of the whole, nutrient-rich foods I consumed. Andrew and I sat around the fire pit listening to the sound of crashing waves while I read trashy novels and books on building bone strength. I learned about calcium-rich foods, made a list, and Andrew shopped accordingly.

My foot felt best first thing in the morning, until I swung my legs over the bed and lowered my feet to the floor. Fresh blood rushed down through my limbs and my right foot would jolt in pain. It would ache and throb the rest of the day. So I lounged and tried sleeping a lot. There was a restlessness, though, a buzz inside me that kept me from fully relaxing.

"You had all this fitness built up and never released it," Dr. Karch said over the phone.

It made sense. Tapering stores energy from training, gathers it so it can be used over the long distance of the marathon. Without the release of racing, kinetic energy was trapped inside me. I tried creative ways to free it. I visualized myself doing a hard workout with Mike on Green Church Road. We set off along the undulating terrain toward the valley, increasing our pace mile by mile. We blew past sage and rabbit brush, and 10 miles later arrived at the van. It was fun but the buzz didn't subside. I grabbed a pillow and screamed into it. That didn't work either.

One morning, I crutched down to the shoreline, and with my eyes focused on the horizon, I let out a few primal screams as loudly as I could. I got a few stares from morning walkers but no relief.

Back in Mammoth, Andrew and I sat in Dr. Karch's office looking at a DEXA scan of my entire skeletal system. Dr. Karch was in his late thirties with a shaved head and a stocky athletic build. "See this dullness here in the images?" he said, pointing to the hollow-looking insides of my bones. "That's the onset of osteoporosis." We were stunned and puzzled. Andrew and Dr. Karch began analyzing. "She's thirty-five, not old enough to be losing bone density," Dr. Karch said. Andrew added that I ate a good diet, ran, and weight trained, all of which supposedly increase bone density. It didn't make sense.

"Could it be connected to the giardia?" Andrew asked.

Three months before Beijing, I'd competed at the Bolder Boulder 10K and had done a training run on a trail above town. I hadn't brought a water bottle so I stopped at a creek, cupped water in my hands, and drank a mouthful to quench my thirst. Weeks later, when the diarrhea wouldn't subside, a test showed I had giardia.

"Sure," Dr. Karch said, and ordered me to have a blood test. They analyzed further. Blood tests showed there was plenty of calcium in my system but almost no vitamin D. "It's odd that you have such low levels when you run outside every day and live at altitude."

We eventually figured out a perfect storm had been brewing in my body. Giardia drained me of nutrients, and when I resumed training, my body grabbed the minerals it needed to function from my bones. I had been unable to replenish vitamin D, a nutrient essential for building bone strength and readily available from the sun, because after multiple bouts of melanoma, I wore long-sleeved shirts, sunscreen, and a hat every workout. So that summer, as my fitness was building, my bones were weakening. One of the lessons from Beijing was that there was a difference between being fit and being healthy. I was one, not the other.

That realization in the hospital allowed me to give more specific attention to healing. I read books on reversing osteoporosis, which focused mostly on exercise and diet. Since exercise wasn't an option at the moment, and I couldn't absorb vitamin D from the sun, I focused on my diet, preparing vitamin-D–rich meals and snacks. At the top of the list was herring, which I ate on pumpernickel toast. Wild salmon and free-range eggs became a staple a few times a week. Organic and local produce offer greater bioavailability, providing more nutrients that the body can readily absorb.

One afternoon, I rested my crutches against the kitchen counter and made a sandwich. I sliced through the ciabatta roll and layered on slices of grass-fed flank steak, topping it with crumbles of Gorgonzola and a fistful of arugula that I'd just picked from the garden. I tucked the sandwich, wrapped in foil, in my backpack along with Kettle Chips and a cold can of Perrier, slung the pack over my shoulder, and crutched outside to the front deck. Balancing on one foot, I spread out my lunch. But just before taking my first bite, the house phone rang. I crutched back and made it to the phone inside. "Hi, Mom," I said.

"Hi. I'm just calling to check in, see how you're doing."

"I'm fine, Mom, same as when you called two hours ago."

"I know, but I'm worried. This is the first time you haven't been able to run, really, ever."

My mom thought I should see a psychologist. I assured her I was fine.

We hung up and I crutched back outside thinking I was fine, really, but that my mom was right. This was the first time in twenty-four years that injury had threatened my return to competitive running. I believed my foot would heal but was less sure if it would let me compete at a high-level again. So why was I fine?

That question turned in my mind as I slowly ate my sandwich and took in the beauty of the tall pines on our street and the grandness of the mountains in the background. The tanginess of the Gorgonzola popped in my mouth and I savored how deliciously it paired with the peppery greens and tender steak. Mid-appreciation, it dawned on me that I was fine because running had prepared me for this moment. It taught me to pay attention to goodness. It gave me the tools of resilience and gratitude, of awe and optimism. And even without running, these were with me. Views would still inspire me, gratitude would always fill me. The positive approach that contributed to my running was ready to strengthen any passion or pursuit. Right now, I was applying it to my health.

I included as many modalities as possible to heal. The cast was off now and I was in a boot, but because I wasn't moving around much, I used acupuncture and massage to facilitate blood flow. I also wore a bone stimulator, a small electronic device that wrapped around my foot. For eight hours a day, it sent little shots of electromagnetic energy through my foot, stimulation that aided the body's own electrical field surrounding the break.

I also called Peter Roth, the intuitive healer in New York whom Terrence had connected me to years ago. Peter had been a source of guidance over the years. His advice was always sage, revealing underlying factors not readily visible. Once, when I couldn't figure out why my hip was sore, he suggested spreading my arms like wings as I slowly walked through a doorway, to stretch out tight pectoral muscles. It might be, he noted, an upper-body issue. It worked. I was curious how he would view my foot injury.

"Isn't it interesting what we think we know?" he said after I told him the whole story. "You thought you were strong and capable before the race, but you were unhealthy. Now with your foot in a boot you are actually healthier because you are giving your body what it needs." I smiled. I was laid up, but already healthier. Simply holding that thought helped me feel stronger.

I wanted my thoughts to be ahead of my healing, directing it to a degree, and I started applying my mind more fully to the process. I pictured my toes moving individually before they were able to. Once the bone fused, I imagined nutrients going to the resealed bone and gently sanding the area, smoothing out the rough edges so there'd be no calcium deposits disrupting my stride.

About two months after the break, I started putting weight on the foot. Once I relearned how to balance equally on both feet again, I graduated to walking around the house. Then I returned to practice with the team. I walked while they ran, starting in secure, stable shoes and working my way down to minimalist shoes to gradually build foot strength. I also did foot exercises while the team did drills. I balanced on disks with my toes spread wide to ensure I wasn't protecting my middle metatarsal, and did towel curls and gentle calf raises. Each day felt like progress.

When my foot fully healed, Terrence encouraged me to increase my distance. "Get out for a two-hour hike," he suggested.

I'd always wanted to hike over Morgan Pass in the John Muir Wilderness south of Mammoth, so I drove along Highway 395 and made the right at a tiny town called Tom's Place. My Jeep climbed in elevation up Rock Creek Road and I parked at Little Lakes Valley trailhead. With a map in one hand and a water bottle in the other, I began the gradual ascent through the glacial valley. The leaves of the aspen trees were just past prime colors, and there was moss on the north side of their trunks. The water in the creek had a mellow flow.

I walked the canyon, craning my neck for views of granite peaks. The trail passed the shores of Heart Lake, Box Lake, and Long Lake. It was so beautiful, I couldn't believe it had taken me so many years to explore the area.

After Long Lake, the trail's pitch steepened. I was 40 minutes into the hike when I arrived at a fork in the trail. Glancing at the map, I realized if I wanted to go over the pass before it was time to turn around, I needed to run. I broke into a light jog and got into an easy rhythm. Endorphins or something of the sort immediately flooded my body. I smiled in appreciation for the high after its four-month hiatus.

The trail crossed the creek, so I stepped across small boulders to get to the other side. That's when the real climbing began. Up the barren switchbacks of Morgan Pass, I felt my chest burn and my pulse quicken. I crested the top and came to a stop at 12,000 feet. The land was so sparse, it looked like the moon. I turned in all directions and was amazed at how gorgeous it was, how far I'd come, and that I was even there. *What a privilege to live among this*, I thought as I raised my arms to acknowledge everything surrounding me. The world was rich and I took in the goodness.

On the descent, I let my stride open up, flying past Gem Lake and through a small boulder field with dry wild grasses. I lifted my head up to take in the changing shadows of the peaks above, my foot caught a root, and I went down hard on both knees. Ha! I laughed, spitting out dirt from my teeth and dusting myself off. The good feeling, however, was unshakable. I washed the blood off my hands and knees in the creek and kept going, hoping to arrive back at the trailhead before the tackle shop sold out of mountain blackberry pie.

19

THE POSITIVE PATH

Knowledge has a beginning but no end.

—ATTRIBUTED TO GEETA IYENGAR

I returned to high-level competition, or at least I tried to. I executed mile repeats at Shady Rest Park, ran long runs with the team, chased the women down Green Church Road, and fended off the men. My foot had full strength and my fitness was high, but there was something flat in my execution.

You just need to race, I told myself. But while I won the Shamrock Shuffle 8K in Chicago and the Great Edinburgh 10K in Scotland, I was more interested in a city tour than competing. There was an absence in the 2009 Chicago Marathon, too. I thought I could win, but the drive to push wasn't there. Running with the pack, I felt like an observer, watching the action rather than inserting myself in it, not running with the heightened charge of racing. At mile 18, I needed a bathroom stop, and when a Porta John appeared, I happily took it. I finished sixth.

My lack of motivation puzzled me. Why, after twenty-five years of chasing the finish line, did winning not seem to matter anymore?

A run around Horseshoe Lake provided the answer. Horseshoe

was an alpine lake at 9,000 feet, the last lake you can drive to in Mammoth. I loved the rawness of the area. Dead trees were scattered on the lake's western shore, felled by the slow and steady release of carbon dioxide seeping from the volcanic activity below Mammoth Mountain, a fact that reminded me of all that goes on under the surface of things. A trail circumnavigated the lake, and I headed into the shaded pine forest. Over the bridges and onto the single track, my career came back to me. I strove for higher goals and used the knowledge in me to get after them. Each workout and race had been part of an upward trajectory of learning and reaching the next level. I'd chased the nation and risen to the top of US distance running. I'd chased the world, and with my London win and time, was ranked number 1 in the world that year. Each season, I knew there was more to learn, more to pull out of myself. Now, with my chance at Olympic gold gone and my fastest days behind me, I didn't see a new peak. Without the underlying drive for progress, training and racing had lost its purpose.

What, then, could renew it? What could draw out the desire to run?

The New York City Marathon had been my first race, and so I thought running it again might have sentimental value that would invigorate me. I signed up for the 2010 race and began building base miles on my own that summer since Terrence and the team were competing in Europe. One morning in Shady Rest Park for mile repeats, I felt more fatigued than usual during my warm-up. I shot off the line anyway, flew past the playground, and at the turnaround was nearly 30 seconds off pace. *Hmm, okay, let's go*, I thought, heading into the return. But the second half was just as slow. I reset mentally and tried again. The result was no better, so I went home.

The fatigue puzzled me. I was sleeping well, though I had been sleeping longer than usual. I'd also been feeling lethargic throughout the day. Was I tired from trying too hard to muster the motivation? Still, last week's speed session was strong. Beijing had taught me that there can be unforeseen things going on inside our bodies, so that afternoon I went to Mammoth Hospital for a blood test. Results would come the next day.

"Maybe you're pregnant," my mom said when we spoke by phone. "That kind of fatigue is typical with pregnancy. I knew I was pregnant with your sister when I was too tired to get out of bed in the morning."

Andrew and I had put off having children because it had never seemed the right time to step away from competition. We'd gotten a little lax with birth control, so I bought a pregnancy test. Andrew watched American David Oliver run the 110-hurdles at a European track meet while we waited for the plus or minus sign to appear. Right after David won, I made the announcement. "We're pregnant," I said with a smile. Andrew shut the laptop and reached to put his hand on my stomach. "Oh, I felt it kick," he teased, and pulled me in for a kiss.

The nurse called the next day, saying she had my blood results and did I want to come in. "No, just tell me if it's true," I said. She laughed, confirming that yes, I was pregnant. "Maybe I should come in then?" No, it's early, she said, make an appointment in a month. I hung up the phone a little bewildered; it felt strange knowing there was a life forming inside me and no one was giving me a written plan on what to do.

My focus easily shifted from training to nurturing the baby. I read *What to Expect When You're Expecting* and *Trees Make the Best Mobiles: Simple Ways to Raise Your Child in a Complex World*, among other books, while preparing the nursery. I ran 30 minutes a day to maintain health, usually up at the lakes or in Shady Rest Park, seeking inspiring views so I could feed the baby the joy of the mountains. The fatigue never fully left and after a month, I started getting side stitches, so I switched to walking. But walking gave me side stitches, too, so I decided to give my body what it seemed to be asking for— rest.

I noted that for a second time, I didn't miss running. I felt a deep gratitude for the sport, but motherhood, perhaps, was my new direction.

"Really, you might not return to running?" a friend asked one night over dinner with Andrew and me.

"I don't know if I'll have the motivation," I said.

"You don't have to know," Andrew said. "Your body will tell you when you're ready to go again, if at all."

There was a peace inside me as we expected our first child. The question of running was there, but it sat with me like an old friend, when your shared history connects you, bolsters you, even though you are unsure if you'll meet again.

A couple of months into the pregnancy, we learned that Aspen had a brain tumor. After a few stressful days of consideration, we made the decision to put her down. She was fourteen years old and had been with me my entire professional career. I was shattered. The physical pain of losing her stunned me and I cried for days. Worried my sadness was harming the baby, I called Peter, the intuitive healer. "Your grief stems from a deep kind of love, love of the highest frequency," he assured me. Peter added that worrying about how my sadness was affecting the baby also came from a place of love. "What you are passing on to your child," he offered, "is life's most powerful gift." Understanding that grief was rooted in love offered comfort amid an uncomfortable emotion.

Coming out of the bedroom one day three weeks from my due date, I gripped the wall. Spasms went up my back and I lowered to the floor. This went on for four days and was so intense, I threw up from the pain. Kneeling on all fours with my belly hanging down offered some relief, but not enough to allow me to carry to term. At the hospital, we were encouraged to forgo our natural birth plan by inducing labor, but it affected the baby's heart rate, so we agreed to an emergency C-section.

Piper Bloom came into our lives the evening of February 21 with a big set of lungs. We heard a little slap, then a wailing cry, and Andrew and I looked at each other with a mixture of relief and pride. The nurse brought our new baby to us and laid her on my chest. "Hi, Piper," I said, feeling the warmth of her body on me. Glancing up at Andrew's tender stare, I fell deeper in love with him and deeply in love with her.

Days later at home, Andrew and I coddled her, fed her, and sang to her. I spent long stretches of time watching her sleep in Andrew's arms, amazed at how immersed one could be in staring at a sleeping baby. It was not, I noted, unlike being entranced in front of a fireplace.

Piper cried a lot and we joked that maybe we should have called her Piper Storm. More frequent feedings seemed to help and when Andrew walked her up and down the stairs, she quieted. Piper, it seemed, liked movement.

One afternoon, I held her in my arms and stepped onto the treadmill in the office downstairs. I punched the buttons to a slow walk and moved with an exaggerated bounce. Piper smiled up at me, closed her eyes, and slept. When Andrew took her gently from my arms, I increased the pace on the treadmill to a light jog. My body tingled from the blood flow. It felt good to move, to get my metabolism going. My stomach still held the staples and stitches from childbirth, but it didn't hurt. I was tired yet invigorated, running a mile in 20 minutes. It wasn't for progress or a medal or win. It was simply movement and it felt good.

So I kept running. I did just what felt right each day. Sometimes that was 10 minutes, others 30, or I opted to walk with Piper and our new dog, Sage, a Neapolitan mastiff. Once, I returned home from a run feeling strong and fast, so the next day I put on a watch and headed out. I ran around the neighborhood and looked at the mile split. I was running 10-minute miles. I laughed at the illusion of speed. Speed wasn't what I had felt. It was joy.

I wasn't sure what returning to running would look like, but I decided to get back into a routine by joining the team at practice. Gradually, my body remembered the rhythm and I found myself charging hills and chasing my teammates. My legs started turning over more quickly and I felt a snap in my stride.

Four months before the Olympic marathon trials, Terrence saw potential in my fitness and built a schedule to get me ready to make my fourth Olympic team. It was a high goal, one I thought might get me excited again. But dividing my focus between running and motherhood was harder than I imagined. I rushed to get out the door to workouts, and afterward, while my team stretched and talked, I hurried back to Andrew and Piper. The remainder of the day, I was immersed with feeding Piper, doing the laundry, cleaning bottles, and playing. Every day I rocked in the chair and read to her, and staged little photo shoots. Once or twice a week, I hopped on the treadmill for a second run. It felt selfish, like an indulgence, and my mind was on Piper crying upstairs. Between 3:00 a.m. feedings and no napping, I was more fatigued than any marathon training had left me. How did parents do this?

On the starting line in Houston for the trials, I hoped my fitness was enough to make the team. I ran with the lead pack that included Desiree Davila, Shalane Flanagan, Kara Goucher, Amy Hastings, and others—strong marathoners all. Around mile 17, as we made our way back toward downtown, the pace got hard. I could've pushed and suffered for it. But I couldn't find it within me to get uncomfortable. I took sixth.

My first thought across the finish line was that I'd failed as an athlete and a mom. I'd cheated putting in the necessary mileage and recovery, and when I ran I felt guilty being away from Piper. I'd never had competing focuses before because I'd built an entire lifestyle that supported my running dreams. Reflecting on my long career and now motherhood, I realized I no longer wanted the lifestyle of a top competitor. Yet, I also wasn't ready to step away. So I allowed the question of running to remain open. What I needed in the moment was a family vacation.

The three of us and Sage took a trip in a rented RV along the length of California's central coast. We took our time in Santa Barbara, headed north to tour Hearst Castle, and camped on the cliffs in Cambria. We headed inland, the RV taking the windy roads with an awkward heaviness, to visit our good friend Doug in Paso Robles. Doug was in his sixties, bald, a successful CPA, and a foodie. His Tuscan-style villa was set among the region's vineyards, and one night he covered his massive dining-room table with large platters of wild boar, caramelized Brussels sprouts, and homemade pappardelle pasta. As we sipped Bordeaux and shiners of decades-old wine, Andrew turned to Piper on my lap and said, "Honey, this is how Kastors camp."

That fall Terrence stopped by to tell us he was taking a coaching job in the UK. "Do you and Andrew want to take over the Mammoth Track Club?" he asked. Some of the team was following him to England, but we could build on the club for the next Olympic cycle.

We talked about it for hours. "Are you ready to be head coach?" I asked Andrew. He responded without hesitation. "This is a dream come true." Taking over the club would build on the coaching that Andrew had been doing locally for years, and as coaching director for the L.A. Marathon. I needed to think through it a little more. My role would be administrative as well as mentoring as I trained alongside the team. And since professional running and motherhood had been difficult to balance, I had some reservations. When I looked at recreational runners, I was amazed at how well they balanced family, careers, and running. Shouldn't I have it easier since running and my career are one and the same? At a race, I asked a father of twins how he did it. He responded quickly: clear priorities. So I set mine. I decided health and family would come first, and running and career would come second. Plus, with Piper now in preschool during training hours, the timing was actually perfect.

Andrew began recruiting promising young athletes and we introduced them to Shady Rest Park and Green Church Road. Andrew sent us off on workouts and I pushed the team in practice, shouting, "Drive, drive, drive" when they charged the hills, hearing Coach's voice in my head. I ran alongside them and when a challenging moment arrived, offered encouragement: "Your only choice is to be stronger than this hill." Andrew pulled up in the van with fluids and advice: "Stay positive in this wind. Your heart and lungs don't know the difference, they only know hard work." It felt like we were paying forward all that we knew.

One Sunday morning in February 2013, just before my fortieth birthday, Andrew sent us off on a 20-mile long run. We were running a new route Andrew had created, which linked together many of our favorite runs. It started from a park in town, ran through Shady Rest, and headed north on a dirt road toward Lookout Mountain before dropping on to a long stretch on Owens River Road. Winter storms had subsided. It was cold, but sunny, a beautiful day. Andrew had staggered the start to make it easier to give fluids and by mile 15, the guys had dropped me. I was far behind them and somewhere in front of the women, in no-man's-land. I took in the view for a bit, my eyes following the sagebrush-covered valley to the peaks beyond. The run became physically challenging and so the mind-wrestling began. My left hamstring hurt, so I focused on the right one. It didn't feel as good as I'd hoped. *Focus on the six inches above your shoulders*, I heard Coach say. But rather than turn to my mind, my focus went to my shoulders, which were hunching up toward my ears.

Why not, I thought, *just hop in the van? You don't need to suffer. The others are putting in the work now.*

I told myself to be positive and thought of Mike's phrase: *Okay, I'm positive this sucks*, which gave me a few minutes of relief thinking of him.

My hamstrings tightened more, pulling for my attention. My ankles felt clumsy and fatigued on the washboard road. *Get out of your body and look around.* But the road ahead seemed long. *You live in a beautiful place, look up for inspiration.*

The sky was strikingly blue, cloudless. *A bald eagle!*

He glided smoothly, effortlessly, overhead. I wondered where he'd come from. *Perhaps the canyon up at Convict Lake. If I were a bald eagle, that's where I'd live. He must be hunting. What if he dives down and catches a fish in the river? I've never seen that before. Actually, I have, on* Planet Earth, *watching back-to-back episodes of eagles, snow leopards, and cave crabs. Nature is amazing. I'm so glad my parents gave me that* Planet Earth *series. I thought for sure I'd get bottles of wine from everyone that Christmas, but they surprised me with that DVD set. I wonder why. . . .*

The van's horn ripped me out of my stream of consciousness. Andrew shouted out the window that I had run over twenty miles.

It was a few minutes of distraction, but my mind had once again taken me out of a place of struggle. It had pulled out my potential in the moment. Every time I reached the crux of a workout or a tough moment in a race, I uncovered deeper layers of strength and optimism, and reinforced what was already there. Growth was constant, self-mastery was never ending. This excited me. My competitive days had a short window, but I could push my mind and strengthen my positivity for a lifetime. How optimistic could I become? How much richer could I build my life? What joy and potential lay ahead?

Pursuing positivity felt infinite, limitless, and in the van, I told Andrew I wanted to get training hard and racing again, push my limits.

"Why?"

"Because that's how I grow and learn. I don't ever want to lose that."

I launched into a full season of tough training and fun racing. Andrew pointed out cross-country had built and challenged me, so why not get to worlds? *Why not?* I competed in nationals and earned a spot on the team. I ran the L.A. Marathon and the following day, headed to Bydgoszcz, Poland, for the world cross-country championships. Run worlds a week after a marathon? *Why not,* I thought, seeing the challenge as a job for my mind to overcome. The race was tough on marathon legs, but I savored the hilly course and the sloppy, windy conditions, letting my mind lead the charge through the mud, and placed thirty-fourth.

Life was joyous and full. I spent time with Andrew and Piper. The three of us went to the park, took gondola rides, and camped at the lakes looking up at the stars. I invited the team over for dinners some nights where I shared an abundance of healthy food I'd spent most of the day preparing.

Andrew recruited more athletes, and I trained alongside the team. It became a game to hunt down the struggle, to get to the point where negativity bubbled and I had to be more resilient, more creative, more optimistic, and more grateful to emerge stronger from it. Every day I got out there so I could apply the mental habits to life more readily. Staying composed in an anxious pack let me keep my wits in L.A. traffic. I could handle a broken foot in the Olympics, and a broken yolk in the skillet. Patience in a long run gave me patience when Piper's flute playing got a bit loud. Seeing all the lessons along the way added to my motivation. I had learned disappointment was rooted in the desire to improve and that under the grief, there was deep love. Resiliency opens doors, and compassion and gratitude can dissolve tension, and enrich any moment.

What more can I understand?

I ran on to see what discovery and life lesson would emerge from the miles ahead.

EPILOGUE

—◼—◼—◼—◼—

Chicago Marathon, 2015

Life is a matter of choices, and every choice
you make makes you.
—JOHN C. MAXWELL

Marathoners give great attention to weather. Ten days out, we refresh the weather app on our phones, noting the anticipated temperature, dew point, and wind trends, beginning to adjust mentally to the conditions, gearing up for a push against the wind or a practice in managing heat. Ten days out from the 2015 Chicago Marathon, where I was aiming to break the American masters (over forty) record, I was not obsessing about weather and fine-tuning race strategy. I was contemplating not racing at all.

I sat in the van at the park with Andrew waiting for the team to arrive. "I can't run Chicago," I said.

Andrew looked shocked, so I listed my reasons. Allergies had compromised some of my training. The smoke from the wildfires had also forced me to forgo some hard miles outside for easy runs on the treadmill. I'd missed three days of training when Piper was sick. Then I'd gotten a version of the flu that seemed to last longer than usual. I was still regaining my strength, I added, and continued suffering greatly from itchy eyes and a runny nose from allergies. I wasn't confident I could finish a marathon, let alone break a record.

"That's not what I see," Andrew said. "You ran four long runs over twenty miles and put in more volume than you've done since having Piper." He pointed out that my training had included 12-mile tempo runs, the longest in a decade; eight 1-mile repeats all under 5 minutes, volume I hadn't done, and times I hadn't hit, in years.

I didn't think I was prepared. Andrew showed me I was. Both were my reality, but only one point of view would let me reach the goal.

I got on pace early in Chicago and told myself to find comfort in the effort. I sang, *This is the rhythm of the night*, and realized, too late, that I'd missed my first fluid bottle. I could worry about it or press on and this choice, and every one after, would affect the outcome. I grabbed a cup of sports drink from a volunteer, crushed the top, and drank it.

My focus alternated between pace and fluids, singing and effort. At the half I was at 1:14:03, 34 seconds ahead of pace. *Celebrate being on pace.* A couple of miles later, a guy drafting behind me accidentally kicked my left foot and I stumbled. For a half a mile, my left foot still felt the phantom contact, adding a hitch to my stride. *Ride it out.* I stutter-stepped to shake the disruption and my stride smoothed out.

At mile 20, I felt strong and amazed to be there, struck as I had been over the years at what a simple shift in perspective delivered. I was on a path toward my best that day, and sent a quiet thanks to Andrew.

Mile 21 was a different story. I crossed the Chicago River, made the left, and as I ran through Chinatown, my legs felt like stiff pistons forcing my hips to take the brunt of the asphalt. My energy drained and I had a flashback to ten years earlier when I'd hit the wall on that same stretch of road. *This is why you're here*, I told myself. It was the refrain I'd been using since the eagle run. *This is where growth begins, find the thoughts to rise to the challenge.*

Every old cell in this body knows how to run this fast for this long. Every new cell, jump on board for a crash course on how it's done.

I put my head down and pushed through the discomfort.

At mile 22, the angle of the sun cast a shadow on my split, so I couldn't tell if I was still on pace to break the record. I chose to appreciate the lack of information, as it meant I was neither elated nor discouraged. Neutral, great.

At mile 23, I hit my lap split and braced myself for a 7-minute mile, confirming the fatigue I felt. It was 5:38. *I'm doing it!* Eternity seemed to pass over the next 3 miles, but the excitement to get the record was a cattle prod, urging me forward. I vowed to smile the rest of the way, a tactic that offered positive energy. My smile may have looked like a grimace, but it came from a place of joy.

I crossed the finish in seventh place having run 2:27:47, a new American masters record. Andrew was standing just over the line with Piper, now four. I went over and gave her a sweaty kiss, which she wiped off, and embraced them both.

The next day as we toured the city as a family, I thought about the power of a single positive choice, how it is the first step into the story we want to create, the outcome we desire. I thought about how every decision that follows builds and expands and *accumulates*. And yet it comes back to the microdecisions we make in any given moment, when we can go in one direction or the other. How on some days, like the eagle run, the positive path is harder to find and we have to be relentless in its pursuit. But a better outlook is always there and well worth chasing. On the other side are potential and possibility.

7 MENTAL HABITS FOR REACHING YOUR POTENTIAL AND LIVING A MORE POSITIVE LIFE

Now it's your turn. This guide is designed for you to follow the same positive-thinking strategies I used to reach my potential as an athlete. Whether you want to run faster, nail a job interview, improve your health, or simply have more energy and enjoy life more, these steps will help guide you mentally and emotionally. The below exercises, adapted from leading positive psychology experts, work to uncover the hidden layers of negativity that are holding you back or weighing you down, while awakening optimism, joy, and belief—the ingredients of a successful and fulfilling life. Why is the approach so effective? Because thoughts not only change the quality of your day and life, but they also change your *brain* (see "Your Brain on Positive Thoughts" below). Use this guide at your own pace and practice the exercises that resonate with you. But I do encourage you to use *all* of them. In the same way that running and strength training combined lead to greater fitness, the full magic of mental work comes from the exercises' collective effect, and from committing to a lifetime of mental conditioning. So grab a notebook and pen, and let's get to work.

Note: This workbook is not intended to replace professional help, as I am not a psychologist. If you struggle mentally or emotionally, please work with a trusted health-care professional.

Your Brain on Positive Thoughts

After I began practicing shifting my thoughts from negative to positive, positive thoughts started coming more quickly and easily. At the time, the change felt instinctual, but it was actually biological. Advances in brain-imaging technology reveal that thoughts can alter the physical structure and function of the brain. In other words, thinking positive thoughts rewires the brain to be more positive, and positive thinking and optimism become more automatic.

The process is similar to how exercise reshapes the body. The more you think positive thoughts, the stronger those neuro pathways become. Dave Smith, Ph.D., a sports psychologist in the UK, describes the process as a bit like walking through tall grass. "The first time, it can be difficult to find the path," he says, "but as you continue to use it, the path becomes clearer, easier to navigate and more instinctual."

I. START WITH PURPOSE

Mental Habit: Create Meaning

"Inventing your dream is the first and biggest step
toward making it come true."
—BIZ STONE

Purpose and *goals* are often used interchangeably, but they're distinct concepts. A goal is an outcome, something you're aiming to achieve, while purpose is the reason you're striving toward that goal. The two work together. Goals provide us with direction while purpose gives our goals meaning and value.

SET A GOAL

Write down a goal, any goal ("nail a job interview/presentation," "clock a personal best in the marathon," "spend more quality time with my family"). Psychologists suggest that a goal have the following four qualities:

- *It has a personal meaning.* When a goal is meaningful to you—when it's personal—you're more likely to prioritize it.
- *It is specific.* A goal without a clear, measurable target or result is like driving without knowing your destination. Clear target: "Leave work by 5:30 so I can spend 30 minutes more a day with my family" is better than "spend more time with my family." Similarly, "run three days a week" is better than "run consistently."
- *It stretches you.* A goal should be high enough to push you, but not so lofty that it paralyzes you. I like my goals to feel slightly out of reach because being a little intimidated by them makes me hunker down and focus on finer details.
- *It has a due date.* If there is no timeline, it's easy to tell yourself, I'll run/write/get home on time/work on that presentation tomorrow.

WHY IS THIS GOAL IMPORTANT?

Answering this question helps clarify the goal's purpose. Keep asking *why* until you reach a core, personal reason. Purpose connects to something you value—health, family, pushing limits, being an example for your kids. When I first started running professionally, I thought my purpose was to get faster. But that was my goal. Reflection helped me understand that what I really wanted was to realize my potential. Improving my speed was also a means of finding a sense of belonging in the elite running community. Uncovering these personal reasons gave me a greater connection to my training and speed goals, which was powerful motivation for training.

Post a reminder of your goal where you'll see it every day. I put Post-it notes on the bathroom mirror or I wear an object, such as a bracelet from a friend. Be creative with chalkboards, posters, colorful pens, or where you place your goal, but the point is that the object represents your goal and is in clear view for multiple daily reminders.

2. BUILD BELIEF

Mental Habit: Instill Confidence

"A man is but the product of his thoughts.
What he thinks, he becomes."
—MAHATMA GANDHI

Often we think of confidence as a trait—someone *is* confident. Confidence, though, is a thinking pattern, a practice of choosing to believe positive statements about yourself and your abilities. Confidence affects not only how we feel but also how the brain acts. When you believe in your goal, and also your ability to achieve it, the systems of the brain fall in line, seeking and then finding proof for your point of view. The opposite is also true: Start with doubt and the brain will give you reason to doubt. So how do you build belief? These exercises provide the mind with the evidence it needs to believe; much of the rest of the guide builds on this foundation of belief.

PLOT YOUR PATH

Writing down the steps you'll take to achieve your goal not only gives you a road map to success, but it also lets you see that the goal is possible, planting the seed of belief in your mind. Make sure each step is an action item: something concrete, measurable, and in your control. And think of these steps as actions, which gives them greater weight in the mind, reminding you they are something you have to *do*.

List four actions you'll take to reach your goal; make sure at least one addresses mind-set. Here are a few examples.

GOAL	STEPS TO GET THERE
Run 4 days a week	(1) Get up 45 minutes earlier two days a week to run; (2) coordinate two runs with your spouse's evening schedule; (3) find a running group to help stay motivated. *Mind-set:* Stop telling myself "I'll do it later" and tell myself to "Do it now."
Increase quality time with family	(1) Drop our phones in a basket before dinner or put them on silent mode; (2) create a list of questions beyond "How was your day?"; (3) institute a family reading hour or a game night once a week. *Mind-set:* Be open to my family's ideas on time together.

WRITE A POSITIVE AFFIRMATION

That is, tell yourself that you're capable, that your goal *is* possible. In psychology, positive affirmations are statements that help you overcome self-sabotaging thoughts while building confidence: *I am capable. I am worthy. I have the courage and strength to do this.* You can adopt any positive affirmation or write your own. Here's a simple approach that I have used often: **Write your goal as a statement in the present tense.** For example, when I was aiming to win the national championship, I wrote "I am a national champion" on a Post-it and put it on the bathroom mirror. The more you identify with your goal—a sub-4-hour marathoner, a writer, a CEO, a kinder person—the more you'll start acting the part. That is, prioritizing the steps you outlined above to get there.

WRITE A BELIEF LIST

A couple years into my professional career, races came with high expectations: defend a national championship, podium on the international stage. Sometimes I wondered if I could meet those expectations, so I gave myself proof by writing this belief list:

- I believe in my coach.
- I believe altitude training will give me an edge.
- I believe the strength of my past training cycles will carry into this new and tougher one.
- I'm willing to adopt new ideas and approaches that will help me grow as an athlete.

Write down at least four reasons why you believe you will reach your goal. The list should include personal qualities about yourself and your approach. Keep this list in a place where you'll see it often.

Adopt a Growth Mind-set

Early in her career, Stanford psychologist Carol Dweck wondered why some of her students shrank from challenges while others dove into them. Her observation led to the idea that there are two primary mind-sets: fixed and growth. A fixed mind-set is one in which you believe that your abilities and talent are what they are (that is, there is no improving them). A growth mind-set is one in which you believe that your abilities can improve through effort and experiment. A number of factors determine mind-set, including genes, relationships, and environment. But the single most important factor is our ability to choose what we believe. When I opened myself to the idea that my running talent was not fixed, but rather within my control to develop, I got to work and my running flourished.

3. REDUCE NEGATIVITY, GROW POSITIVITY

Mental Habit: Reinforce Positive Thinking, Optimism

"Positivity changes how the mind works. . . .
It widens the span of possibilities that you see."
—BARBARA FREDRICKSON

Use the proven techniques below to trade in worry, doubt, and fear for confidence, belief, and trust.

PAY ATTENTION TO THINKING PATTERNS AND CHANGE NEGATIVE THOUGHTS TO POSITIVE

Noticing your thoughts and feelings is a form of *mindfulness,* a term positive psychologists consider ground zero for positive thinking. "Mindfulness," wrote Barbara Fredrickson, Ph.D., in her book *Positivity,* "can literally sever the link between negative thoughts and negative emotions." When we slow down enough to be present and aware, we're able to see that negative thoughts are reflexive and temporary, and that we can choose positive ones instead. Here's how:

- *Designate a set period to pay attention to your thoughts.* The best time for this is when you're performing your action steps outlined above in "Plot Your Path." For example, runners would commit to noticing their thoughts during a run. How do you "notice" your thinking? Simply put the idea in your mind as you head into the task, and you'll likely find your mind obeys. If it needs a nudge, pause a few times and ask yourself: What am I thinking? What are the *undercurrents* of thoughts behind what I am doing?

  The more frequently you reinforce positivity in the mind, the more automatic and habitual positive thinking becomes. Over time, positive thoughts start jumping into your head, and your mind becomes an advocate for what you're trying to accomplish.

- *Observe your thoughts with curiosity, rather than judgment.* Be aware that negative thinking comes in many forms: worry, fear, or anxiety about a point in the future; self-criticism and focusing on inabilities or flaws; regret and guilt; blaming others, and excuses.

- *Every time you catch yourself thinking negatively, replace the negative thought with a positive one.* Contrary to what many of us want to believe, the mind cannot multitask. If you're focused on something positive, negativity falls away.

- *Repeat!* The mind naturally falls back into negative patterns, so guide it back to being positive. When I first got started, I suspect I shifted my thinking a hundred times a day. It takes discipline and mental energy, but the positive energy it creates, and the profound sense of belief it generates, is life changing.

Here are some examples of my negative thoughts and the positive alternative I found.

MY PESSIMIST	MY OPTIMIST
I'm too tired to run.	A short run will wake me up.
I don't have time to run.	I have control over my schedule and priorities.
I won't be able to finish this workout.	I get to test and learn from my limits today.
I hate hills.	I'm getting stronger with each climb.
I'm pathetic!	(Okay, notice my own self-pity here.) I want so much more, but I'll give my best now in order to get there.
I can't beat these girls.	I'm in charge of whether I run my best today.
I don't belong here.	I've earned my spot on this starting line.

MAKE CHOICES, NOT SACRIFICES

Each day, we face multiple decisions that will move us either toward our goal or away from it. Spend time finishing emails at work . . . or get home in time for dinner with the family. Join friends for drinks . . . or get your workout in. Making these types of decisions was a struggle for me at first because my FOMO meter ran high! But once I started viewing these decisions as *choices* rather than sacrifices, the emotional tug-of-war ended. Taking charge of my decisions made me feel empowered and more committed to my goal. It also made me more creative in time management (have one drink and then go home; write five emails and do the rest after dinner with family). Since your day is the sum of your choices, conscious decision-making helps make each day one you can feel good about.

WORK THROUGH NEGATIVE EMOTIONS

When we increase our ability to manage and move beyond negative emotions, we open the door to progress.

The first step with any emotion—worry, fear, doubt, disappointment—is to give yourself permission to feel it. Denying an emotion buries it in the body and mind, and it will inevitably rear up later in some dramatic fashion. When you feel a negative emotion, pause and take a few deep breaths. Name and acknowledge the emotion, which helps normalize it and reduce its intensity and power. Then work through it using the following five tools.

- *Seek understanding.* We talk about some emotions as being negative or bad, but all emotions serve a purpose if we seek to understand them. Examine the emotion for what's underneath it. Ask yourself why you feel fear, frustration, irritation, or whichever emotion you are feeling. For me, doubt and disappointment became reminders that I *cared* about the workout or the race. When my dog Aspen died, I came to see that deep love was at the root of my grief. Seeing the underlying positive reason for a feeling can help release its grip.
- *Balance the feelings with facts.* Checking your emotion against reality can diffuse it. For example, if a bad workout left me worried I wouldn't meet my goal, I would look at my log and

see the accumulation of good workouts, and I realized one bad one didn't negate that.

- *Apply reason.* Step back and think through the entire situation (both sides of the story), then put it into perspective. Focus on recognizing what you can and cannot control.
- *Take action.* I rank taking action as the best thing you can do to manage emotions. The action plan you created above is an ideal tool; checking something off your list of steps, particularly related to your emotion, is connected to your goal. The best thing I ever did when I was worried about meeting my goal was to complete my workouts and runs. Those were the best actions I could take toward my goal, and the accomplishment quieted my doubts and fears. The main point: taking action when tough emotions arise can help you move beyond them—rather than allowing the feeling take the lead, you take control yourself.

4. EXPAND THE GOOD

Mental Habit: Encourage Feeling Good

"I will greet this day with love in my heart."

—OG MANDINO

Research shows that cultivating positive emotions opens us to a wider range of possibilities and solutions. We are more resilient, creative, and industrious. Positive emotions also build on themselves, creating what Barbara Fredrickson calls an "upward spiral" and I call "the path to our potential."

TAKE IN THE GOOD. EVERY. DAY.

Our brains evolved to have a negative bias, meaning our survival instinct has hardwired our brain to focus on the negative, which is one reason a single mishap can turn an otherwise good day into a negative one. Positive emotions, unfortunately, don't get recorded automatically. Unacknowledged, they slip by. To counter this, neuropsychologist Rick Hanson, Ph.D., author of *Hardwiring Happiness: The New Brain Science of Contentment, Calm, and Confidence*, suggests pausing for ten to twenty seconds a few times a day to "take in the good." Consciously observing and *feeling* positive emotions—pleasure, satisfaction, awe, joy, love—prompts the brain to record the feeling.

WRITE A DAILY GRATITUDE LIST

Gratitude is one of the most powerful of human emotions. When I started writing a gratitude list, I wasn't trying to better my running, yet that's what happened. When we're grateful, we're immersed in goodness, and our brain is, too. Gratitude activates regions in the brain associated with the neurotransmitter dopamine, one of the body's feel-good chemicals. It's also associated with greater resiliency, optimism, motivation, better sleep, lower anxiety, fewer aches and pains, and overall better health.

To bring more gratitude to your life, **keep a daily gratitude list for a week or longer.** You can keep a written list or do it mentally (on a run, at the grocery store, while cooking dinner). And follow positive psychologist Shawn Achor's advice: Include at least three items. Why three? Because research shows it takes three to five positive thoughts or feelings to counter negativity. Avoid repeating the same items because it challenges you to look for gratitude in unexpected or surprising places.

KEEP
CALM
AND GET YOUR
GRATITUDE
ON

CREATE STRATEGIC JOY

Achor's book *The Happiness Advantage* includes one of my favorite quotes about positivity and performance: "Even the smallest shots of positivity can give someone a serious competitive edge." You can create these small shots of positivity yourself, a practice I call strategic joy. Strategic joy is doing something intentionally to foster positive feelings: Wearing a fun running outfit because you feel good in it. Calling your spouse midday for a smile. Looking at a picture of your kids on your desk before a presentation.

I used to dread long runs because I always got my butt kicked by my male training partners, so I started baking fresh scones and reading the Sunday *Times* before those workouts. By deliberately doing something I enjoyed beforehand, I would go into long runs with a positive frame of mind. Or as Achor says, by adding "a quick burst of positive emotion, [we improve] our ability to function at our best."

HAVE A SECOND HELPING OF JOY

We often think we'll be happy when we get that job, have a baby, clock a personal best in the marathon. But Achor's research teaches us that life satisfaction—being happy now—is one of the most important predictors of productivity and performance. When we are joyful, we have no resistance, and a well of energy is available to us. **So, do something each day that brings you joy.**

The "something" doesn't need to be a big thing, just something specific and personal: saying hello to a neighbor, sending a good article to a friend, buying your spouse a favorite snack. I like looking for and then writing an inspiring quote on our family chalkboard or taking a walk with family members on a pine-canopied trail. After you do your joy-generating task, stop a moment and "take in the good"—be grateful for that moment.

APPRECIATE THE PEOPLE IN YOUR LIFE

It's no surprise that in the Harvard Grant Study, one of the longest-running studies on well-being ever conducted, the most important factor for happiness was love. Acknowledging and nurturing relationships is among the most powerful means of creating positive emotions—building resilience, optimism, and hope in others and ourselves.

Make a list of the people and groups who love and support you and whom you love and support. If you feel compelled, let them know how much their support means to you. Recognizing these people is an act of gratitude. It also gives your individual pursuit a deeper purpose. To run with the love of those around you is to feel this generous, motivating, potential-building, and life-expanding emotion. ♥

Why Positive Emotions Are Powerful

In 1996, when I was experimenting with my thoughts in Alamosa, Colorado, psychologist Barbara Fredrickson was at the University of Michigan studying positive thoughts and emotions. Fredrickson was one of the pioneers of the then-emerging science of positivity psychology, the study of happiness, or what makes us thrive. Previous research had determined that fear, anger, and disgust help keep us safe—the fight-or-flight instinct honed long ago by our ancestors. Fredrickson wanted to know if positive emotions such as gratitude, joy, and love served any purpose beyond making us feel good.

Her findings were groundbreaking. Unlike negative emotions, which narrow our thinking, positive emotions open us to a wider range of possibilities and solutions. We become more resilient, creative, optimistic, and industrious. *From an evolutionary perspective then, survival was not just of the fittest, but of the happiest.* Our more positive ancestors were likely the ones building new tools and developing the skills that allowed them to stay alive.

5. BE ANALYTICAL

Mental Habit: Practice Self-Study

> "He who knows others is learned;
> he who knows himself is wise."
>
> —LAO-TZU

LOOK AT YOUR EXCUSES—THEN LOOK TO YOURSELF

"I don't have time." "It was raining." "I was waiting on so-and-so at work." We all make excuses for a missed deadline, workout, or sub-par performance. But when we place blame outside ourselves, we give away our power. Only you can control you, so by taking ownership of your role in a situation or outcome, you put yourself in the driver's seat.

Sometimes, our excuse is real. We *don't* have time. The weather *was* bad. Sure, but when we take the time for a deeper investigation, we uncover the small or big solution that can help us progress.

In the chart opposite, I map out a few examples from my career for reference.

LOOK AT YOUR (BAD) HABITS

Identify a habit that's undercutting your progress; ask yourself why you do this, and find a solution. Some common ones: staying up too late; not speaking up at work; saying yes too often; skipping self-care (your workout, healthy eating).

LOOK AT YOUR LANGUAGE

As you become more skilled at switching negative thoughts to positive ones, pay attention to your language in *all* areas of your life, both in your speech and your thoughts. Are you speaking positively, about yourself and others? Where in your speech do you bring negativity into your day (or others' day)? How is your tone? Sometimes, our words might be fine, but our tone is off, sounding sarcastic or condescending.

SITUATION	REASON	A CLOSER LOOK	SOLUTION
Slowed a lot at the end of long run.	Not fueling enough.	Yes, but also, I *expect* to slow down, so I am allowing myself to.	Experiment with more fluids. Set a goal to run the last 2 miles of every long run at faster pace; find the thought/mantra to help me do it.
Took second at Olympic marathon trials when my fitness and times indicated I would win.	Poor breakfast, bonked.	I'd taken the win for granted and therefore hadn't focused on the basics, like fueling.	Check my attitude, always. Remember: respect the distance, respect your competitors.
Sudden calf strain threatened to call off my season.	I can't find one.	Maybe fear that my best isn't good enough is manifesting in physical ways.	Realize that it's worth following through with my season is the only way to find out my potential. Calf healed in two days upon working through this.

Once, shortly after Andrew and I moved in together, I was rushing out the door and yelled, "Don't forget to take out the trash!" Andrew said, "Whoa, it would sound so much nicer if you said, 'Please remember to take out the trash.'" He was right. It was far less nagging to use "please remember" instead of "don't forget."

Using positive language in your speech can help you foster positive energy around you. It can also help you improve your skills and build confidence. After the encounter with Andrew, I eliminated "don't" from my self-talk to profound effect: Instead of thinking *Don't lose contact* in a workout, I thought *Stay attached* or *Maintain contact*. It shifted the tone from reprimanding to cheerleading, and I felt the energy shift in my body. *Don't fade on the hill* became *Power up this hill*. *Don't stop* became *keep going!*

LOOK AT YOURSELF

In taking charge of managing my thoughts, I learned that I was also taking charge of constructing who I wanted to be. So I selected traits I wanted to embody, rated myself on how well I lived that characteristic, and worked on areas of weakness. Use the list below to honestly rate yourself, and in doing so, identify areas to work on. This acknowledging helps during critical decision-making moments. Ask yourself: Who do I want to be right now? Revisit this exercise every now and then to see if you traits are improving.

Ratings: 1—Not me at all; 2—This is me sometimes; 3—I'm average at this; 4—I do this most of the time; 5—This is absolutely me.

Committed (no excuses; you don't let yourself off the hook)

1 2 3 4 5

Focused (your priorities are clear and your choices reflect them)

1 2 3 4 5

Accountable (you take responsibility for your actions and their outcomes)

1 2 3 4 5

Positive (you seek solutions, learn from setbacks)   1 2 3 4 5

Present (you focus on one task at a time)   1 2 3 4 5

Growth seeker (you look for ways to improve; take feedback constructively)

1 2 3 4 5

Confident (you believe in yourself)   1 2 3 4 5

Identity/Worth (you talk kindly to yourself; believe in your own value; are defined by who you are, not by outcomes)

1 2 3 4 5

(Fill in the blank—for example, persistent, kind, caring)

1 2 3 4 5

Improve Your Thoughts, Improve Your Health

Positive thoughts and emotions not only make our days feel better, but they also make us healthier. Positive emotions like gratitude are linked to higher levels of heart and bone health, a stronger immune system. They also reduce the presence of stress-related hormones in the body, such as cortisol. In one widely acclaimed study, social psychologist Sheldon Cohen surveyed subjects on how they were feeling—happy, calm, and energized or sad, depressed, and unhappy. He then injected everyone with the cold and flu virus. Controlling for multiple factors (including depression and self-esteem), the subjects who were experiencing positive emotions reported fewer and less severe symptoms than those who were stressed or feeling down. A recent study by positive psychologist Barbara Fredrickson found that people who felt they had a sense of direction and meaning in their lives had greater antibody and antiviral gene expressions in their blood—meaning their immune systems were more robust.

6. REBOUNDING

Mental Habit: Build Resilience

"Success is falling nine times and getting up ten."
—ATTRIBUTED TO BON JOVI

It's impossible to overemphasize the importance of resilience. Injury, a bad day, rejection, poor performance, defeat, or simply a yolk breaking in the skillet are all part of life. These are the moments when positivity does its best work. The following are a few ways I've bounced back.

HONOR THE EMOTION

When I broke my foot in the middle of the Olympic marathon in 2008, I had a good long cry and acknowledged that my body breaking in the middle of the Olympic Games truly sucked. So when I hear someone shrug off disappointment with "It's okay, I'm fine," I want to tell him it's okay to *not* be fine for a moment. *Making something positive when it's not is denial, not positivity.* It's okay to walk away and punch the sky if you need to. Let it be raw and real for a bit. The trick is to not let it weigh you down for long. Honor the emotion, but avoid wallowing in it.

FIND THE LESSON

It may be a cliché to say we can find a silver lining in disappointment, but doing so helps us accept and move on from a letdown. Acknowledging what went right and opening yourself to learning how to do better can build excitement to move forward again.

CONNECT WITH OTHERS

Studies show that people who turn away from friends and loved ones when they're disappointed or discouraged take longer to bounce back than those who rely on caring and supportive relationships to get through rough patches. Reach out.

7. EXECUTE, DAY AFTER DAY

Mental Habit: Maintain Steadfast Positivity

> "[We must be] firm in the knowledge that there is nothing so
> satisfying to the spirit, so defining of our character,
> than giving our all to a difficult task."
> —BARACK OBAMA

The greatest lesson I learned is that one positive turn of thought can lift any given moment, and that turning thoughts positive moment after moment, day after day, leads to a positive life. In doing so, you are not only moving toward your goals, but building character, stronger relationships, greater success, and more stable happiness. How to keep it going:

Keep a positivity calendar. What we write down or record increases our commitment to a practice. Record your positivity practice in a way that makes sense to you. It could be a big "P" for the days you practiced being positive, an emoji, or just highlighting the day in yellow. Enjoy the journey while unlocking your potential.

Return to this workbook, year after year. I'm always surprised and delighted by what I discover about myself and the world as I continue to practice positivity. It is my hope that the journey keeps you learning and growing.

ACKNOWLEDGMENTS

Writing this book required an amazing team of people. I am overcome with gratitude as I type each of their names.

Paul and Heleana Drossin: thank you, Dad and Mom, for introducing me to the sport and offering years of support while I pursued it. The greatest challenge was not being able to talk on the phone every day while I wrote. Now, let's chat!

To my sister, Lesley, for being supportive and proud of everything I do—always. I hope this book inspires you, Aaron, Ari, and the little girl on the way.

Thank you to my husband, Andrew, for supporting my every stride and believing I had a story to tell. I love you, the journey we are sharing, and the abundant life we've created.

Thank you to my daughter, Piper, for giving me deeper purpose. If this book helps you grow in even the most minuscule way, it will have been worth it. I cherish sharing time together, and you were so generous and patient to give me the great length of time it took to write this book.

Thank you to my coauthor and friend, Michelle Hamilton, for listening, asking the right questions, truly understanding, and writing with clarity and devotion. I'm forever indebted. And thank you, Gary Pienkowski, for giving Michelle the time, space, and support to do this project, even when a year became two, then three.

To Coach and Caroline Vigil, for believing in me and my goals, even when they were more like wishes. I am forever and most grateful for the values you instilled in me and my life; this book is my way of paying it forward.

Thank you, David Hale-Smith and Liz Parker, at Inkwell Management, for believing in this book and putting it in the right hands.

We're grateful to Kevin Doughten, our editor, for pushing us to greater understanding and toward a richer story. This book would not have gotten to the finish line without you. Thank you to our star-studded team at the Crown Publishing Group for getting behind this project: Julie Cepler, Kathleen Quinlan, Melissa Esner, Tammy Blake, Kathryn Santora, Tricia Boczkowski, Molly Stern, Rachel Willey, Patricia Shaw, Norman Watkins, Songhee Kim, and Jon Darga.

A million thanks to all the coaches who held my hand through the discovery of this sport: Sal Pratts, Vicki Fox, Bill Duley, Lance Harter, Milan Donley, Joe Vigil, Terrence Mahon, and Andrew Kastor.

Thank you to my sports agent, Ray Flynn, "Uncle Ray," for being my advocate in everything, everywhere, all the time.

Thank you to ASICS, my sponsor of almost two decades, for the mission of supporting a *sound mind* and *sound body*. I'm inspired to live by your values every day.

Thank you to Bruce and Jan Kastor, for your love and support, and for coming to Mammoth and playing with Piper during critical editing time.

Thank you, Cheryl Wood, for the depth of your friendship and for introducing me to the art of character development in writing and in life.

Thank you, Liz, Bob, Doug, Susan, Mary, Issi, Heather, Brandee, and Magnolia, for helping in your million generous ways as I worked on this book. You are all true friends to know I needed a sanctuary of quiet space to type, and you helped pull up the slack of my being "absent." After I type these final acknowledgments, I look forward to thanking you in person in a big, big way.

Thank you, Scott Jurek and Marshall Ulrich, for connections and direction when the book process was still undiscovered. Your endurance inspires me—because it took that of an ultrarunner to finish this book.

Many thanks to Farley Chase, Peter Flax, Tish Hamilton, and Monica Prelle, for early input. I feel privileged to have been offered your expertise and wisdom.

Thank you, Amby Burfoot and Cristina Negron, for critical moral support. And to Tara Weaver, who is in a category all her own. Your wisdom on writing, your strength and cheerleading, enabled us to keep going.

I'm grateful to the following for their help in digging up facts and photos: Adam Schmenk, Jill Geer, Glen McMicken, and Michael Scott with USA Track & Field; David Monti, *Race Results Weekly*; Mark Butler, BBC Athletics Statistician; Peter Ciaccia and Stuart Lieberman, New York Road Runners; Jason Henderson, *Athletics Weekly*; Joy Ekema-Agbaw, Arkansas Razorbacks Communications; Mark Evans, Crescenta Valley Cross-Country; Ed Fox, *Track & Field News*; Tim O'Rourke, LA84 Track & Cross-Country Coaching Education Program Coordinator; Marc Bloom, David Lassen, John Ortega, Mike Glaze, and Kirby Lee, whose articles I relied on; the Chicago Marathon; Ryan Lamppa for history of *Running USA*; Roger Robinson for history of the marathon; John Barnhart, Stylecraft; Victor Sailer, PhotoRun; Dan Cruz, Competitor Group.

Thank you to the media for asking critical questions that encouraged me to reflect. Thank you again for your support and for documenting history so I may confirm the accuracy of my memory.

We're indebted to the work of psychologists, researchers, and authors Shawn Achor (*The Happiness Advantage*), Barbara Fredrickson (*Positivity*), and Martin Seligman (*Learned Optimism*, *Authentic Happiness*), whose work gave us the necessary understanding and framework for sharing my story. Shawn also gave generously of his time in an interview; thank you, Shawn, we're grateful.

Thank you to the Greater Good Science Center for its comprehensive and clear presentation of the core elements of positive psychology; particular thanks to science director Emiliana Simon-Thomas, Ph.D., for her time.

Thanks to Dave Smith, Ph.D., a sports psychologist at Manchester Metropolitan University, and Greg Chertok, M.Ed., sport psychology consultant at Telos Sport Psychology Coaching, for your time and expertise.

A heartfelt thank-you to Anita Head and Ed Pienkowski, for opening your home and providing space for a much-needed Tahoe writing retreat.

Thank you, Matt and Gracie Hammer, of Black Velvet, for not charging me rent when I pulled long hours at your coffeehouse, even when, on those longer days, I traded in my coffee mug for a wineglass.

Thank you to my Mammoth Track Club teammates, for understanding my no-show days were because I was working toward the finish line of this book. I'm back and I'm ready to go the distance together.

Thank you, members of the Montana Women's Run and the Red Power Divas in San Jose, California, for testing a workbook version of this book: Mike Adams, Sandy Butler, Lisa Carnicom, Bethany Christensen, Megan Fallon, Alyssa Francis, Suzanne Goodman, Christina Gomer, Pamela Heldenbrand, Amber Nordahl, Rosalinda Savercool, and Jeannette Lau Yamada.

And a shout-out to Skype, for giving us authors a platform on which to connect daily.

ABOUT THE AUTHOR

DEENA KASTOR is an Olympic medalist and the American record holder in the marathon. She lives in Mammoth Lakes, California.

MICHELLE HAMILTON is a health and fitness journalist. Her work has appeared in *Runner's World, Bicycling, Women's Health,* and other publications.